INSURGENT IDENTITIES

INSURGENT IDENTITIES

Class, Community, and Protest in Paris from 1848 to the Commune ❦ ❦ ❦ ❦ ❦

ROGER V. GOULD

THE UNIVERSITY OF CHICAGO PRESS

Chicago and London

Roger V. Gould is assistant professor in the Department of
Sociology and the College at the University of Chicago.

The University of Chicago Press, Chicago 60637
The University of Chicago Press, Ltd., London

© 1995 by The University of Chicago
All rights reserved. Published 1995
Printed in the United States of America

05 04 03 02 01 00 99 98 97 96 95   1 2 3 4 5

ISBN: 0–226–30560–0 (cloth)
0–226–30561–9 (paper)

Library of Congress Cataloging-in-Publication Data

Gould, Roger V.
Insurgent identities : class, community, and protest in Paris from
1848 to the Commune / Roger V. Gould.
p.   cm.
Includes bibliographical references and index.
1. Social classes—France—Paris—History—19th century.
2. Protest movements—France—Paris—History—19th century.
3. Group identity—France—Paris—History—19th century.
4. France—History—February Revolution, 1848.
5. Paris (France)—History—Commune, 1871. I. Title.
HN438.P3G68   1995
305.5′0944′36—dc20   95-14101
CIP

Contents

7

Conclusion
195

Appendix A

Statistical Analyses of June 1848 and Paris Commune Arrests
207

Appendix B

Methodological Concerns
213

Bibliography
229

Index
243

Acknowledgments

In a variety of respects, the production of this book has been as much a collective effort as any of the events described here. The dissertation research that was the starting point for the present study took shape through discussions with Roberto Fernandez, Patrice Higonnet, Peter Marsden, Theda Skocpol, and Harrison White. Funding for that research was generously provided by the Council for European Studies, the Social Science Research Council, the Krupp Foundation, and the French government through its Chateaubriand Fellowship program.

Numerous colleagues at the University of Chicago and elsewhere influenced my thinking in ways that I fear the final product reveals only imperfectly. James Coleman, Roberto Fernandez, Edward Laumann, Peter Marsden, Doug Mitchell, William Sewell, Jr., and Theda Skocpol offered much-needed advice on the book's overall conception. Resources for repeated trips to French archives came from the Social Sciences Division of the University of Chicago and the National Endowment for the Humanities. During its various phases, elements of the work in progress (and its author) benefited from the comments of and conversations with Andrew Abbott, William Axinn, Gary Herrigel, John Padgett, Moishe Postone, William Sewell, and members of the University of Chicago Workshop on Organizations and Statebuilding. Both Chip Heath and Amy McCready read and criticized the entire manuscript with a rare combination of lucidity and constructiveness. Anonymous reviewers at the University of Chicago Press and elsewhere provided fresh insights when my own began to grow stale. Craig Calhoun's comments on the first few chapters helped to a degree that even managed to outstrip his intentions.

Given the perspective I adopt in the pages of this book it would be utterly inappropriate to neglect the informal network context of my work over the past four years. In France, Masumi Iriye, Daniel Jamous, David O'Brien, Christophe Quétel, Jean-François Tricaud, and Mikal Ziane afforded hospitality and comradeship on myriad occasions. On three continents, Bob, Lois, and Tony Gould offered equal doses of encouragement and nonacademic perspective. Whether in Chicago or elsewhere, Amy McCready has been a comforting and sustaining presence whose absence would have had consequences I could not hope to enumerate.

Collective Identities and Social Conflict in

Nineteenth-Century France

ERHAPS no nineteenth-century society inspired more fear among conservatives, or hope among revolutionaries, than France. Between 1830 and 1871, mass uprisings centered in Paris (usually assisted by war or economic crisis) toppled two monarchies and an empire, and shook the foundations of two republics—a record unmatched in any other Western nation. Even Karl Marx, who for reasons of both personal and historical caprice vacillated at various times on the question of whether German, English, or French workers were the most politically mature and class-conscious, consistently saw in France's working class the clearest signs of an impending proletarian revolution.[1]

Each new upheaval, moreover, seemed to contemporary observers to make a cataclysm (of the emancipatory or apocalyptic sort, depending on one's outlook) ever more certain. In January 1848, one month before revolutionary crowds swept away the July Monarchy, Alexis de Tocqueville warned the Chamber of Deputies that working people were becoming increasingly radicalized:

> Do you not see that, little by little, ideas are spreading among them,
> opinions that do not call simply for the abolition of this or that law,
> or ministry, or government, but of society itself, for the destruction
> of the foundations on which it rests?
> . . . Such, gentlemen, is my profound conviction; I believe that,
> at the present moment, we are sleeping upon a volcano.[2]

Although other commentators on the right saw less evidence of cognition in the popular agitation of the period, viewing it instead as social disintegration brought on by drink and general moral decline among the "inferior classes," they were

1. Karl Marx, "Address of the Central Committee to the Communist League" [1856], *The Marx-Engels Reader,* edited by Robert C. Tucker (New York: Norton, 1978), p. 578; for discussion of the revolutionary potential of English workers, see *The Poverty of Philosophy* (New York: International Publishers, [1847] 1963); on German workers, see "Critical Marginal Notes on 'The King of Prussia and Social Reform'" [1844], *The Marx-Engels Reader,* pp. 128–29.

2. Alexis de Tocqueville, *Oeuvres complètes,* vol. 1, p. 372.

no less apprehensive about France's future. Radicals, meanwhile, saw these events as an enlightened endorsement by workers—not just in France but throughout Europe—of their plans to overthrow and remake the social and political order.

The social revolution of 1848 was short-lived, however, and (apart from the resistance to the coup d'état of 1851, in which Louis Napoleon Bonaparte dismantled what was left of the 1848 republic) signs of strife were rare until the strike waves of the 1860s and the insurrections of 1871. In May of that year, as the people of Paris were clearing the streets of the thousands killed during the army's repression of the Commune, Marx wrote that the French working class had at last reached the level of socialist consciousness that was necessary for the abolition of capitalist society, a consciousness that had been lacking in 1848:

> The cry of "social republic" with which the Revolution of February [1848] was ushered in by the Paris proletariat, did but express a vague aspiration after a republic that was not only to supersede the monarchical form of class rule, but class rule itself. The Commune was the positive form of that republic.
> . . . Its true secret was this. It was essentially a working class government, the produce of the struggle of the producing against the appropriating class, the political form at last discovered under which to work out the economical emancipation of labor.[3]

Though the details of the story have undergone considerable revision, the master narrative furnished by Marx's plentiful and insightful analyses remains the orienting axis of modern scholarship on nineteenth-century social conflict, both in France and elsewhere in Europe. In this narrative, the growth of capitalist production and its attendant effects on workers contributed to a century-long set of transformations, the ultimate outcome of which was a working class conscious of itself as a class.[4] The central expression (and source) of this emerging consciousness is taken to be social protest; and the revolutionary upheavals of 1830, 1848, and 1871 (as well as 1831 and 1834 in Lyon) are therefore seen as critical moments in a process that also depended, naturally, on strikes, the formation of producers' cooperatives and resistance societies, and public demonstrations. The

3. Karl Marx, *The Civil War in France* (New York: International Publishers, 1940), pp. 56–60.

4. See, e.g., Ira Katznelson, "Working-Class Formation: Constructing Cases and Comparisons," pp. 3–44, in *Working-Class Formation: Nineteenth-Century Patterns in Western Europe and the United States*, edited by Ira Katznelson and Aristide Zolberg (Princeton: Princeton University Press, 1986).

protagonists of these struggles, most authors now agree, were skilled and semi-skilled handicraft workers rather than the proletarian factory workers Marx imagined; but they were nonetheless engaged, knowingly, in the struggle of labor against capital. Although contemporary feminist and poststructuralist scholars, to be discussed later in this chapter, have begun to chip away at the class-centered account, their arguments have concentrated on the culture and conflict of everyday life. Perhaps because of their apparent resonance with the rhythms of the class-formation narrative, revolutionary upheavals have remained relatively untouched by this critical enterprise.

William Sewell has furnished the most comprehensive and convincing account of the emergence of class consciousness in France between 1830 and 1848.[5] The influence of the pre-1789 "corporate idiom" on workers' identities, he argues, prevented labor militants from articulating a class-centered account of their struggle until the 1830s, when the rhetoric of "association" provided a link between the solidarity of craft groups and the individualism of post-Revolutionary French political culture. By reinterpreting craft solidarity (and thus workers' organizations) as the product of free association between autonomous citizens, and by advocating a "democratic and social republic" governed by trade associations, the activists and worker-journalists of the 1830s and 1840s made it possible for workers to see themselves simultaneously as individual citizens and as members of the working class. As a result, Sewell argues, "the July revolution of 1830 had caught the workers unaware and incapable of articulating an independent program until it was too late, [whereas] the February revolution of 1848 immediately provoked a massive class-conscious workers' movement, not only in Paris, but in cities throughout France."[6] Moreover, this emerging class-conscious movement "set the pattern for the French working-class and socialist movement through and beyond the Commune."[7]

Any master narrative, by definition, elides certain elements of the story of which it is a rendering in the interest of placing the remaining, and presumably more central, elements into a coherent interpretive framework. In the present case, the most significant feature of the story that is missing from the class-

5. William H. Sewell, Jr., *Work and Revolution in France: The Language of Labor from the Old Regime to 1848* (New York: Cambridge University Press, 1980).

6. William H. Sewell, Jr., "Artisans, Factory Workers, and the Formation of the French Working Class, 1789–1848," in Katznelson and Zolberg, eds., *Working-Class Formation*, p. 65.

7. Ibid., p. 67.

formation narrative is the profound dissimilarity between the kinds of protest that occurred in France in 1871 and those that occurred in 1848. One of the core arguments of this book is that the pervasive class awareness to which numerous historians have attested in the activism of 1848—and by class awareness I mean, specifically, the conviction on the part of participants that the February Revolution and the popular agitation surrounding it were principally directed toward the replacement of capitalism with a social order ruled by and for workers— reappeared in 1871 in only diluted form. The "communal revolution" that took place in Paris between March and May of 1871 was, I intend to show, much more a revolt of city dwellers against the French state than of workers against capitalism. To be sure, the majority of the insurgents were indeed workers, and the French state was, among other things, a staunch defender of capitalism;[8] but it was not as workers that they took up arms against the state, and it was not as a defender of capitalism that the state earned their enmity. That this was the case is not refuted, but only made more noteworthy, by the fact that the ranks of the insurgent movement were populated by as many workers as were those of earlier uprisings.

This claim ought not to be understood as a challenge to the view that by 1848 militant French (and above all Parisian) workers had successfully articulated a distinctly class-based, if not Marxian, understanding of the struggle they were engaged in—an understanding that many acted on, and died for, in the June insurrection of 1848. On the contrary: some of the evidence I will present in the chapters that follow is intended to defend that view against a number of recent criticisms by historical sociologists. My point, rather, is that the very clarity and robustness of the class awareness permeating the events of 1848 make its faintness in 1871 a puzzle in need of resolution. If class struggle was at the root of the radical mobilizations of 1848, how can we make sense of its relative marginality during the Commune?

✺ Revolutionary Contrasts ✺

The differences between the two revolutionary uprisings were expressed in at least three visible ways that the master narrative of class formation teaches us to overlook. First, the event that precipitated the Revolution of 1848, the govern-

---

8. Not, however, of laissez-faire capitalism. The heavily Saint-Simonian outlook of financiers, industrialists, and state officials during the Second Empire will form part of the subject of chap. 3, with particular attention to its effect on the transformations of Paris between 1852 and 1870.

ment's decision to cancel a "reform banquet" organized by a number of prominent socialists and republicans, constituted a direct confrontation between the
state and a movement for social and political change. In contrast, the uprising
that led to the proclamation of the Commune was sparked by the government's
attempt to fulfill the terms of an armistice by seizing the artillery of the Paris
National Guard in a military operation. Moreover, these differences of conjunc-
ture paralleled differences in the underlying conflicts leading to revolution: while
the mounting unrest of 1847–48 focused on France's economic woes and the
plight of the worker, that of 1870–71 revolved around the war with Prussia and,
more particularly, around the perception that the French government had abandoned Paris to the mercy of Bismarck's armies. Other grievances surfaced in both
cases, of course, and these were inevitably pulled into the vortex of debate in
political clubs and the popular press. But, as I shall show in subsequent chapters, the two uprisings had unmistakable—and unmistakably different—orienting axes.

Second, the demand that the state recognize the "right to work" (*le droit au
travail*) was as absent from the demonstrations and public pronouncements of
1870–71 as it was pivotal to the agitation of February–June 1848. In 1848, just
hours after King Louis-Philippe had fled Paris, the Provisional Government, at
the urging of the socialist Louis Blanc and of the vociferous revolutionary crowds,
issued a decree (written by Blanc) according to which it would "guarantee labor
to all citizens." Three days later, again in response to mass demonstrations in the
streets, the young republic's leaders created the Government Commission for the
Workers (*Commission de Gouvernement pour les Travailleurs*), a veritable laborers' parliament pledged to reform the organization of work.

No such impulse possessed the insurgents of 1871, despite an unemployment
crisis of comparable proportions in Paris. While the leaders of the Communal
Council knew enough to create a Commission of Labor and Exchange and to
issue a variety of pro-labor decrees, there was comparatively little popular
clamor either to demand or to applaud these measures.[9] Even though the Commune's Delegate to the Labor and Exchange Commission, Leo Frankel (a socialist

9. The only notable exception (others included announcements in the newspapers praising the
Commune for its various social reforms) was the demonstration by bakery workers in appreciation of
the decree abolishing night work. The mildness of the social-revolutionary tenor of 1871 is underscored by Frankel's comment that this measure—itself hardly revolutionary by modern standards—
was "the only truly socialist decree passed by the Commune." Stewart Edwards, *The Paris Commune,
1871* (London: Eyre and Spottiswoode, 1971), p. 258.

printer and member of the Paris chapter of the International), received a variety of petitions and proposals from individuals and workers' organizations, his work in this capacity must have seemed terribly lonely when compared to the endless procession of delegations, representatives, petitioners, and committees that streamed through Louis Blanc's commission at the Luxembourg Palace in 1848. The majority of the Commune's social measures—apart from the long-debated decrees eliminating back rents and overdue bills—bore the mark of top-down reforms and in a number of instances triggered little public response from Parisian workers.

Third, the bloody confrontations that ended the two uprisings (the "June insurrection" of 1848 and the *semaine sanglante,* or "bloody week" of May 21–28, 1871) were manifestly different affairs, despite a number of real similarities. The June uprising occurred because the government had issued an order signaling its intention to close the National Workshops, ringing down the curtain not only on the immediate source of livelihood of tens of thousands of Parisians but also on the sacrosanct project of guaranteeing the right to work—the February Revolution's key achievement in the eyes of most workers. Insurgents set up barricades throughout the working-class sections in the eastern half of Paris, attempting to seal off an area that encompassed the Saint Lazare railway station, the Hôtel de Ville (the seat of city government), and the hotbed of revolutionary activity known as the Faubourg Saint Antoine. Three days later, however, the French army and the Mobile Guard had routed the insurrection, killing fifteen hundred and imprisoning twelve thousand.

In May 1871, on the other hand, the locus of conflict was not the *quartiers populaires* of eastern Paris but the entire city, and the enemy came from outside the city's walls—from Versailles, where the National Assembly, the government, and the French army were temporarily based. From March 18 onward, events unfolded as a struggle not between the working class and an unresponsive republic, but between the "people" of Paris (along with that of several other cities), on one hand, and the French state, backed by a conservative peasant population, on the other. In the popular press and in the mouths of the urban insurgents, the army of Versailles typically became *les ruraux* ("the rurals"), and the barricades intended to keep them out were erected all over the capital, not just in predominantly working-class areas. After nine weeks of municipal independence—an independence of which the idea of *la Commune,* despite its multivalence as a symbol, was generally seen as the expression and guarantor—the revolutionary movement in the capital was crushed in a display of savagery unlike anything the

French had ever experienced.[10] It was for Paris as a whole that the revolutionaries fought, and it was Paris as a whole that the army reclaimed for France. For the defenders of the Commune, then, the street fighting of this final week was a war between Paris and the "Government of National Treason" (the sobriquet applied to the provisional government that had negotiated the peace with Prussia), not a war between the workers and the bourgeoisie or its lackeys.[11]

In short, these two Parisian revolutions began differently, ended differently, and were understood by their protagonists as thoroughly different kinds of struggles—or, to put the same point another way, they were struggles between protagonists who understood *themselves* differently. Whereas the insurgents of mid-century fought and died on the barricades in defense of their status as workers, those of 1871 did so as members of a besieged urban community. It will be the burden of this book not only to demonstrate the depth of this difference but also to explain it in terms of transformations that took place in Paris in the interval between these two revolutions. If an urban consciousness divorced from the notion of class struggle served as the rallying point of urban revolt, I argue, this can only have happened because of radical changes in the urban environment itself.[12]

✦ Critical Urban Sociology and the Question of Class Struggle ✦

There is one group of scholars who, unlike social historians and historical sociologists, have placed the "urban" in "urban protest" at center stage, and who have thus implicitly recognized the contrast between 1848 and the Commune. I refer, of course, to the urban sociologists and radical geographers who, since the early 1970s, have firmly rejected the liberal empiricism of mainstream urban studies in favor of a "critical" approach to the analysis of urban space. To be more precise, writers such as Manuel Castells and David Harvey, and before them Henri Lefebvre, have argued forcefully for an understanding of the urban process in

10. The Terror, for example, claimed an estimated 17,000 lives in the space of a year and a half. The figure for the *semaine sanglante* of May 21–28, 1871, is somewhere over 20,000.

11. The forces of order, however, seemed to harbor a different view. Although the authorities' representations of the insurgent movement contained the inevitable images of foreigners, thieves, and criminals, the Communards' most fearful trait, in the eyes of elites, was their supposed disregard for property.

12. I do not mean to imply that 1871 was the first time an urban identity furnished the basis for radical mobilization; earlier centuries provide numerous examples (including the French Revolution of 1789) to refute such a claim, both in France and elsewhere. What was distinctive about the Commune was that it was the first urban uprising with a communitarian focus to occur in the capitalist era and in a city where violent class conflict had already become a tradition. It is the contrast with 1848 that makes the Commune surprising, not the importance of an urban identity as such.

terms of the connection between city life, transportation, and land use, on one hand, and the logic of capitalism, on the other. According to these scholars, liberal urban sociology and its policy-oriented cousin, urban planning, have been blind to the fact that their own practices and the urban problems they purport to address are generated by forces implicit in the process of capital accumulation and the extraction of surplus value. Social scientists who study the city, from Wirth, Park, and Burgess to the Urban Institute, have pursued a meliorative approach to a set of problems in city growth and development that are not mere unintended consequences but, rather, intrinsic to the nature of cities in capitalist society. Urban blight, homelessness, poverty, unemployment, and crime are not isolated rough spots on the path to prosperity; they are true contradictions in the Marxist sense, and their elimination in one domain will only make them resurface somewhere else. Indeed, for Harvey and Castells (particularly in his early, Althusserian incarnation), the "urban process" consists of precisely this cycle of investment, crisis, and state intervention to avert crisis by stimulating further investment. While they differ in their emphasis—Harvey on the state's effort to shore up the falling rate of profit by encouraging investment in the "built environment," Castells on the state's role in organizing "collective consumption" to ensure social reproduction—both strive to situate explanations of urban growth and change in the broader context of Marxian political economy.

It should come as no surprise that instances of urban protest generally, and of urban insurgency in particular, have received considerable attention in the work of these scholars and their followers.[13] In the radical framework, urban social movements (including riots, rent strikes, squatters' groups, neighborhood preservation groups, and movements for affordable housing) are both shaped by and profoundly threatening to the urban process under capitalism. Consequently, radical social scientists argue that these movements provide analytical insight into the contradictions at the heart of the capitalist city and, in keeping with the dialectical tradition, an expression of the emancipatory forms of social life that might replace capitalism.

Although these arguments typically focus on contemporary movements, the Paris Commune of 1871 remains a touchstone—sometimes explicit, at other

13. See, for instance, David Harvey, *Consciousness and the Urban Experience* (Baltimore: Johns Hopkins University Press, 1985); Manuel Castells, *The City and the Grassroots* (Berkeley: University of California Press, 1983); Stuart Lowe, *Urban Social Movements: The City after Castells* (New York: St. Martin's Press, 1986).

times implicit—for the efforts of radical geographers and urban sociologists to achieve a theoretical purchase on the connection between capitalism and urban protest. In *The City and the Grassroots,* Castells devoted a chapter to the Commune in order to give weight to his claim (one might say his recant) that urban movements cannot be reduced analytically to struggles among classes. Harvey's *Consciousness and the Urban Experience* includes a 160-page study (a monograph, really) of Paris between 1852 and 1870, followed by a chapter on the building of the Basilique du Sacré-Coeur, the monument built in the heart of Montmartre in expiation of the "terrible year" of 1870–71 (and known to tourists not for its funereal origin but for its panoramic view of the capital). And the intellectual godfather of critical urban studies, the Marxist philosopher Henri Lefebvre, made the Commune the subject of a book-length history and the archetype of *la révolution urbaine* in his book of that title.[14]

The reasons for the Commune's centrality in the minds of these scholars are straightforward. First, it was, by any measure, the largest and most intense urban uprising ever seen in the West. With something between fifty thousand and one hundred thousand Parisians in arms (pitted against one hundred thirty thousand in the Army of Versailles), the Commune mobilized more people than has any urban movement before or since—and for a type of insurgency whose dire risks (of death or life imprisonment) were conspicuously clear to all. Second, it was the first such uprising in which specifically urban issues—concerning rents, municipal autonomy, local and democratic administration of the National Guard, and so forth—became a focus of public debate. And, third, all of this happened immediately following a ten-year period of massive, state-sponsored construction and renovation in the capital, including the annexation of eighteen suburban towns, a complete overhaul of the sewage system, and the clearing away of hundreds of buildings to make way for major new thoroughfares. The largest urban revolution in modern history occurred on the heels of the first experiment with urban planning in an industrial city.

The Commune thus stands as a coveted prize for any sociological theory that claims to make sense of the relationship between urban protest and the place of

14. Henri Lefebvre, *La proclamation de la Commune* (Paris: Gallimard, 1965); *La révolution urbaine* (Paris: Gallimard, 1970). The former work has been completely ignored by writers on urban social movements, perhaps because it casts the Commune as a movement driven by a desire for spontaneity more than by an "urban consciousness." In Lefebvre's later work, the issue of spontaneity has been folded into the notion of the urban way of life as a reaction to the flattening of space and social relations by capitalism. See Henri Lefebvre, *La production de l'espace* (Paris: Gallimard, 1973).

the city in capitalist society. This explains the enormous lengths to which Harvey has gone to demonstrate that, despite all the attention paid to community during the 1871 uprising, it was fundamentally a class-based movement. To the extent that the issues of municipal autonomy and urban space *were* salient during the event, he argues, it was only because of the "contradictory" effects of the Second Empire's attempt to ensure the free circulation of capital in Paris while maintaining the imperial tradition:

> That many felt at home with the idea that there was a community of class as well as a class of community was not an ideological aberration: it had a real material base. What was perhaps more surprising was the way many evidently felt not only that community and class provided compatible categories and identities but that their synthesis was the ideal toward which any progressive civil society must strive . . . Yet it was also true that the conceptions and realities of both community and class underwent a very rapid evolution as the Second Empire progressed. Haussmann's works and the transformation of the Parisian land and property market upset traditional notions of community as much as they upset the sociospatial structure, and transformations in financial structures and labor processes had no less an impact upon the material basis of class relations. It is only in terms of such confusions that the extraordinary alliance of forces which produced the Paris Commune—the greatest class-based communal uprising in capitalist history—can be fully appreciated.[15]

If the insurgents of 1871 saw themselves as members of an urban community, in other words, this was merely an artifact of the way capitalism had transformed the urban environment; moreover, it was the intertwining of class and community, not community itself, that underlay the unique (i.e., nonclass) features of the insurrection.

Castells, in his rejection of the structural-Marxist orientation of his pathbreaking earlier work, adopts the opposing stance: that it is the notion of urban meaning, articulated *independently* of class solidarity, that makes sense of the Commune (as well as other instances of "urban social movements"). The debate over rents, the demand for municipal liberties, and the reclamation of the city center through the building of barricades were, on this account, constitutive of the communal movement rather than epiphenomena of the effects of capital accumulation on the city and its residents. For Castells,

---

15. Harvey, *Consciousness and the Urban Experience*, p. 154.

if we are entitled to consider the Commune as an urban social movement, this is because it was primarily a municipal revolution, as we have tried to argue. By municipal revolution we mean a popular mobilization aimed at radically transforming the political institutions that represented the local society, both in their internal organization and in their relationship to the central state . . . For the Commune of Paris, the city was essentially a particular political culture, a form of popular democracy, articulating grassroots democracy and representative democracy to reorganize the nation by the connection between successive levels of political delegation.[16]

If there is a positive point underlying Castells's argument, it must reside in the way the term "urban meaning" is understood; otherwise, asserting that urban movements are explained better this way than in class terms amounts to nothing more than naming a residual category. In the case of the Commune, Castells argues, a new version of "urban meaning" formed in response to the conflict between the city's residents and a specific set of institutional actors: the paternalistic, controlling Church, the centralized bureaucratic state, and the real-estate speculators who took advantage of Haussmann's rebuilding projects to get rich while remaking the city's "spatial forms." It was the contingent interplay of these social forces, not a constellation of forces in the service of capital, that provoked the radical response of urban revolt.

Since 1983, then, the key figures in critical urban studies have collectively forged a significant debate about the principles underlying urban social movements—a debate in which the balance of explanatory power has been for various reasons tied to the test case of the Paris Commune. Broadly speaking, the issue is whether the distinctly urban focus of the 1871 uprising can be viewed as a by-product of the relationships between the working class, capital, and capital's relatively autonomous servant, the state or, instead, as a completely independent dimension of collective action influenced but in no sense determined by the logic of capital accumulation (in either its straightforward or contradictory aspects). Whatever the answer, writers like Harvey and Castells have made it clear that the issues of community, municipal autonomy, and control over urban space permeated the events surrounding the Commune so thoroughly that to ignore them on theoretical grounds alone would be indefensible. The urban character of France's last revolution was quite real and therefore merits retrieval from the dustbin of history.

16. Castells, *The City and the Grassroots*, p. 25.

Unfortunately, the conceptual approaches employed in this debate are no better suited than is the class formation narrative to resolve the "puzzle" I have described. According to Harvey, the Commune was an urban revolution only insofar as the process of capital accumulation was deflected from its underlying logic by the interaction of this logic with the vagaries of French history. His extensive research on Paris under the Second Empire is intended to explain *away*, more than to explain, the differences between the Commune and France's earlier upheavals. For his part, Castells insists that urban struggles are *intrinsically* about city life, in the sense that they are invariably conflicts over "urban meaning," where the content of that term is established through political and cultural battles in particular historical settings.[17] If we choose the former analytical strategy, we are committed to finding class struggle at the heart of any conflict. But if we elect for the latter, we are a priori enjoined from relating urban protest to any other sort of social process: urban upheavals are by definition about defining the urban, and nothing more. In place of the teleology of class formation, in short, radical geographers offer either a sophisticated Marxist reductionism, on one hand, or an antianalytical historicism, on the other. The first perspective determines the explanation for the differences between 1848 and 1871 before empirical research begins; the second denies the legitimacy of "explaining" the difference at all.[18] This dilemma exactly parallels the unsatisfactory choice between structuralist and culturalist understandings of class, which I will discuss below.

In the next section of this introduction, I offer a simple conceptual framework for talking about (and studying) collective action that does not prejudge the crucial question of what protest is about but, rather, makes the question the subject of empirical investigation. I then set out a theoretical model, expressed in the terms of the conceptual framework, that links this issue—what a case of protest is about—to the networks of social relationships in which potential protesters are implicated. Subsequent chapters will apply the model (and its language) in an effort to make sense of the contrasts between the upheavals of 1848 and 1871. In light of the foregoing discussion, the justification for an approach that acknowledges the multiplicity of bases for conflict should be transparent: unless the language a theory uses to talk about social conflict is essentially agnostic

---

17. Castells, *The City and the Grassroots*, pp. 318–22.

18. Ira Katznelson discusses a number of these concerns in *Marxism and the City* (Oxford: Clarendon Press, 1992). His main goal, however, is to incorporate the issue of urban space into the study of class formation rather than to study the spatially defined community as an alternative basis for protest.

about conflict's "real" basis, the statements it makes about the connection between that basis and any other aspects of social life are unfalsifiable. And if that
is the case, empirical research will not be much help in deciding whether the
theory is any good.

For the same reason, I should hasten to note that at no point in this book will
I claim to offer a comprehensive interpretation of something like *the* doctrine
underlying the Commune or the Revolution of 1848.[19] On the contrary, it would
seem to be one of the essential features of any revolutionary uprising that what it
is about is (at least initially) contested not only by scholars but by those swept up
in it. When the French army retreated from Paris on March 18, after its attempt to
seize the National Guard's cannon had provoked a popular rising, it took only a
few hours for activists—the Friends of Order and militants alike—to placard the
city with their hastily composed interpretations of the event. It did not escape
anyone at the time that what people might conclude about what was happening
would have tremendous consequences for what would happen; it should not escape modern analysts either.

Collective Identity and Protest

Rather than construct a pair of monolithic and therefore reifying interpretations,
then, I propose to determine the extent to which the various competing and contemporaneous "versions" of these two revolutionary mobilizations succeeded in
motivating people to participate in them. To this end, I shall permit myself exactly one theoretical construct not already prevalent in the social-scientific literature on protest; it concerns what I shall call a *participation identity*. By this I
mean the social identification with respect to which an individual responds *in a
given instance of social protest* to specific normative and instrumental appeals. In
earlier work, I have argued that individuals participate in collective action for
two reasons, one involving interests and the other norms.[20] The problem for actors

19. Various such efforts have, naturally, been mounted. See Edward S. Mason, *The Paris Com-
mune: An Episode in the History of the Socialist Movement* (New York: Macmillan, 1930); Charles
Rihs, *La Commune de Paris, sa structure et ses doctrines* (Geneva: Droz, 1955); Jacques Rougerie, *La
Commune, 1871* (Paris: Presses Universitaires de France, 1988).

20. Roger V. Gould, "Collective Action and Network Structure," *American Sociological Review*
58 (1993): 182–96. The importance of collective identity in protest movements is now widely accepted. See, e.g., William Gamson, *The Strategy of Social Protest*, 2d ed. (Homewood, IL: Dorsey,
1990); Alain Touraine, *The Voice and the Eye* (New York: Cambridge University Press, 1981); Alberto
Melucci, *Nomads of the Present* (Philadelphia: Temple University Press, 1989). While many of the
writers who focus on the issue of collective identity do so in reference to the so-called new social
movements, I think it is unreasonable to assume that the role of collective identities in movement

involved in mobilization is to convince potential participants that, given their social situation, they are both likely to benefit from and, as a result, obligated to contribute to the collective effort. For instance, a coal miner who joins a union because of an appeal to solidarity among mine workers has, from the point of view of the unionization drive, responded to a mobilization effort framed in terms of an occupational participation identity. As someone who works for a mining operation, he or she stands to gain from a successful attempt to unionize; and the fact that this is so implies (in the presence of norms of fairness) that it would be wrong to remain idle while other miners contributed to the unionization drive. These are the essential components of any attempt to mobilize support among the constituents of a movement.[21]

When someone responds positively to an appeal to solidarity, then, he or she has acknowledged membership in the group whose boundaries are defined by the terms of the appeal. In other settings, he or she may accord priority to the identity of parent, child, tenant, debtor, member of an ethnic group, U.S. citizen, or any other social role; and these may in some circumstances directly compete with occupational identity.[22] What the term "participation identity" refers to is the particular identity whose normative and practical implications are relevant for successful recruitment in the case under consideration.

Observing that various collective identities may be relevant to individuals at different times and in different contexts directs attention to two equally interesting (and probably inseparable) questions: where does the range of candidate identities come from in the first place, and what determines which candidate (if any) predominates in actors' interpretations of collective action? In this work, I wish to avoid the reductionist tactic of assigning causal priority either to existing

---

mobilization is a new development. On the contrary, I would claim that the idea of belonging to an aggrieved group is, and always has been, constitutive of participation in social protest. What is distinctive about movements of the post-1968 era (e.g., the environmental, feminist, and gay rights movements) is the degree to which they self-consciously make collective identity an explicit focus of debate and goal of mobilization. For a similar argument, see Craig Calhoun, "'New Social Movements' of the Early Nineteenth Century," *Social Science History* 17 (1993): 385–428.

21. A notable exception is the "conscience constituent," someone who contributes to a movement despite the fact that he or she will derive no material benefit from its success. The participation identity of such a person clearly differs from that of a potential beneficiary insofar as the reasons for contributing are different. For a typology of supporters of a social movement, see John A. McCarthy and Mayer N. Zald, "Resource Mobilization and Social Movements: A Partial Theory," *American Journal of Sociology* 82 (1977): 1212–41.

22. Of course, some participation identities may be overlaid on or linked positively with others. For example, appeals to patriotism during wars are often tied to the role of family protector.

identities or to the social interactions they inform in determining the shape of social conflict. Instead, I hope to demonstrate the merits of a theoretical perspective according to which collective identities undergird normative commitments to social protest, but are at the same time the product of the very social relations that are both affirmed and forged in the course of protest. The collective identity of workers *as* workers only emerges if the social networks in which they are embedded are patterned in such a way that the people in them can plausibly be partitioned into "workers" and "nonworkers"; but once this is possible, social conflict between collective actors who are defined in terms of this partition will heighten the salience and plausibility of the partition itself.[23] The intensification of the boundary's cognitive significance for individuals will, in other words, align social relations so that the boundary becomes even more real.

If this argument about the connection between collective identities and social conflict is sensible, then it follows that one of the most important things ideologies do is to render a schematic image of the world in terms of collective actors. In its simplest form, for example, revolutionary socialist ideology portrays social relations as fundamentally determined by the dominant mode of production; the mapping of individuals into collectivities that this portrayal implies leads to a rigid partition into capitalists and workers (usually with a number of residual categories). By highlighting production relations, in other words, such an ideology represents other allegiances (to the nation, to ethnic groups, etc.) as incidental, or perhaps as fabrications that the ruling class deploys to distract workers from their true interests.[24]

In practice, of course, insurgent ideologies are endowed with considerably more nuance and complexity than this depiction suggests; but I maintain that a mapping of individuals into collective actors (both protagonists and foes) is always present in mobilization efforts. Examples abound in the anticolonialist rhetoric of Frantz Fanon, Gandhi, and their republican precursor, Toussaint-Louverture; in the "moral economy" language of nineteenth-century English arti-

---

23. This is, of course, the essence of Marx's argument about the impact industrial conflict would have on workers' class consciousness. See "Wage Labor and Capital" in *The Marx-Engels Reader,* pp. 203–17.

24. Essentially the same strategy characterizes orthodox Marxist social science: "false consciousness" is the consequence of workers' failure to see their true interests through the mystifications of class relations proffered by the dominant class and accounts for the absence of revolutionary action in advanced capitalist societies. For the moment I am focusing on the use of this line of argument as a tactic for mobilization; in the next section I take up the issue of its relevance for sociological explanation.

sans; in the Puritans' self-portrayal as "saints"; and, most recently, in "identity-oriented" social movements that demand recognition of alternative lifestyles, sexual orientations, or conceptions of gender.[25]

In general, then, mobilizing ideologies provide a conceptual, "reduced-form" account of the world that (1) identifies key types of social relations that are crucial for understanding a set of grievances, and (2) assigns individuals to collectivities based on the similarity of their position in the system of social relations as defined by (1). Socialist ideologies represent workers (or peasants) as similarly exploited by similar capitalist employers (or landlords); the basis for the appeal to solidarity among workers, in other words, is the fact that the abstract categories "labor" and "capital" furnish a framework within which a multitude of social relations, and the people implicated in them, suddenly appear homologous. (Naturally, conservative ideologies also cluster workers and employers into two groups, the difference being that the employment relation is in this case seen as cooperative or paternal rather than exploitative. Either way, the partitioning is the point of departure for appeals to solidarity.) The homology, in turn, justifies the argument that collective action benefiting some members of the group (at least with regard to the grievance in question) will benefit all other members, making it incumbent on them to contribute their fair share of effort.

Readers familiar with the network tradition in sociology will have observed that at the core of my argument lies the idea of "structural equivalence"—a relation among pairs of individuals that obtains if they are tied in equivalent ways to equivalent others, regardless of whether they are tied to one another. As anyone who has examined social networks knows, there are always multiple ways (none of them perfectly satisfying the formal definition of structural equivalence) of partitioning actors in a network into equivalence classes defined in this way—a fact that has proved immensely frustrating for scholars working in this area. But in the realm of social movements, this is precisely the point: mobilizing appeals compete with one another precisely because there are many ways in which people can view their social position relative to others. This is true not only because people linked by a particular set of social relations can be divided into subgroups in a variety of ways that satisfy the equivalence criterion equally well; it is also

25. See, e.g., Frantz Fanon, *The Wretched of the Earth* (New York: Grove Press, 1963), esp. pp. 118–99; Mohandas K. Gandhi, *Indian Home Rule* (Madras: Ganesh, 1922); Gareth Stedman Jones, *Languages of Class: Studies in English Working-Class History, 1832–1982* (Cambridge: Cambridge University Press, 1983); Michael Walzer, *The Revolution of the Saints: A Study in the Origins of Radical Politics* (Cambridge, MA: Harvard University Press, 1965).

true because different kinds of social ties are accorded dramatically different amounts of salience from different ideological standpoints. The issue of conflicting loyalties (between friend and kin, family and employer, nation and church) is resolved as much through a ranking of the relations within which these loyalties are expressed as through a ranking of the actors implicated in these relations.

Appeals to solidarity in social conflict confront, therefore, a basic indeterminacy in the dimensions along which the relational basis of solidarity can be defined, with a corresponding indeterminacy in the placement of group boundaries.[26] The social categories (class, race, nation, and so on) within which individuals see themselves as aligned with or against other individuals depend on the conceptual mapping of the social relations in which they are involved and on the partitioning of people into collectivities whose boundaries are logically implied by this mapping. Only rarely will diverse types of social relations line up so perfectly that the same collective actors will emerge regardless of the type of relation considered; on the other hand, when this does occur, the absence of cross-cutting collective identities should lead one to expect very high levels of mobilization indeed.[27]

Despite my focus on the variable character of participation identities, however, I do not claim that the choice of a mapping and the group boundaries it implies is arbitrary. On the contrary, the fact that appeals to solidarity in social conflict are consistently relational means that the persuasiveness of movement ideologies to real people is constrained by the patterns of their social relations.

26. A noteworthy example of militants consciously wrestling with just this issue can be found in the history of the Knights of Labor. Debates within local chapters of this "producerist" labor organization revolved around whether the enemy was large enterprise or employers in general. If the former, small employers would constitute natural allies; if the latter, only wage workers would be offered membership. The answer depended on the choice between a worldview in which the central evil was the purchase of wage-labor in general and one in which only monopolistic employment relations were seen as exploitative. See Victoria Hattam, *Labor Visions and State Power: The Origins of Business Unionism in the United States* (Princeton: Princeton University Press, 1993); Kim Voss, "Disposition Is Not Action: The Rise and Demise of the Knights of Labor," *Studies in American Political Development* 6 (1992): 272–321, and *The Making of American Exceptionalism: The Knights of Labor and Class Formation in the Nineteenth Century* (Ithaca: Cornell University Press, 1993).

27. This statement presupposes the absence of serious external constraints on collective action. Innumerable cases (including South Africa, Brazil, Central America, and the United States for much of its history) demonstrate that economically oppressed ethnic groups can be kept quiet for very long periods through a combination of surveillance, terror, and opportunistic use of the law. It is self-evident that the presence of coextensive group boundaries is not by itself sufficient to ensure radical mobilization; but it seems equally clear that, when mobilization does occur in these contexts, it is often marked by an especially virulent sort of hatred.

An appeal to solidarity will only succeed to the degree that the collective identity it invokes classifies people in a way that plausibly corresponds to their concrete experience of social ties to others. This does not just mean that individuals must be able to see their own social connections as concrete instances of the abstract model implied by an ideology; they must also perceive the social connections of their putative peers as equivalent to their own. Potential recruits to a social movement will only participate if they see themselves as part of a collectivity that is sufficiently large and solidary to assure some chance of success through mobilization. A significant source of the information they need to make this judgment is the very same set of social ties the ideology deems relevant: these social relations are not only the basis for mutual obligation, in other words, but also the mechanism for mutual recognition of shared interests (and of recognition of this recognition, and so on). Regardless of how plausible a conceptual map of oppression may be to one person, he or she will see little hope for change in the absence of direct contact with others whose lives are similar in relevant respects and who may consequently respond affirmatively to mobilization efforts.

This line of reasoning leads to two considerations that (if the reasoning is borne out by evidence) must inform the study of any instance of collective action. First, students of collective action ought to be as sensitive to the impact of short-term events as they are to underlying structural variables; and second, formal organizations should be considered as pivotal not only to the mobilization of resources but to the formation of collective identities on a larger scale than would otherwise obtain. A few moments' reflection will demonstrate why these statements are implied by the preceding argument.

If it is accepted that people typically juggle multiple roles in their daily lives and that each role can tie a person to a different set of others (as well as set him or her against a different set of adversaries), then it follows that short-term events can profoundly alter the priorities assigned to these various roles. Feuds between siblings vanish in the face of a sudden threat from outside the immediate family; lifelong friendships are torn apart in times of war by the demands of one's clan, tribe, nation, or church.[28] It is no accident that the deep anguish brought about by the tensions between multiple allegiances is a recurring theme in the literary

28. An example of a strictly hierarchical form of this process was noted by Evans-Pritchard in his study of Nuer social organization. Among the Nuer, levels of allegiance (family, clan, lineage, tribe) were completely nested: people who were allied with each other at any given level would remain so at higher levels. In general, we should expect collective identities to overlap considerably less neatly than this image suggests. E. E. Evans-Pritchard, *The Nuer* (Oxford: Oxford University Press, 1940).

traditions of numerous cultures. What often appears senseless to outside observers, or even to participants—for example, the fact that political turmoil can turn friendly neighbors into blood enemies seemingly overnight—merely reflects the dependence of social obligations (or, more precisely, their relative importance) on current circumstances. During periods of economic prosperity in agrarian societies, extended kin relationships are less salient, relative to voluntary friendships, than in periods of famine. Likewise, deaths—particularly of prominent persons—entail for the kin of the deceased immediate recognition, as well as ritual reaffirmation, of the social relations constituting the kin group.[29]

The contingent ranking of social relations and of the group boundaries they induce implies that collective identities depend significantly on critical events. A dispute between two individuals ramifies into a full-fledged group conflict if each can call on a significant number of allies; those with ties to both may be forced to choose a side.[30] Imminent changes in taxation, political rights, or property rights generate confluences of interest among people who may have preexisting, though relatively inactive, social ties to one another.[31] Such events may also highlight or deepen interests that were already shared. For instance, a wage cut or work speedup may matter more as a fresh opportunity for employees to see their interests as congruent than as a source of anger or resentment in its own right; this distinction explains why apparently minor transgressions by employers can provoke work stoppages followed by major demands on the part of workers.[32]

In brief, critical events can set the stage for mobilization not because they create collective identities where none existed before but because they rearrange the priority ranking of social identifications that already matter to people in varying degrees. Insofar as meaningful group boundaries are predicated on the presence (and perception) of common patterns of durable social ties, it would be surprising to find new collective identities emerging purely on the basis of suddenly convergent interests. If events increase the likelihood of collective action, it is

29. Arnold van Gennep, *The Rites of Passage* (Chicago: University of Chicago Press, 1960), pp. 146–65.

30. See, e.g., Christopher Boehm, *Blood Revenge: The Anthropology of Feuding in Montenegro and Other Tribal Societies* (Lawrence: University Press of Kansas, 1984), pp. 171–73.

31. At the same time, the *absence* of such ties among actors with newly congruent interests makes the role of "broker"—an actor with ties to disconnected others—critical for collective action. See Roberto M. Fernandez and Roger V. Gould, "A Dilemma of State Power: Brokerage and Influence in the National Health Policy Domain," *American Journal of Sociology* 99 (1994): 1455–91.

32. For an example of this sort of incident, see Rick Fantasia, *Cultures of Solidarity* (Berkeley: University of California Press, 1988), chap. 2.

because they crystallize collective self-understandings—not by forging new ones but by attaching new significance to old ones.

The importance of formal organizations for the creation of *new* collective identities follows directly from this dependence of identities on patterns of preexisting social ties, as I shall now demonstrate. If group boundaries are only plausible to the degree that they identify sets of people with (1) similar patterns of social relations to others *and* (2) a sufficient level of internal social contact to ensure mutual awareness of this similarity, then the collective identities relevant to mobilization should generally be quite local in their level of inclusiveness. What aspect of a dispute over grazing rights with a local landlord would suggest to the peasants of a pastoral village that their conflict was a single instantiation of a broader struggle between "the peasantry" and "the nobility"? In the absence of significant amounts of interaction across villages, it seems overwhelmingly improbable that peasant uprisings against landlords would rely on participation identities on a larger scale than individual villages, or in some cases "marketing areas."[33] Even if militants appeal to collective identities that range more widely than existing social networks, such appeals will have less force than localistic ones—and what force they do have will be parasitic on the more narrowly defined relational base from which they are abstracted.

In general, we should expect collective self-representations that succeed in mobilizing people to include the largest possible number of people fulfilling condition 1, subject to the scale constraint imposed by condition 2. Condition 1 in effect sets a lower bound on the scale of participation identities because larger numbers of potential participants will almost always be beneficial to mobilization, especially when rates of participation are likely to be low (as a result of risk, the temptation to freeload, etc.). Appeals to solidarity will therefore emphasize the breadth of the group identified as sharing a common fate.[34] Condition 2 im-

---

33. The cases of rural rebellion in nineteenth-century China and in France during the Great Fear of 1789 are highly instructive in this regard—as is the contrast between the latter and rural mobilization against Louis Bonaparte's coup d'état in 1851. See Philip A. Kuhn, *Rebellion and Its Enemies in Late Imperial China: Militarization and Social Structure, 1796–1864* (Cambridge, MA: Harvard University Press, 1971); John Markoff, "Literacy and Revolt: Some Empirical Notes on 1789 in France," *American Journal of Sociology* 92 (1986): 323–49; Georges Lefebvre, *La grande peur de 1789* (Paris: Armand Colin, 1970); Ted W. Margadant, *French Peasants in Revolt: The Insurrection of 1851* (Princeton: Princeton University Press, 1979).

34. The story is actually a bit more complicated. Because similarity is a continuous variable, broad group boundaries will in general encompass more heterogeneous sets of people than narrow boundaries; and this means that, if the force of an appeal depends on the similarity of the people it targets, broadening the boundary may have a negative impact on the appeal's persuasiveness. I main-

poses an upper bound on scale for the simple reason that the social contacts necessary for mutual recognition of comparable social position (structural equivalence) will be scarcer, the wider the net cast by the boundary. (In future chapters, I will use the term "minimally inclusive collective identity" to refer to a group boundary that meets these criteria simultaneously.) Indigenous patterns of social interaction limit the scale, as well as the content, of the collective identities governing mobilization.

Precisely for this reason, formal organizations—including clubs, correspondence committees, and militias—can exert an enormous influence on the scale at which group identities are convincing to potential participants in collective action. In the literature on social protest, organizations matter principally as mechanisms for coordinating action and mobilizing resources (human and otherwise) through the application of incentives; their impact on social interaction tends to go unnoticed, largely because the social ties thought to facilitate mobilization are assumed to exist prior to the formation of such institutions. Craig Calhoun, for example, insists that the radical activism of early-nineteenth-century English workers stemmed almost exclusively from the informal social organization of artisanal communities:

> The growth of working-class collective action depended on the social integration of working-class communities. Protest movements before the 1820s and 1830s did not depend to any significant extent on formal organizations. Such formal bodies as there were generally added a dimension of increased organization to social bonds which went on both before and after them. The radicals were linked to each other by kinship and personal friendship, as neighbors and co-workers. Their political mobilizations followed these lines; they were not distinct from them.[35]

In contrast, Calhoun argues, the trade unions of later years succeeded only in producing reformism because the industrial workers they represented lacked the indigenous social "connectedness" necessary for radical collective action.

---

tain, however, that in most cases the groups that could be identified as similar by mobilization appeals (steelworkers, peasants, women, dairy farmers, etc.) are very large relative to the networks of social relations in which individuals are embedded. Consequently, condition 2 is the "limiting factor," in the sense that homogeneity should not decrease with scale until well after the point at which levels of within-group social interaction begin to decline.

35. Craig Calhoun, *The Question of Class Struggle: Social Foundations of Popular Radicalism during the Industrial Revolution* (Chicago: University of Chicago Press, 1982), pp. 174–75.

Yet this contrast passes over what may be the most interesting situation: formal institutions that link previously isolated collectivities, each with its own plausible group identity. Because organizational structures are enacted (frequently by powerful elites), rather than "crescive" or emergent, they have the unusual potential of fostering contacts that cross the boundaries established by the routines of everyday life. An unintended consequence of formal organizations, in other words, is the creation of social ties that encourage the recognition of commonalities on a scale considerably broader than would be expected on the basis of informal social networks alone. Interaction produced by formal organizations consequently raises the ceiling on participation identities imposed by condition 2. The constituent elements these new groups comprise are very likely informal communities of various sorts (thereby determining, in conjunction with critical events, whether the broader collective identification is based on occupation, class, region, or some other category); but the jump in scale that formal institutions permit is possible precisely to the extent that such institutions *fail* to follow the patterns established by preexisting social ties.[36]

In the foregoing discussion I have sketched a theoretical model of the relationship between collective identities, networks of social relations, critical events, and the mobilization of collective action. Although some of the subsidiary propositions included in it draw on stylized facts from social science research, as a model it merely makes a set of predictions that follow logically from its presuppositions. However plausible (or implausible) it may appear, the theory's usefulness depends on a demonstration that its predictions are consistent with empirical evidence, and in a way that does not rely on post hoc, and thus tauto-

36. In the work just cited, Calhoun outlines a theory of radical collective action that my argument resembles in a number of respects. In particular, he argues that "for class action to take place, the component units of the class, such as communities and crafts, must be strong, but their in-group association must not so completely predominate over their affiliation with other groups that they are not densely knit into a web of class relations" (ibid., pp. 176–77). I would point out three significant differences between this argument and the theory I have outlined in the preceding pages. First, because he focuses on class conflict, Calhoun's argument does not address the variable content (ethnic, religious, economic, etc.) of collective identities, considering variation in scale only. In contrast, I have tried to emphasize that the same people may respond in different situations to appeals of very different types. Second, the recognition of this contingency leads me to highlight the dynamic role of critical events, whereas Calhoun's theoretical framework relies on comparative statics. Third, by noting the variability of identity content and by distinguishing between informal social relations and the interaction fostered by formal organizations, I have called attention to the effects of multiple (and cross-cutting) social networks. Calhoun, on the other hand, aggregates diverse types of social ties into the unidimensional conception he terms "community." Indeed, the literature on social movements almost invariably discusses social networks in this undifferentiated manner.

logical, interpretations of that evidence. To this end, the next section will specify the relationship between the general, abstract language of the model and the empirical case considered in this book, namely, Parisian insurgency in the mid–nineteenth century. It will also relate my approach to the ways in which social scientists have tried to understand class, class conflict, and urban protest in industrializing Europe.

Class Formation, Class Consciousness, and Urban Revolt

E. P. Thompson's landmark work, *The Making of the English Working Class*, is usually credited with achieving, at least in the realm of labor history, what Western labor movements could not: the emancipation of the working class. By insisting, in a memorable phrase, that the English working class was "present at its own making," Thompson provided a framework for discussions of class and class conflict that dispensed with the assumption of an objectively defined set of interests which workers had to recognize and act upon before they could be deemed "class-conscious." Whereas structural or "scientific" Marxism took as its point of departure the existence of a class structure that determined workers' true interests once and for all, Thompson's culturalist alternative proposed that workers took an active role in the articulation—which was not far removed from the creation—of those interests. If the militants of the industrial revolution had not succeeded in overthrowing capitalism, Thompson suggested, at least their historians could spare them the tyranny of structuralism.[37]

For students of labor militancy, this argument made it legitimate to abandon the search for explanations of why most working classes in the West (Germany being the single prominent exception) "failed" to achieve the revolutionary class awareness orthodox Marxism had expected (even demanded) of them.[38] Instead,

37. It hardly needs pointing out that this tyranny has had consequences as brutal as those engendered by capitalist production. The model of class formation orthodox Marxists have used to explain labor movement reformism derives directly from Lenin's contrast between "revolutionary" and "trade-union" consciousness. The most useful property of this and other accounts of false consciousness is that they justify trampling on the expressed wishes of those whose interests they purport to identify. See V. I. Lenin, *What Is to Be Done?* (New York: International Publishers, 1969); John Foster, *Class Struggle and the Industrial Revolution* (London: Weidenfield and Nicolson, 1974); E. P. Thompson, *The Poverty of Theory and Other Essays* (London: Merlin Press, 1978).

38. For a sensitive discussion of this issue, see Aristide Zolberg, "How Many Exceptionalisms?" pp. 397–455, in Katznelson and Zolberg, eds., *Working-Class Formation*. Two studies which explicitly made this point with regard to France were Edward Shorter and Charles Tilly, *Strikes in France, 1830–1968* (Cambridge: Cambridge University Press, 1974), and Bernard Moss, *Origins of the*

social historians followed Thompson in exploring, even celebrating, the rich diversity of the working-class experience in nineteenth-century Europe, confident that the varying types of collective action they were uncovering all merited inclusion within the rubric of "class struggle." If militancy and the rhetoric surrounding it could take a seemingly endless variety of forms, this did not mean that the working class had strayed from the path laid out for it by the march of history. On the contrary, Thompson's culturalist view of class authorized seeing this variety as evidence of workers' creative potential in defining and responding to the experience of industrialization.

Ironically, however, this revolution in social history eventually succeeded in subjecting the protagonists of nineteenth-century upheavals to a new tyranny, albeit a more backhanded one. No matter what they said or did, it seemed, artisanal laborers, factory workers, and domestic outworkers somehow contributed to the class struggle. Broadside ballads, friendly societies, absenteeism, even forms of recreation and styles of speech or dress that made the bourgeoisie uneasy—all manner of words and deeds could now be labeled as protest and registered as weapons in the fight against industrial capitalism. Simply by virtue of earning a wage, the subjects of social history have repeatedly been impressed into service by their chroniclers. Until recently, therefore, it appeared that the true interests of the working class were still determined largely by the relations of production, if not by modern researchers; workers merely had a little more latitude in their choice of responses.

The years since 1980 have witnessed a second emancipation of sorts. Scholars in a variety of disciplines have begun to focus on the multitude of ways in which alternative dimensions of identity contributed to or competed with class in limiting, encouraging, or shaping social protest. Ira Katznelson's study of American cities showed that the separation of home and work made room for cross-class political organizations based on patronage and ethnicity even as workers were mobilized for explicitly class-conscious (if reformist) activity at the factory.[39] Gareth Stedman Jones attacked Marxist interpretations of Chartism by disclosing its roots in the English radicalism of the eighteenth century.[40] Joan

French Labor Movement: The Socialism of Skilled Workers (Berkeley: University of California Press, 1976).

39. Ira Katznelson, *City Trenches: Urban Politics and the Patterning of Class in the United States* (New York: Pantheon, 1981).

40. Gareth Stedman Jones, "Rethinking Chartism," in Jones, *Languages of Class*, pp. 90–178.

Scott and Louise Tilly, among others, have forcefully argued that gender relations and visions of the family profoundly complicated the impact of industrialization on nineteenth-century French laborers, sometimes allying female with male wage-earners and at other times highlighting the divergent interests of women and men.[41] Patrick Joyce suggests that, in England, the categories of "people" and "nation" were lively competitors with class throughout the nineteenth century and into the twentieth.[42]

Historians and sociologists have, generally speaking, drawn two lessons from these challenges to the story of class formation (although it bears mentioning that the two lessons are occasionally conflated). The first lesson is a corollary of the chief insight of the "new social history." Researchers of the 1960s and 1970s demonstrated that protest that did not take the form of proletarian revolution could nevertheless be reasonably interpreted as class-based; the new generation of scholarship acknowledges that such protest *can* be "about" class but insists that this is not *necessarily* the case. If the protagonists of social history could choose how to construe the experience of class formation, they could also choose not to construe industrialization in class terms at all. As fruitful as it may have been to relax the definition of class so as to accommodate the real world of the early industrial era, it is important to recognize that the concept loses all its analytical bite if stretched to encompass everything we can observe about the lives of ordinary folk. If class was a "happening," to use Thompson's term, it was by no means the only one.

The second lesson is a metatheoretical inference based on the first one— though not everyone responsible for the first has embraced the second.[43] If the diversity of responses to social change can be attributed to the creative potential of human agency and if this agency occurs principally through the construction

41. Louise A. Tilly, "Women's Collective Action and Feminism in France, 1870–1914," pp. 207–31, in Louise and Charles Tilly, eds., *Class Conflict and Collective Action* (Beverly Hills: Sage, 1981); Louise A. Tilly and Joan W. Scott, *Women, Work, and Family* (New York: Holt, Rinehart, and Winston, 1978); Joan W. Scott, "On Language, Gender, and Working-Class History," *International Labor and Working-Class History*, no. 31 (Spring 1987), pp. 1–13; idem., *Gender and the Politics of History* (New York: Columbia University Press, 1987).

42. Patrick Joyce, *Visions of the People: Industrial England and the Question of Class, 1848–1914* (Cambridge: Cambridge University Press, 1991).

43. Of those who have pointedly declined to go this second step, I would call attention above all to Ira Katznelson and Charles Tilly. See Katznelson, "Working-Class Formation: Constructing Cases and Comparisons"; Charles Tilly, *The Contentious French* (Cambridge, MA: Harvard University Press, 1986).

of representations (of work, gender, the market, the household), then—so the reasoning goes—social scientists may comfortably renounce the search for structural explanations of the phenomena they study. Variation in outcomes, many researchers have concluded, is far more sensibly explained in terms of cultural innovation than in terms of material factors like capital concentration, patterns of landownership, and control over hiring practices. Because any such structural features of the social world are invariably mediated by discursive and interpretive practices, it is the latter which merit analytical attention. Indeed, the most radical version of the culturalist view denies even that the former exist independently of human acts of interpretation: "'Language,'" writes Joan Scott, "not only enables social practice; it *is* social practice."[44]

It should be clear that the approach adopted here takes the first of these two lessons quite seriously. Indeed, the possibility of multiple dimensions of identity is the basis for the comparison between 1848 and 1871 that forms the crux of this book: unless one recognizes in advance that these two revolutionary upheavals could in principle have been based on fundamentally different participation identities, the contrast can yield only minimal theoretical insight. (Recall the objection I raised to Harvey's structural-Marxist account of the Commune.) But it should be equally evident, given the model of collective identities outlined in the previous section, that I do not accept the second point (see especially pages 17–18, in addition to my comments on Castells). It is, of course, the case that capitalist production, labor markets, work-discipline, and social ties, like anything else, do not affect social life without first being interpreted, often in creative or imaginative ways, by historical agents. But it surely does not follow from this that what is being interpreted has no systematic effect on the behavior of these agents or that the cultural schemata they use reveal most of what one needs to know to make sense of this behavior. To draw such a conclusion would be as misguided as trying to understand visual perception without bothering to learn about light or its interaction with physical objects. The fact that scholarly observers must (like everyone else) avail themselves of some conceptual framework to

44. Joan Scott, "A Reply to Criticism," *International Labor and Working-Class History*, no. 32 (Fall 1987), p. 40 (emphasis in original). When pressed, Scott takes pains to emphasize that her notions of "language" and "discourse" include much more than speech and text: "By discourse I do not mean utterances, or 'words' . . . but whole ways of thinking, of understanding how the world operates and what one's place is in it. And not only ways of thinking, but ways of organizing lives, institutions, societies, ways of implementing and justifying inequalities, but also of refusing them." With such an inclusive notion, Scott is surely right that "language is social practice." But this inclusiveness also makes the point thoroughly banal.

discuss the phenomena they study changes nothing: even with multiple herme-neutic levels, the world is not, as the philosophers are fond of saying, interpreta-tion "all the way down."

What does this epistemological commitment mean for the present work? It means, primarily, that deciding what kind of participation identity is central to any given instance of mobilization depends both on the group boundaries people explicitly invoke in their calls for action *and* on the observable characteristics of the individuals who end up acting. The fact that most of the participants in an insurrection can be identified as workers does not necessarily mean that "worker" was the key identity framing their actions. Conversely, frequent calls for solidarity among workers do not by themselves warrant the conclusion that mobilization is based on class: we need to know whether substantial numbers of workers responded to those appeals. Needless to say, within the conceptual framework I have set forth, the same considerations apply for identities based on gender, ethnicity, race, region, or anything else.[45]

My argument in this book can thus be restated as follows. In 1848, insurgents in Paris responded to a participation identity based on class. The vast majority of them were wage-earners, and this fact was central to participation in the revo-lution: they justified their actions, both to themselves and to others, using a con-ceptual framework that explicitly tied their grievances and demands to their sta-tus as exploited workers in a social system understood as capitalist. The June insurrection was a revolt against the French Provisional Government and Con-stituent Assembly, but only because the latter were accused of trampling on the right to work and were consequently standing in the way of the emancipation of the working class.

The participation identity that drew people into the insurgent movement in 1871 was, on the other hand, the urban community (as the name "Commune" itself makes clear).[46] This does not mean principally that the issue of municipal

45. Note that these are statements about the conceptual framework, not about things in the world. I am not suggesting that purely subjective (or purely objective) notions of class or gender are wrong, only that they will not be very useful in explaining the differences between various instances of mobilization.

46. *Commune* in French means "community," "town," and "commune." Ever since the revolu-tion, it also referred to the radical democratic body that governed Paris during the Jacobin period of 1789–92. This multiplicity of interpretations was crucial for the emergence of the Commune as a rallying cry for dissent in Paris during the Franco-Prussian War of 1870–71, and for the factionaliza-tion among Blanquists, Jacobin republicans, and Proudhonian socialists that partly paralyzed the revolutionary government in the capital between March and May 1871.

independence vis-à-vis a centralized state was the dominant theme underlying the events of that year (even though that may have been the case, given some reasonable account of what the notion of a "dominant theme" refers to); what it means is that, when massive numbers of Parisians joined insurgent National Guard battalions and risked their lives on barricades, they did so for specific reasons that had much more to do with their self-conception as inhabitants of a city than with their self-conception as workers.

In contrast to purely culturalist or structuralist accounts, then, an argument about participation identities focuses simultaneously on the discursive behavior of activists and on patterns of mobilization. The ecological distribution of insurgency, the particular tactics chosen, the social characteristics of participants, and the terms in which calls to action are couched are all relevant to deciding what sort of collective identity was central to an instance of protest. Moreover, because the theory sketched in the previous section includes propositions about the impact of social networks on collective identities, the research presented in later chapters also examines observable patterns of social interaction both prior to and during protest. The question I aim to answer, in other words, is not, "What were the differences between the discursive practices that characterized these two revolutions?" nor is it, "What structural and material changes led to the behavioral differences between the two revolutions?" The question is, "What structural and material changes led to the differences between the two events in the way discursive practices influenced insurgent behavior?" What had happened to social life in Paris prior to 1871 that made the class identity that had been so powerful in the Revolution of 1848 so secondary during the Commune?

In the remainder of this work, I will investigate the roots of protest in Paris between 1848 and 1871 in an effort to demonstrate and explain the dramatic differences between the insurrections that began and ended this period. Rather than presuppose either the reducibility or the primacy of "urban consciousness," I shall show that the patterns of behavior that distinguished the two uprisings cannot be understood without recognizing the relative salience of class as a participation identity in 1848, and of the urban community in 1871. I shall trace this difference to the fact that the massive rebuilding of the capital rearranged networks of social relations within the working population—not, as many have argued, by segregating workers from the bourgeoisie and thereby forging a universal class identity but by integrating some workers into strongly residential neighborhoods while leaving others firmly tied to their craft enclaves and the world of work. The paradox of the Commune was this: it was the former group that predominated in the ranks of the insurrection, while the latter—those who, because of their corporate traditions, had long been the stalwarts of artisanal activism—remained, relatively speaking, on the sidelines.

✦ Methodological Remarks ✦

The next five chapters are arranged more or less chronologically. Chapter 2 examines the French Revolution of 1848, demonstrating the centrality of class and pointing to its connection with the organizations and institutions within which workers were mobilized politically. Chapter 3 details the profound changes in the physical and social character of Paris between 1848 and 1870, and chapters 4 and 5 relate these changes to developments in the nature of social protest in the capital during that period. In particular, chapter 4 shows that industrial collective action depended on the clustering of certain craft groups in the center of Paris, whereas chapter 5 reveals that public meetings became a form of protest principally in the residential neighborhoods of the periphery. Finally, chapter 6 describes the tragic events of 1871, showing that the Commune relied on neighborhood rather than class as the central collective identity and network basis for mobilization.

In addition to the order in which chapters appear, the events and developments outlined within each chapter are frequently presented in narrative form. I want to make it absolutely clear at the outset, however, that these narratives play no analytical role in the book's theoretical argument.[47] Events are discussed in chronological order for purely expository purposes. The analytical constructs used to make sense of the empirical context of nineteenth-century French insurgency come from the theoretical model presented in the present chapter, not from a model of social process based on the notion of "emplotment." Indeed, one of the points I am trying to make in this work is that a focus on relatively durable patterns of social ties, albeit in interaction with such short-term events as war or state collapse, does a better job of accounting for differences between 1848 and the Commune than does the conceptual framework of class formation—a framework that is founded on the use of narrative as an explanatory device. I do not

---

47. Increasing numbers of social scientists argue that narrative is an essential analytical tool rather than a mere means of telling stories. See, for example, Andrew Abbott, "Conceptions of Time and Events in Social Science Methods: Causal and Narrative Approaches," *Historical Methods* 23 (1990): 140–50; George Steinmetz, "Reflections on the Role of Social Narratives in Working-Class Formation: Narrative Theory in the Social Sciences," *Social Science History* 16 (1992): 489–516; Margaret R. Somers, "Narrativity, Narrative Identity, and Social Action: Rethinking English Working-Class Formation," *Social Science History* 16 (1992): 591–630.

mean to suggest that narrative is not in general a useful form of social science research, only that the primary example of the narrative approach in this particular substantive area falls short in key respects.

A second methodological point concerns the use of evidence. Many of the claims made in this book take the form of general assertions meant to summarize the behavior of large numbers of people. One example is the assertion that labor protest was more likely when practitioners of a specific trade lived near each other and socialized together after work. Such assertions are intrinsically about quantities, in that they refer to such phenomena as levels of residential clustering and the relative preponderance of coworkers in individuals' sets of friends. Other claims concern the general tendencies of certain classes of protest to either reinforce or depend on one or another collective identity—for instance, the argument that public meetings from 1868 to 1870 lent credibility to the collective identity of urban neighborhoods as significant political actors opposing the state. Even when the data supporting this sort of assertion are discursive, the nature of their support for the assertions is still in one sense quantitative: according to the definitional conditions I have laid out, protest is not taken to be dominated by the collective identity of class unless participants mention class solidarity *relatively often* in their comments, pronouncements, and exhortations. (Note that this condition is necessary but not sufficient.) Independent of whether such a criterion is analytically useful is the question of whether the available evidence warrants the conclusion that it has been met; and it is therefore worthwhile to state in advance what my procedures for deciding this sort of question are.

Where possible and appropriate, I have endeavored to collect information on a large scale regarding the backgrounds and actions of Parisians in general and participants in protest in particular. Aggregate levels of mobilization, the occupational and geographical distribution of arrestees, and overall patterns of informal association (as reflected in marriage registers) are used as evidence because they reflect broad patterns in the social lives and behavior of nineteenth-century Parisians—and because my theoretical approach regards particular collective identities as significant for protest only if they succeed in guiding the behavior of many people. This approach to evidence grants a privileged status to quantities (total arrests, class composition of neighborhoods, and so on), but for a reason: in the framework I have set out here, mass mobilization is *by definition* a process involving large numbers of individuals, and meaningful statements about it must therefore refer at least some of the time to the numbers of individuals involved.

I shall not, however, present overtly quantitative evidence regarding the degree to which appeals to the distinct collective identities of class and neighborhood predominated in pamphlets, posters, speeches, and other verbal media. Instead, I shall present documents I take to be typical of the kinds of appeals many participants in public debates made, on the basis of a thorough reading of the available sources. My implicit contention is that other knowledgeable and reasonable scholars examining the same sources would conclude that these selections and my interpretations of them are not idiosyncratic. Given the argument made in this book, it would not be terribly useful to go further and present a systematic accounting of the locutions used in public discourse in 1848, 1871, and the intervening years, even if such an enterprise were practical. The reason is that appeals based on a specific collective identity need not numerically swamp other sorts of appeals to be regarded as significant for mobilization: what is necessary is that they be sufficiently widespread to make plausible the claim that large numbers of people might have responded to them. (Whether many people *did* respond is decided with reference to evidence about mobilization levels.) I have already indicated that it is important to be aware of the multiplicity of interpretations—and, more specifically, of appeals to collective identities— that political activists of various stripes offer during moments of political opportunity. The implication of this awareness is that one should not expect to decide what protest is about by looking for unanimity in the way would-be leaders characterize it; more is to be gained by investigating the relative effectiveness of *diverse* characterizations in promoting collective action.

Class Mobilization and the Revolution of 1848

FRANCE HAD no shortage of professional revolutionaries in the 1800s, but they tended to capitalize on, rather than initiate, the nation's most significant insurgent moments. The career of Auguste Blanqui, the inveterate militant whose many stints in prison earned him the title *"l'enfermé"* ("the locked-up one"), is probably the most eloquent expression of this pattern: having failed to pull off a coup d'état in 1839, Blanqui was imprisoned until 1848, when he returned to Paris just in time to play a prominent role in the first weeks of the February Revolution. Arrested again in May, he missed the massive uprising of June and emerged from prison in 1859, only to be locked up once more from 1861 until he escaped to Brussels in 1865. He was similarly to miss the events of 1871: following another abortive coup attempt in Paris in October 1870, he was arrested in the provinces in March 1871—one day before the March 18 uprising in the capital led to the proclamation of the Paris Commune.

Other militants in Paris were scarcely better prepared for the Revolution of 1848 than was Blanqui. To be sure, radical groups abounded in Paris at the time, including Etienne Cabet's loosely knit Icarian socialist followers, a shadowy collection of republican secret societies, and the organizers of outdoor banquets at which thousands of Parisians listened to prominent radicals and reformists delivering lengthy "toasts" concerning political and social questions. But none of these groups, nor their popular leaders, intended to bring about a revolution in February 1848. When King Louis-Philippe abdicated the throne and fled France in disguise on the morning of February 24, it was presumed by many that his grandson would ascend the throne, with the young prince's mother, the Duchesse d'Orléans, serving as regent. It was not until late in the evening that crowds surrounding the Hôtel de Ville, the traditional site of revolutions in France, were able to pressure the leaders of the moment into proclaiming the

Republic.[1] Even then, there was no agreement either in the streets or among political figures as to what kind of revolution had just taken place.

But over the next four months, workers in Paris settled with increasing confidence on a singular and genuinely novel interpretation of the events in which they were participating: the Revolution of 1848 was to be *their* revolution, to be protected from the clutches of the bourgeois traitors who, with Louis-Philippe in the lead, had appropriated the July Revolution of 1830 for themselves. And because the extension of political representation was thus synonymous with the enfranchisement of workers, political revolution would inevitably bring social revolution in its train. The force of this conviction—or, conversely, of the disillusionment that resulted when the hopes on which it rested were shattered by the Provisional Government—was to be measured by the unprecedented scale and violence of the uprising of June.

My purpose in this chapter is to provide some insight into the reasons why the initial confusion about the meaning of February 24 soon crystallized—for a sizable number of people, at least—into a vision of revolution by and for the workers. In pursuing this objective, I intend not so much to present an original interpretation as to highlight elements of the 1848 revolution that are significant for a comparison with 1871, namely, the degree to which the various issues of craft, class, the urban community, and the state were salient in the words and actions of participants. An overriding factor in the emergence of class as a core mobilization identity, I shall argue, was the expansion of the suffrage from a narrow, propertied electoral base to include nearly all adult men—an overnight transformation that defined the laboring poor as occupying a common status with respect to the emerging republic. The proper means of exercising this new status, moreover, was debated and hammered out in the tumultuous setting of neighborhood clubs and workers' associations. In Paris, where the most active workers' societies held their nightly meetings in the heart of the city's traditional industrial sections, the heady world of electoral politics rapidly became welded to the world of work.

A second central factor this chapter will highlight is an aspect of the events

1. It was one of the peculiarities of the revolutionary tradition, dating from the original French Revolution of 1789, that new governments were formed at the Hôtel de Ville. Even when the point of political contention was an institution of national government, for instance the Chambre des Députés, the revolutionary repertoire called for the crowd's relocation to the seat of municipal government to proclaim a new regime. This ritual reflected above all the overwhelmingly central role the city of Paris played in French national politics. See Charles Tilly, *The Contentious French.*

of 1848 that scholars have more frequently neglected. Even more than the clubs, which frequently mixed fraternal, classless views of the world with progressive social demands, the formation of the National Workshops and of the Luxembourg Commission created two new institutional settings within which the laboring poor of Paris could perceive themselves and each other for the first time as *workers* pure and simple—not as plain citizens nor as shoemakers, stonemasons, or tailors, but as manual laborers.[2] This fact, together with the explicit and official linkage of the Workshops with the government's guarantee of the right to work, left little room for Parisians to see the institution's abolition in June as anything but an attack on the working class as a whole. It was the shared organizational experience of participation in the Luxembourg Commission and the National Workshops, just as much as their symbolic significance, that made the June insurrection into a class war.[3]

The February Revolution

It is difficult to overstate the euphoria that engulfed the people of Paris when they discovered, on the morning of February 25, that they had toppled the July Monarchy. What had begun earlier that week as a protest against the cancellation of a banquet had quickly become a movement to force the dismissal of the hated Prime Minister, Guizot; but a brief outbreak of violence in which fifty protesters were killed, hastily followed by the ouster of Guizot, only fueled the angry ambitions of the crowds in the streets, and as the barricades went up, the eighteen-year-old Orléanist regime unraveled overnight. After the Republic was proclaimed from the balcony of the Hôtel de Ville, late in the evening of February 24, it would have been hard to persuade anyone in the cheering crowd that any limits remained to the prospects for human happiness. Placards posted throughout the city the next day, like this one printed by the editors of the Fourierist

2. I do not intend to suggest here that historians have ignored the National Workshops as such (which would be ludicrous) but, rather, that their role as a setting within which trade boundaries were overcome has not received attention.

3. Mark Traugott, in his comparison of the June insurgents and the personnel of the Mobile Guard, the central force behind the repression of the uprising, similarly points to the role of organizations as determinants of political behavior. However, he focuses on the differences in the way material grievances were addressed by the administrative authorities for the two organizations, arguing that unanswered demands in the National Workshops led to the radicalization of its personnel. In contrast, I am interested in the reasons why, given this radicalization, the conflict was understood in class terms. The implications of Traugott's study for my argument are discussed toward the end of this chapter. See Mark Traugott, *Armies of the Poor: Determinants of Working-Class Participation in the Parisian Insurrection of June 1848* (Princeton: Princeton University Press, 1985).

newspaper *La démocratie pacifique,* joyously welcomed the new political order and the worldwide transformations it would bring:

Long Live the Republic!

The Republic of 1792 destroyed the old order.
The Republic of 1848 must constitute the new order.

General amnesty.—Break with the past.—Abolition of the death penalty.

National sovereignty through universal suffrage. Freedom of speech, freedom of the press, freedom of petition, freedom of election, freedom of association.

Property respected.—The right to work guaranteed. Labor organized and liberally compensated. Fraternal union between employers and laborers . . .

The clergy democratized.—Election of Bishops by the priests.

Abolition of war. Independence for all nationalities.—Holy Alliance and confederation of peoples.

Peace and happiness on earth. Order based on liberty. All questions of order and justice resolved through free association. No more constraint, no more force, no more violence. Government by persuasion and by love.[4]

Amidst this mood of wild optimism, however, public interpretations of the event displayed a sense of urgency, a suspicion that "the people" needed to make a passionate and concerted effort to safeguard the republic. The radical workers' newspaper, *L'atelier,* warned its readers, "They must not conjure away [*escamoter*] the Revolution of 1848, the way they conjured away the Revolution of 1830." This phrase was frequently repeated over the next four months—though with some notable transformations in the way the word "they" (along with its implicit complement, "we") was understood.

Interpretations of the February Revolution, and the calls for action based on these interpretations, were thus colored from the very beginning by the perception of the July Revolution of 1830, the three-day upheaval that had definitively swept away the Bourbon dynasty, as having been derailed from its republican trajectory by Louis-Philippe and his monarchist allies. Much of the basis for this perception had been formed, moreover, in the pages of the workers' press in the

4. Reproduced in Alfred Delvau, ed., *Les murailles révolutionnaires de 1848,* 2 vols. (Paris: E. Picard, 1868), vol. 1, p. 32.

months immediately following the July Revolution. Given the public praise workers had received for their prominent role in the overthrow of the reactionary Bour-
bons, whose avowed goal had been to eradicate all traces of the Revolution of
1789 and of Napoleonic rule, the decidedly elitist character of the new regime
came as a particularly bitter shock. The powers of the legislative assembly were
expanded, and the new electoral law lowered the property tax qualification for
voter eligibility, but even so the enlarged electorate comprised only 167,000 voters in a country of 35 million. At roughly the same time, the new government
made it abundantly clear that the principles of liberal political economy were
going to be taken very seriously—which meant that working-class collective action would be severely restricted on the grounds that it would interfere with individual liberties. Harsh repression of strikes and the quick passage of laws limiting the freedom of association left no uncertainty about the rigid stance the July
Monarchy intended to adopt toward laborers' demands.

The consequence, of course, was that French workers felt betrayed by the
propertied classes on the political and the social fronts simultaneously. What this
implied was that republican demands for the enfranchisement of "the people"
were now linked to calls for social reform on behalf of workers, because the
boundary that differentiated between voters and nonvoters was barely distinguishable from that which separated employers from wage-laborers. Thus Auguste Colin, a Parisian printing worker, wrote in a pamphlet entitled *Le cri du
peuple* that capitalists had replaced the nobility as the dominant class, leaving
only wage-earners to defend the principles of the revolution:

> Despotism, tyranny, and arbitrary rule . . . had begun to emerge from
> the shadows, when suddenly the enlightened, heroic population of
> the capital of the civilized world rose up in indignation. Vengeance
> was in our hearts and on our lips, and in three days nothing remained
> but the memory of everything that had for so long been used to forge
> our chains. Such was the magical effect of the cry, LIBERTY.
>
> . . . The people reasonably expected that those in whom they had
> placed their confidence would realize the hopes that had led them to
> conceive the miracle that the cry of LIBERTY had produced.
>
> Wrong! The people accomplished all, and nothing will be done
> for it. Those whom we had for so long believed to be our defenders
> have deceived us; they made common cause with us only so long as
> they suffered from the same proscription that we bear. . .Because

they mixed their appeals with ours, we thought them our friends! What fools we were! We lived without ambition, we wanted nothing but contentment through our work, and we imagined ourselves the subject of the solicitude of these rich capitalists and grand entrepreneurs made wealthy by our arms. But it was not we who occupied their thoughts, it was the product of our labor; and if they could procure it without our help we would become as worthy of their disregard as we were for the "men of parchment" [i.e., the nobility]. We threw off the yoke of the aristocrats of nobility, only to fall under the domination of the aristocracy of finance.[5]

It was also in the aftermath of the 1830 revolution that bourgeois republicans began to include in their political programs what became known as "the social question," and workers began to flock to republicanism in small but significant numbers. This latter shift in particular was clearest in Paris, though similar patterns have been observed for other French cities: in 1834, according to police records examined by Alain Faure, two-thirds of the Paris chapter of the militant republican Society of the Rights of Man (Société des Droits de l'Homme) were workers.[6]

But while political events furnished the impetus for the emerging awareness among workers of "the working class" (*la classe ouvrière*) as a collective actor with joint interests, these same events dictated that the institutional framework for concrete working-class militancy would follow craft divisions. In the absence of state-sponsored social reforms and in the face of the first impulses toward modern capitalist production, French workers learned on their own, through small-scale, local struggles, to build the organizations that formed the basis for the labor movement throughout most of the century. Militant workers, many of them influenced by the ideas of Saint-Simon and Fourier (and, in the 1840s, by the writings of Pierre-Joseph Proudhon, Louis Blanc, and Etienne Cabet), wrote

5. Auguste Colin, *Le cri du peuple* (Paris: Imprimerie de Démonville, 1831). Reprinted in *Les révolutions du XIXe siècle*. Vol. 4, *Naissance du mouvement ouvrier, 1830–1834*, 12 vols. (Paris: EDHIS, 1974).

6. Alain Faure, "Mouvements populaires et mouvement ouvrier à Paris, 1830–1834," *Le mouvement social*, no. 88 (July–September 1974), pp. 51–92. For evidence concerning other cities, see Yves Lequin, *Les ouvriers de la région lyonnaise, 1848–1914* (Lyon: Presses Universitaires de Lyon, 1977), 2 vols.; Ronald A. Aminzade, *Class, Politics, and Early Industrial Capitalism: A Study of Mid-Nineteenth-Century Toulouse* (Albany: State University of New York Press, 1981); John Merriman, *The Red City: Limoges and the French Nineteenth Century* (New York: Oxford University Press, 1985).

pamphlets and founded newspapers dedicated to the articulation of a cooperative socialist vision of society—a vision in which producers' cooperatives would compete with and gradually supplant capitalist employers, and in which political matters would be directed by a federation of independent trade associations. Simultaneously, the strike waves of 1830–33 spurred workers in numerous trades all over France to form "resistance societies," temporary strike committees which often evolved into permanent mutual-aid associations (sociétés de secours mutuels).[7] Like their old-regime counterparts, such societies provided their members with sick benefits, funeral costs, and occasionally pensions for widows; and, like the confraternities of the eighteenth century, they organized along craft lines. In short, both the utopian and the practical sides of labor militancy under the July Monarchy regarded the craft group as the basic unit of struggle and progress.[8]

The conceptual innovation that the July Revolution of 1830 provoked—a view of wage-earners as a collectivity with a common interest vis-à-vis property-owners—consequently remained quite distant from the lived experience of labor protest for all but a tiny group of radical working-class autodidacts. So long as there was no republic, the link forged between republicanism and workers' demands had few implications for the concrete practices and organizational entities of the labor movement. However real this early version of working-class consciousness may have been for the militants of the Society of the Rights of Man, it maintained a largely abstract existence throughout the eighteen years of the July Monarchy.

Hence the combination of euphoria and unease in the streets of Paris in February 1848. The proclamation of the Republic was now synonymous with the enfranchisement of working people; and this fact, combined with the crushing consequences of a fifteen-month-old recession, meant that the new government

7. Indeed, the authors of these publications and strike militants were often the same people. In Paris, for instance, the tailor Grignon wrote a number of pamphlets on association while organizing a massive two-month tailors' strike in 1833. He was also a prominent member of the Paris chapter of the Society of the Rights of Man, and helped found several mutual-aid societies. See his Réflexions d'un ouvrier tailleur sur la misère des ouvriers en général, la durée des journées de travail, le taux des salaires, les rapports actuellement établis entre les ouvriers et les maîtres d'ateliers, la nécessité des associations d'ouvriers comme moyen d'améliorer leur condition, reprinted in Naissance du mouvement ouvrier, 1830–1834.

8. For an extensive treatment of the ideology of this emerging movement, see Sewell, Work and Revolution in France. Detailed studies of industrial conflict in the same period include Jean-Pierre Aguet, Les grèves sous la monarchie de juillet: Contribution à l'étude du mouvement ouvrier français (Geneva: Droz, 1954); and Alain Faure, "Mouvements populaires et mouvement ouvrier à Paris."

would have no choice but to develop a serious political approach to the social question. At the same time, hardly anyone in the working population had a clear sense of what ought to be done with this opportunity. The concrete proposals concerning labor that emerged in the first days of the Provisional Government, and their organizational consequences, accordingly took on an unprecedented level of significance in the ensuing months.

Chief among these proposals (not in concreteness but in scope) was the demand that the government acknowledge the existence of a remarkable new right: the right to work. At approximately noon on February 25, a group of Parisian workers forced their way into the room in the Hôtel de Ville where the members of the Provisional Government were deliberating. One of them, a young machinist named Marche, read aloud a message from several editors of *La démocratie pacifique* that, following their usual breathless pattern, demanded

Organization of labor, the right to work guaranteed.
Minimum living standard assured to workers and their families in case of sickness; relief from misery for workers deprived of employment, by means chosen by the sovereign nation.[9]

Although only two of the Provisional Government's eleven members, Louis Blanc and the worker known as Albert, were sympathetic to the demand, the cheers of support from the milling crowd contained undertones sufficiently menacing to force its acceptance. Before the workers' delegation withdrew, Blanc drafted a decree by which

The Government of the Republic commits itself to guarantee the existence of the worker by labor.

It commits itself to guarantee labor to all citizens;
It recognizes that workers should associate among themselves to enjoy the legitimate benefits of their labor.[10]

In two days, France had gone from a conservative constitutional monarchy to a republic dedicated to the "right to work"—a right made all the more powerful

9. Quoted in Rémi Gossez, *Les ouvriers de Paris. Bibliothèque de la Révolution de 1848*, vol. 24 (La Roche-sur-Yonne: Société de l'Histoire de la Révolution de 1848, 1967), p. 11.
10. *Murailles révolutionnaires*, vol. 1, p. 36.

by its complete novelty on the political scene.[11] The simultaneity of this decree with the announced extension of the franchise could only reinforce the popular perception, first articulated in the early 1830s, that constituting a republic entailed above all the recognition of both social and political rights for workers.

Three days later, the Minister of Public Works, Pierre Marie, announced the creation of "National Workshops" in the form of large-scale public works projects. In the official decree, Marie wrote, "Workers of Paris! You wish to live honorably through labor; be assured, all the efforts of the Provisional Government will be directed at helping you to accomplish this wish . . . Workers! After the victory [of February], labor is yet another shining example you have to offer the world, and you shall offer it."[12] Although Marie and the more conservative members of the Provisional Government saw the undertaking as a temporary measure designed both to relieve the economic crisis through public expenditure and to exert some control over the mass of unemployed,[13] Parisian workers and activists on the left interpreted the National Workshops as the tangible expression of the promise made in Louis Blanc's February 25 decree. Additional support for this interpretation came from the apparent connection to Louis Blanc's well-known socialist tract, *L'organisation du travail,* in which he had advocated the formation of "social workshops" (in essence, producers' associations) as a solution to the rampant exploitation and competition characterizing capitalist society.

The Workshops expressed the common destiny of laborers in a less rhetorical manner as well. Although the initial plan envisioned shops organized by trade, with seamstresses and tailors making uniforms for the National Guard, construction workers building bridges and highways, and so on, the lack of actual work meant that in practice Workshop members were thrown together in brigades regardless of occupation. Most of the assignments, when there were any, consisted of make-work excavation projects with no clear purpose and requiring no particular skill.[14] The organizational context of the government's attempt to deliver on

11. The editors of *La démocratie pacifique* had called for recognition of *le droit au travail* at least a year earlier; but at no point had this demand become the topic of serious public debate, either in Paris or elsewhere.

12. *Murailles révolutionnaires,* vol. 1, p. 151. Although the projects were officially national in scope, as the name suggests, it was only in Paris that the program went into effect on a significant scale. Not surprisingly, Paris was also the sole locus of insurrection when closure of the Workshops was announced in June.

13. See the report of Pierre Marie to the National Assembly: Assemblée Nationale, *Compte rendu des séances* (Paris: Imprimerie de l'Assemblée Nationale, 1849), vol. 1, p. 60.

14. Report of Ulysse Trélat, Ministre des travaux publics, to the National Assembly, *Compte rendu des séances,* vol. 1, p. 285.

its guarantee of work to all laborers, through no one's intention, temporarily cut across trade barriers for an enormous mass of Parisian workers.[15] Consequently, when the authorities closed the Workshops in June, they set off a conflict in which tens of thousands of Parisians saw their joint interest as deriving exclusively from their common status as laborers.

And it was not only wage-earners who saw the Workshops as a major commitment on the part of the state to the working class. The bourgeois press in Paris immediately pounced on the measure as the clearest sign that the revolution had gotten out of hand—which is to say, out of middle-class hands and into the control of pro-labor radicals. Moderates and conservatives alike voiced the fear that the enrollment of massive numbers of the unemployed would amount to the formation of a working-class army dedicated to rebellion and disorder. Their anxiety became all the more acute as official reports indicated that the number of workers enrolled (fifteen thousand in March, over one hundred thousand by mid-May) was growing far more rapidly than the number of available work assignments, though everyone continued to receive daily payments; in conservative eyes, the government was spending huge sums of money to encourage laziness, and it seemed likely to many that this would lead to unruliness. One article in the journal *L'Assemblée Nationale* claimed that the Workshops comprised "20,000 bandits, most of them escaped convicts . . . allied with 80,000 workers paid by the State to learn the art of revolt in the idleness of the wine-shop."[16]

This crystallization into class terms of debate over the National Workshops coincided with similar processes occurring in the administration of the National Guard, France's civilian militia force, and in the political arena. As a citizen army, the National Guard could not remain the elite bourgeois institution it had been under Louis-Philippe, and its rolls were therefore opened when the Republic was proclaimed. Service in the militia force was now demanded of all males between the ages of twenty-five and fifty, and arms and uniforms would now be provided by the state rather than paid for by individual guardsmen. Moreover, once enrollment lists were closed in early March, the newly formed Guard battal-

15. To be more precise, the mixing of workers from diverse trades was unintentional only with regard to actual work assignments. Emile Thomas, the young engineer who directed the Workshops until late May, made a point of assigning *idle* members to brigades in a way that minimized contact among workers of the same trade. His explicit goal in so doing was to forestall "coalitions among workers of the same profession, which could lead to serious or even dangerous difficulties." Emile Thomas, *Histoire des Ateliers Nationaux* (Paris: Michel Lévy, 1848), p. 53.

16. Quoted in André-Jean Tudesq, *Les grands notables en France (1840–1849)*, 2 vols. (Paris: Presses Universitaires de France, 1964), vol. 2, p. 1077.

ions were to proceed with democratic elections of their officers—with potentially radical consequences, given that the reorganization of the National Guard explicitly linked the issue of political enfranchisement with that of social equality.[17] Dozens of newly formed political clubs, many of them with explicitly socialist or pro-labor leanings, immediately set about the task of drawing up slates of candidates for both elections. In an announcement entitled "Appeal to the Workers" that appeared on walls and in numerous newspapers, the Club Républicain des Travailleurs-Libres (Republican Club of Free Laborers) declared that

> the clubs are the living barricades of Democracy . . . It is by means
> of the clubs, the second National Assembly, ever in session, always
> acting, that the new social order will be built . . . Laborers! As mem-
> bers of the sovereign, each one of you has a mission to fulfill, and
> you well know what it is. If you are not already active in this new
> crucible of opinion, come to us, and we will act in concert.[18]

The demand that workers should not merely choose their representatives but that the representatives themselves should come from the working class quickly emerged as a dominant theme in many club meetings. One of the leaders of the Club des Travailleurs Unis (Club of United Laborers), a chimney sweep named Moriot, published a broadside insisting that the catastrophe of 1830 would recur if workers failed to organize an electoral strategy:

> Workers, my brothers in labor, in probity and in poverty, let us unite!
> . . . We shall elect our own representatives, shunning those who were
> not on our side *before* the revolution, rejecting the timid, equivocal
> allegiance of the latecomers. We alone, soldiers of the barricades,
> we who feed the nation, we who are after all the true People, we alone
> can truly defend the rights and the liberty of the People. The workers
> of the Department of the Seine [i.e., the Paris region] must nominate
> as deputies twenty workers, chosen from their own ranks. The work-
> er's blouse must enter the National Assembly without shame or
> fear.[19]

With elections only weeks away, then, radical political activists attempted a discursive fusion of the working class with the People, upon whose sovereignty

17. See Peter Amann, *Revolution and Mass Democracy: The Paris Club Movement in 1848* (Princeton: Princeton University Press, 1975), pp. 81–88, for a detailed treatment of club debates concerning the National Guard.

18. *Le peuple souverain, journal des travailleurs,* March 26, 1848, p. 2.

19. *Murailles,* vol. 2, p. 468.

the Republic was based. Bourgeois leaders experienced in politics were too closely tied to the treachery of 1830 and the July Monarchy to merit the trust of the "true" people. In such a political climate, it is not surprising that workers who announced their candidacy for a National Guard post or a seat in the National Assembly routinely referred to their membership in the "laboring classes" as a critical asset. It was a hallmark of the brand of republican socialism developing during the revolution that a working-class background implicitly guaranteed one's devotion to the Republic:

> Citizens:
>
> Several comrades have been so kind as to nominate me to the rank of deputy battalion commander. The importance of this function led me at first to decline; but once they had pointed out to me that the purpose was to bestow an honor upon the class of laborers, I decided that it was my duty to accept . . .
>
> A simple worker, I have been a zealous National Guardsman, because I have always thought that it is in the ranks of the citizen militia that one could serve in the interests both of liberty and of order . . . A diligent worker and sincere patriot, I duly present myself for election by my comrades of the 4th battalion.
>
> Long Live the Republic!
>
> Etienne Bacon, typographer[20]

This invocation of social class in the context of a battalion election is especially noteworthy when it is recalled that National Guard units were organized residentially (a detail to which I shall return in chap. 6). Localistic appeals might have seemed much more appropriate, all the more so given that political clubs as well depended on a significant neighborhood clientele. Yet the distinctive nature of the moment, above all the dramatic entry into the political realm of a huge number of people whose principal shared trait was nonpossession of property, moved hundreds of activists to rely on a group identity that was simultaneously broader and more exclusive: broader, because it reached beyond the immediate boundaries of craft and neighborhood, and more exclusive, because it highlighted the division between property owners and the newly assertive "laboring classes." The formal organization of electoral politics produced a minimally inclusive col-

---

20. *Murailles,* vol. 1, p. 475.

lective identity that spanned trade boundaries but marked workers as politically distinct from other segments of "the people."

In sum, the sudden and sweeping enfranchisement of workers led to an upsurge in political activity construed not merely as the exercise of the will of the people but as collective action *by workers*. Both the National Assembly and the National Guard were seen as doubly bourgeois institutions in the sense that they had in the past provided representation for, and would very likely continue to be dominated by, property holders. Only concerted action in political clubs and workers' associations (the membership of the former very often overlapping with the latter) could forestall a repetition of 1830 and ensure a firm linkage between the twin goals of political and social transformation.[21]

At the same time, workers in Paris fully expected to undertake some of the task of remaking the social order on their own, through the creation of radically new institutions more suited than parliaments to resolving the question of the "organization of labor." One day after the general decree on the right to work, Louis Blanc—again supported by clamorous crowds filling the plaza outside the Hôtel de Ville—pressed the other members of the Provisional Government to create a Ministry of Labor. As a concession, he was granted a Government Commission for the Workers whose object was the formulation of a theoretical approach to "the organization of work"; but as a "standing committee . . . with the express and specific task of concerning itself with workers' problems," it would have no formal authority. Blanc himself would act as chairman, the omnipresent but wordless worker Albert was chosen for the position of vice-chairman, and the Luxembourg Palace, former site of the aristocratic Chamber of Peers, was designated as the commission's meeting place.

Despite its largely symbolic role, the Luxembourg Commission came to epitomize what the February Revolution was about for Parisian workers. Each trade in the capital was asked to appoint a delegate who would become a regular member of the commission, and a number of prominent socialist writers were invited to sit in on its meetings. Within a few days, the halls of the stately palace were flooded with delegations from trades all over the city, filing petitions, grand proposals for the reorganization of labor, and requests for the arbitration of disputes. The most immediate practical consequence was that the establishment of the Luxembourg Commission shielded the more conservative members of the government from working-class agitation on a daily basis by offering the crowds a sym-

21. For a more extensive discussion of the election issue, see Amann, *Revolution and Mass Democracy*, chaps. 3–5; Gossez, *Les ouvriers de Paris*, pp. 249–259.

pathetic forum on the other side of the Seine. Ultimately more important, however, was the fact that the creation of Blanc's commission gave workers the clear impression—enshrined in the very wording of the official decree—that, along with the vote, they had received recognition from the French Republic as a legitimate group with interests and problems of special importance to the nation. The *Journal des travailleurs*, a newspaper founded by the commission's worker-delegates, announced in its first issue that the revolution of February 24 was only the first step:

> After the last paving stone was replaced, fresh from the barricades and still red with our blood, one might have thought for a moment that the revolution was achieved. A few days later we realized that no revolution deserved the title until it had benefited those who had made it. In a word, February 24 was merely the political prologue to a grave drama whose conclusion would be the complete, radical emancipation of the producers.
>
> . . . Let us be more precise. We desire—we, the laborers, we who not only sacrifice our life for the defense of the rights of the nation but also suffer its most tyrannical, implacable, incessant miseries— we desire, we say, that nothing which we produce be taken from us, we want the proclamations of the RIGHT TO WORK to become a reality.
>
> We desire that our daughters no longer be condemned by hunger to sell their love for a bit of bread and dishonor . . .
>
> We desire that *association,* in all its forms, become the sole and unique flag that rallies all laborers.
>
> We desire that the *word* and the *idea of exploitation* of man by man be effaced from all governmental institutions.
>
> We desire that *solidarity* become a fact.[22]

In this and the dozens of other short-lived workers' journals that sprang up between February and June, the implications of the revolution's first few days were spelled out starkly and with deadly seriousness. The Luxembourg Commission, together with the extension of the franchise, lent political and organizational solidity for the first time to workers' conception of themselves as a single social class.

The clearest evidence of the novelty of this conception and the continuing reliance of collective action on preexisting patterns of social ties is the ease with which workers' activities and debates lapsed into the trade-bound patterns that

---

22. *Journal des travailleurs,* no. 1, June 4, 1848, p. 1. (Emphasis in original.)

had characterized industrial militancy under the July Monarchy. In the massive street demonstration of March 17, organized by Parisian clubs and workers' societies to show support for the Provisional Government and the Republic while calling for a postponement of elections, workers marched behind banners identifying their particular trade. Likewise, the flurry of organizational activity sparked by the creation of the Government Commission for the Workers focused on the formation of mutual-aid societies and producers' cooperatives whose membership, in keeping with tradition, respected occupational boundaries.[23] From the perspective of the theory spelled out in chapter 1, this behavior is unsurprising. Even as political events and formal organizations create new forms of interaction, preexisting social relations play a major part in mobilizing collective action—provided that the loyalties these ties engender have a content that is relevant to the political events in question. In 1848, the debate over the right to work necessarily highlighted the importance of workplace social ties, which were thus critical for mobilization. What Luxembourg and the Workshops did was to show workers that the same loyalties and the same demands were mobilizing people in all crafts at once.

If it was natural that the early efforts at organizing in March centered on the formation of trade-specific workers' associations and the election of trade delegates to the Luxembourg Commission, it might not seem obvious that mobilization around the upcoming elections should have followed the same lines. Yet this is just what happened: prompted in part by agitation like that of the Club des Travailleurs Unis, the worker-delegates to the Luxembourg Commission constituted themselves as a Central Committee of Workers of the Department of the Seine and called for the "corporations" comprising the workers in each trade to nominate one of their own as a candidate for the National Assembly, with the final selection to be made by the committee.[24] Only the intervention of Louis Blanc, who exercised considerable influence over the Luxembourg delegates, persuaded them that a strategy of representation by trade would produce division rather than unity. His March 28 speech to the delegates brought home the point that political action by workers must be *class* action:

23. This tradition linked the corporate worldview of the *ancien régime* to the continued relevance of the "corporate idiom" in the nineteenth century, as evidenced by the currency of terms like "corporation" and "corps d'état" to describe craft groups. Sewell, *Work and Revolution in France,* chaps. 2 and 8.

24. *Murailles,* vol. 1, pp. 361–63.

> You are up against a class that knows much better the workings of elections, and this class has understood perfectly well that, to ensure victory for its candidates, it must vote with the greatest possible unity . . . You must start from the principle that you are not here as forgers, joiners, tailors or machinists, you are here as men of the people, as brothers who wish to achieve the emancipation of the people.[25]

As Blanc saw, the craft group loomed large as the basis of solidarity in the minds of many militants, the result of years of activism in which the shop floor was the only venue for protest. Prior to the February Revolution, labor struggles depended on the work-based social ties of craft groups and on the minimally inclusive identities these groups implied. And while social relations within crafts continued to mobilize workers for the collective action of 1848, it was the creation of a set of entirely new organizational entities—the Luxembourg Commission, the popular republican clubs, a democratized National Guard, and the National Workshops—that enabled the workers of Paris to act collectively *across* crafts and with the perception that by doing so they were asserting their existence as a social class.

♦ The June Days ♦

If class consciousness emerged in the organizational crucible formed by the elections, the Luxembourg Commission, and the National Workshops, the closure of the latter in June provoked class war. When the National Assembly abolished the one official institution that had put into practice the Provisional Government's solemn promise of a guaranteed livelihood, working people in Paris abandoned hope of the "democratic and social republic" they had envisioned in February, and rose in insurrection.

This rupture between the middle class and the workers hardly came as a surprise, however. The election of April 23 had put in place a National Assembly with decidedly moderate leanings: only eighty of nine hundred places went to republicans of the left, and only one of the twenty worker-candidates nominated by the Central Committee of Workers of the Seine managed to win a seat. The implications of this disappointing outcome for the left were lost on no one, and conservatives in the National Assembly rapidly proceeded with a campaign to

---

25. Quoted in Gossez, *Les ouvriers de Paris,* p. 254.

roll back the social measures of February and March. On May 10, one week after its inauguration, the Assembly replaced the eleven-member Provisional Government with an Executive Commission purged of Louis Blanc and Albert. During the same session, Blanc's proposal on the floor of the Assembly to create a "Ministry of Labor and Progress" met with widespread derision and was voted down by an overwhelming majority.[26]

The principal target for the forces of reaction was, however, the increasingly disquieting and expensive National Workshops, whose ranks were now swollen to 115,000. Plans to close the rolls and to begin transferring younger male members into the army had already been formulated when, on May 15, demonstrators who had assembled for the Fête de la Concorde—initially a show of support for the republican movement in Poland—set off an attempted coup d'état by deviating from their planned path, bursting into the National Assembly, and briefly seizing control of the session.[27] The fact that an estimated 14,000 members of the National Workshops had participated in the morning's demonstration reinforced conservative views that the continued presence of work brigades in Paris posed a serious threat to order—even though the vast majority of those enrolled were still largely loyal to the regime and had taken no part in the day's activities.[28] From that day onward, the fate of the Workshops was sealed, and efforts to speed their abolition only radicalized those in the rank and file who had previously supported the government. In late May and early June, police officers in the capital reported that sizable groups of workers were assembling in the streets in the evening, debating politics, shouting revolutionary slogans, and expressing their general dissatisfaction with the turn of events.[29] The Assembly reacted by pass-

26. *Compte rendu des séances,* May 10, 1848, vol. 1, p. 112.

27. It was at this point that Auguste Blanqui and several other leftist leaders attempted to take power, leading the crowd to the Hôtel de Ville to proclaim yet another revolutionary government. A number of them, including the veteran radicals Armand Barbès and François Raspail, were promptly arrested by loyal National Guard battalions under the command of the republicans Lamartine and Ledru-Rollin; Blanqui slipped away unnoticed but was arrested a few days later.

28. Donald McKay, *The National Workshops: A Study in the French Revolution of 1848* (Cambridge, MA: Harvard University Press, 1933), pp. 70–73; Traugott, *Armies of the Poor,* pp. 26–27.

29. Maurice Agulhon, *1848, ou l'apprentissage de la république, 1848–1852* (Paris: Editions du Seuil, 1973), p. 67. In some cases, to the consternation of many, workers in the streets shouted, "Vive Bonaparte!" They were referring to Louis Napoleon Bonaparte, the expatriate nephew of the first Emperor of the French who, after attempting unsuccessfully to overthrow Louis-Philippe, was now back in Paris to try his hand at republican politics. Bonapartist sentiment throughout France reflected the fairly widespread conviction that the nation's difficulties could be resolved by a strong, heroic leader—a conviction which was to result in Bonaparte's election as president in December 1848 (see chap. 3).

ing a new law restricting the right of public assembly, provoking a spate of protests in the workers' press. The editors of one journal denounced the measure as the act of "blind bourgeois" using the National Guard to disrupt peaceful workers' gatherings. "The street," they wrote, "is the first, the most sacred of all the clubs. What do you want, *Messieurs les bourgeois?* The people do not have access to your gilded, ornate salons. The porte St. Martin, the porte St. Denis, the Bastille, these are its meeting places . . . The blouses [i.e., workers' shirts] were there yesterday, they will be there tomorrow."[30] The rupture was nearly complete. The bourgeoisie controlled the political process so long as it took place indoors; the "people," now indistinguishable from the "workers," had no choice but to take politics into the streets.

The insurrection of June 23–26, coming as it did at the end of a series of setbacks for the workers' movement, followed the inexorable logic of despair rather than that of shock and outrage. The National Assembly announced on June 21 that Workshop members aged eighteen to twenty-five would be required to enlist in the army, while older members would be shipped to the provinces where they would be assigned to work projects. The palliative of provincial work assignments was all the more galling to Parisians in light of the news that the Assembly had also formed a special committee to draw up plans for the complete dissolution of the workshops. Marie, the Minister of Public Works, rebuffed a delegation of angry workers by assuring them that those who did not comply with the new orders would be forcibly removed from the capital. By noon the next day, nearly one thousand barricades had sealed off the eastern section of the city.

In the four bloody days that ensued, an insurgent force numbering somewhere between 10,000 and 20,000 confronted 37,000 regular army troops and 15,000 members of the Mobile Guard in a fierce street battle. The authorities arrested 5,000 people during the fighting, to which were added another 6,000 suspected insurgents in the aftermath; although precise figures for such events are chimerical, most scholars estimate that the number of insurgents killed was close to 2,000, with at least 1,000 wounded. The savagery of the conflict, which was to be surpassed only by the civil war that put an end to the Commune, testifies to two things: the acuteness with which the June insurgents felt the loss of their "democratic and social republic" and the government's very real fear of the revolutionary cataclysm this loss might unleash.

An explicit comparison of the June insurrection with the upheaval of 1871

30. *L'organisation du travail,* June 5, 1848, p. 1. See also the angry editorials in *Le tocsin des travailleurs,* June 6, 1848, p. 1, and *Le travail,* June 8, 1848, p. 1.

appears in chapter 6. For the moment, the key question is just how salient the participation identity of "worker" was in drawing Parisians into the fighting of June 23–26. Given the language in which criticism of the government was cast in late May and early June, an interpretation of the June Days as an uprising of people who understood their actions as the actions of workers hardly seems risky. Still, evidence of a less circumstantial sort is desirable. As I pointed out in chapter 1, demonstrating the relevance for mobilization of a given participation identity requires two types of evidence. In the present context, the first includes indications insurgents explicitly gave about their understanding of what they were doing and why. The second involves patterns of insurgent activity that reveal whether this understanding actually affected behavior on a significant scale— specifically, by mobilizing at a disproportionately high level those sorts of people to whom the collective identity corresponded.

To begin with, there is no doubt that a disproportionate number of the participants in the insurrection were affiliated with the National Workshops and that this affiliation furnished the *reason* for their participation. Although the figures are not precise, analyses of judicial records from the uprising have indicated that nearly half of those arrested were enrolled in the Workshops at the time of the announced closure.[31] Moreover, insurgents publicly linked their participation to Workshop membership: police reports from June 22 noted that the angry crowds marching through the center of Paris carried banners identifying the National Workshop brigades to which they belonged. Many of these banners adorned the barricades of the next day.[32] Other banners expressed the insurgents' view of their struggle in more general terms but with chilling simplicity: "Work or Death!" In the pages of *Le tocsin des travailleurs,* one of the few workers' newspapers to continue printing after the start of the uprising, the insurgents were just "the workers" (although, once again, "the people" appears to have had the same meaning):

> Yesterday, the beginning of the closure of the National Workshops
> brought a number of the workers to their feet. Their march through

31. Traugott, *Armies of the Poor,* pp. 122–24; Charles Tilly and Lynn H. Lees, "The People of June, 1848," in *Revolution and Reaction: 1848 and the Second French Republic,* Roger Price, ed. (New York: Barnes and Noble, 1975), p. 194. Using a sample of 104 trial dossiers, Traugott estimated that 43 percent of arrestees were Workshop members. Tilly and Lees, using a similarly small sample ($N = 123$), reported a figure of 53 percent.

32. See Tilly and Lynn H. Lees, "The People of June, 1848," pp. 170–209; Roger Price, ed., *1848 in France* (Ithaca: Cornell University Press, 1975), pp. 107–9.

the streets of the capital, banners flying, heightened the sense of everyday misery among the mass of the people. This morning the barricades went up. Let no one say that this is the result of a conspiracy. The people are suffering, the insult perpetrated against them is like no other in Europe; never, under Louis-Philippe, were so many injuries heaped upon the workers as under the National Assembly of the Republic . . . The workers on the barricades have none of the élan of February, but a dark resignation. *Better to die from a gunshot,* they say, *than from hunger.*[33]

François Arago, a renowned astronomer and member of the Executive Commission, wanted to hear for himself what the people on the barricades had to say. Just prior to a bloody battle at the Place du Panthéon, he inquired of two men, "Why are you rising against the rule of law? Why build barricades?" The bitter response of one was, "We've been promised so much, and they haven't delivered—we won't take our pay in words any more." The other demanded, "Why do you reproach us, Monsieur Arago? You have never been hungry, you do not know what misery is!"[34] The plight of those who were forced to live by earning a wage, and the callousness of those who were not, were plainly central to the uprising in the minds of many.

The spatial distribution of insurgent activity, and its relationship to sociodemographic patterns, provides another source of insight into what the uprising was about. As I mentioned, the barricades built on June 23 covered the eastern half of the capital; indeed, the fighting was almost exclusively confined to this section, traditionally seen as the city's working-class area. The map (fig. 2.1) indicates that, like the fighting, arrestees' residences were heavily skewed to the east. We may conclude that, in terms of socioeconomic composition of the rank and file, this was a workers' uprising. Note that there is no danger here of an ecological fallacy (i.e., inferring that insurgents were workers merely because they lived in districts with many workers): the trial documents indicate that the arrestees were overwhelmingly wage-earners.[35]

The striking thing about the pattern of arrests is not, however, that more arrests occurred in working-class districts (though that is, of course, the case). If

33. *Le tocsin des travailleurs,* June 24, 1848, p. 1.

34. Quoted in Rémi Gossez, "Diversité des antagonismes sociaux vers le milieu du XIXe siècle," *Revue économique* 7 (May 1956), p. 441.

35. Tilly and Lees, "The People of June, 1848," pp. 190–92; these authors present a useful discussion of the validity of trial documents for studies of insurgent participation.

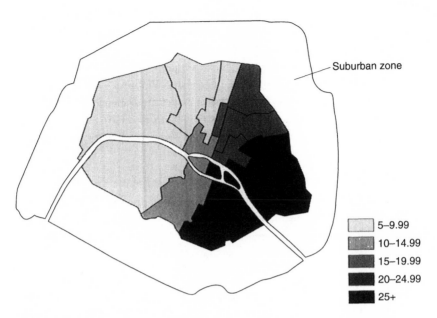

Suburban zone

5–9.99
10–14.99
15–19.99
20–24.99
25+

Figure 2.1 Arrest rates (per 1,000) by district, June 1848. Note that arrests in suburban areas averaged 4 per 1,000 but were higher in the northeastern suburbs (marked by arrow). Arrests here totaled 18 per 1,000.

the idea that the June insurrection was a workers' uprising is interpreted narrowly to mean that workers were the primary group fighting on the barricades, then arrest rates per capita should have been higher in districts with more working-class people, simply because there were more "eligible" insurgents in those areas; and we should then observe a roughly linear relationship between total arrests and size of the working-class population.[36] As figure 2.2 indicates, there were indeed more arrests in *arrondissements* where the population was more

36. I am assuming, of course, that total arrests reflect reasonably well the rates of actual participation in various districts of the city (and I will make the same assumption in my discussion of the Commune). This assumption seems warranted to the extent that arrest patterns closely match impressionistic accounts of where the fighting took place as well as documented reports on the location of barricades. Note that I have *not* assumed, and do not need to assume, that the total number of arrests is equal to the total number of insurgents living in each area of the city. All that is necessary to make these analyses meaningful is a reasonably close correlation between arrest patterns and patterns of actual insurgent participation. That is, the number of arrests must be more or less proportional to the number of participants in the uprising.

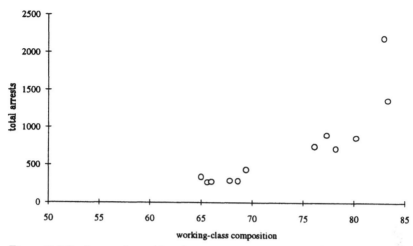

Figure 2.2 Total arrests by working-class composition of Paris *arrondissements*, June 1848.

heavily composed of workers. But the pronounced curvature in the graph shows that something more complicated occurred: areas with the most working-class inhabitants experienced even more arrests than one would expect on the basis of their larger pools of potential insurgents. Indeed, figure 2.3 shows that the relationship only becomes linear (and strikingly so) when working-class composition is plotted against the logarithm of total arrests; and the clarity of the linear pattern that emerges in this figure indicates that the class composition of districts accounts for almost all of the variation in arrests. In other words, the pattern of arrests is almost completely summarized by the following statement: *people participated at higher rates in those districts where the population was largely working class.* Workers on the whole were far more inclined to join the uprising than nonworkers; but workers who lived in the most exclusively working-class districts (above all, the eighth and twelfth *arrondissements*) were even more likely insurgents than workers in areas with more mixed populations.

The most satisfactory way to demonstrate this pattern is, of course, a multivariate analysis. Appendix A presents results of a regression of total arrests (by *arrondissement*) on total working-class population and on working-class composition. Despite their correlation with each other and despite the small number of observations, these two factors exert positive, significant, and independent effects on total arrests, confirming the impression given by the two figures. In these analyses, total working population and class composition together account for

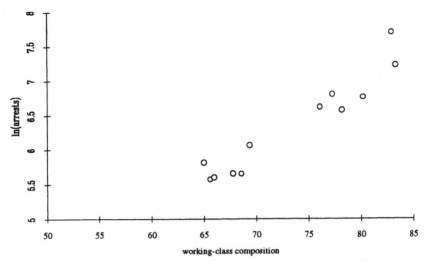

Figure 2.3 Total arrests (logarithmic scale) by working-class composition of Paris *arrondissements*, June 1848.

more than 90 percent of the variation in total arrests; even allowing for the fact that twelve observations do not provide an enormous amount of variation to explain, this is a remarkable result.

To restate the point, the uprising appears—judging from what is admittedly, but inevitably, an ecological analysis—to have been most effective in mobilizing those workers who in their daily lives were surrounded by other workers. The industrial area of eastern Paris, an urban environment that in other circumstances might (and did) favor attachment to craft groups, became a crucible for class action when a set of large formal institutions brought wage-earners from diverse trades into contact with one another for overtly political reasons. The pattern of insurgency that resulted, along with the tendency of sympathetic contemporaries and the participants themselves to see the phrases "the workers" and "the insurgents" as synonymous, shows how crucial the participation identity of "worker" was to the insurrection of June 1848.

Relatively little is known about the day-to-day process of mobilization and recruitment—information that would be invaluable in determining just what kinds of social relationships were important in drawing people into, as well as pulling them out of, the fighting. (The research I report on insurgent participation in the Commune, discussed in chap. 6, is much more helpful in this regard.) Nevertheless, several details point to the conclusion that, even more than in the radical agitation of the previous two months, work-oriented social networks mattered a great deal, while other sorts of social ties did not. As I observed earlier, banners of National Workshop brigades proliferated on the barricades, indicating that the process of mutual encouragement and cajoling that is indispensable for mobilization occurred principally when these groups were formally assembled, not when they were gathered informally near their homes. The first crowds to assemble on June 22 and 23 also comprised large numbers of Workshop members, some coming from a confrontation with the Minister of Public Works in his office, others having just received their final pay allotment.[37] In addition, data compiled by Tilly and Lees demonstrates a strong correlation, net of other factors, between the presence of workers' societies in a neighborhood and the rate of insurgent participation there, indicating that work-based social relationships exerted a positive influence on mobilization levels. On the other hand, the presence of political clubs appears to have dampened rates of participation in the insurgent effort.[38] This difference suggests that the social relationships contributing to radical mobilization were those that specifically involved work-based loyalties.

Furthermore, the other major organization that might have served to mobilize people into the insurrection, the National Guard, did not do so: in the western half of the city, National Guard battalions generally answered the *rappel* to take part in the repression, whereas the more "popular" battalions in the east generally failed to respond, either to put down the uprising or to join it. Because its battalions were recruited by district, the National Guard militia was the quintessential neighborhood organization in nineteenth-century Paris. As I shall subsequently show, this fact played an enormously important role in the insurgent mobilization of 1871; in 1848, however, it was associated with opposition to the uprising in the west and passivity in the east. However significant neighborhood ties might have been to the solidarity of these militia units, they contributed little to the radical mobilization of June.

The lesson to draw from the available evidence is not that the insurgents were predominantly workers or that many were threatened by the impending closure of the National Workshops (though, again, both of these statements are certainly true). After all, only a fraction of the working-class population of Paris, and a fairly small proportion of Workshop members, actually took part in the fighting; so the mere fact of being a worker or a National Workshop brigade member was

37. Roger Price, ed., *1848 in France*, pp. 107–9; Tilly and Lees, "The People of June, 1848," pp. 182–83.

38. Tilly and Lees, "The People of June, 1848," p. 200.

not enough to make most people join the insurgent effort. Rather, what is important is that, for those who *did* take part, the dominant account of why they were fighting was linked to their self-understanding as workers. It was their status as workers that, by virtue of the March 25 decree, entitled the insurgents to a livelihood guaranteed by the state; and it was the four-month process during which this status emerged as salient that enabled them to feel collectively betrayed by the government's attack on the "right to work." Because of this conceptual understanding of the conflict, finally, social relationships forged in the workplace, in the National Workshops, and in workers' associations proved to be the most consequential basis for insurgent recruitment.

⁺ℳ Class Mobilization ℳ⁺

The verbal and nonverbal behavior of Parisian militants during the 1848 revolution establishes the prominence of "worker" as a pivotal collective identity drawing National Workshop members and others into the political turmoil of the spring, and above all into the insurrection of June. But does this conclusion really justify the claim that insurgent mobilization was "class-based," as I argued in chapter 1? Perhaps my focus on participation identities is just a definitional sleight of hand, a ploy that highlights class while pushing competing interpretations offstage. Three points bearing on this possibility must be considered. First, as I have noted, the term "people" appeared over and over in the course of the 1848 revolution, suggesting that class may not have been the only dimension along which collective actors were ranged. Second, what is one to make of the fact that the rank and file of the forces of repression resembled the insurgents in a number of respects? Third, the use of barricades to seal off a well-defined area of the capital city during the insurrection implies a spatially defined collective self-understanding that corresponds in important ways to the notion of "community" that I have mentioned with regard to 1871, and to which I shall return in chapters 5 and 6. I will address these issues in order, demonstrating why they do not vitiate the particular class-struggle account of 1848 proposed here.

Once historians like Jules Michelet and Alphonse Lamartine, writing in the 1830s and 1840s, had restored the French Revolution of 1789 to an honored place in France's political culture, it was perhaps inevitable that the concept of "the people" would play a recurring role in the upheavals of the nineteenth century. The symbolic link between the republican idea of the sovereign people and the historic battles against "tyranny" that France had fought under the Directory and then under Napoleon continued to inspire rhetoric and political action half a century later, as the May 15 demonstration for the people of Poland showed. Moreover, a considerable amount of the political activities undertaken in popular societies in February, March, and April revolved around the republican ideals of political equality and representation (for males, that is) as much as they focused on radical socialist proposals like the right to work. Among the 203 societies that Peter Amann has identified in Paris during the revolution, names like Club du Peuple or Société des Amis du Peuple (Club of the People, Society of the Friends of the People) are about as common as labor-oriented names such as Club des Travailleurs or Club de la Fraternité des Ouvriers (Club of the Laborers, Club of the Fraternity of Workers); the vast majority of names included such keywords as "democratic," "republican," "fraternal," and "equality," revealing the wide-spread appeal of French revolutionary rhetoric.[39] Consequently, it is at least plausible that "the people," a tacitly gender-specific but potentially class-neutral collective identity rooted in the revolutionary tradition, played a significant role in the mass mobilization of June.

If the fate of the popular societies after the elections of April is any indication, however, this was not the case. Following the dramatic defeat of radical candidates on April 23, republican popular societies in Paris drifted ever further from those activists who were determined to appropriate the February Revolution for the working class. The fiasco of the demonstration and attempted coup of May 15 definitively convinced most club activists who were still wavering that mass action in the streets should be avoided at all costs.[40] A few weeks later, the radical paper Le Père Duchêne printed an announcement of a gigantic Banquet of the National Workshops, involving "fraternizing and discussions concerning the interests of the proletarians." Plans for this first banquet quickly merged with an independent effort, a Banquet of the People; the organizers, some of them affiliated with a militant club from Belleville, anticipated that the bargain "five-sous" (25 centimes) admission fee would draw a crowd of 300,000 people. But rather than rally to this cause, whose stated purpose was to recapture the radical effervescence of February, the most prominent popular societies (including the Société des Droits de l'Homme and the Club de la Révolution) immediately launched a campaign to cancel the event. They embroiled the organizers in a

39. Amann, Revolution and Mass Democracy, pp. 353–69.

40. Peter Amann, "The Paris Club Movement in 1848," in Roger Price, ed., Revolution and Reaction, p. 128.

lengthy struggle over the appropriate date (proposing indefinite postponement, in fact), wearing down the enthusiasm of the banquet's supporters until the movement simply collapsed.[41]

The implication of the banquet episode is straightforward. The more moderate clubs, whose membership drew on a broad spectrum of social strata, touted a republican version of the February Revolution as a victory of the People, employing a collective identity that blurred distinctions based on socioeconomic standing. The elections of April, with their resounding rejection of working-class candidates, flatly refuted any further efforts to represent the revolution as founded on cross-class consensus, above all with respect to the "social question." In the face of clear indications that urban middle-class and rural voters had no interest in upholding the right to work, or for that matter its institutional realization, the National Workshops, radical mobilization could no longer rely plausibly on "the people" as a participation identity—unless the term were transformed into a synonym of "the workers." And this is exactly what occurred: once the Workshops were abolished in June, "the people" had none of the optimistic inclusiveness that had characterized the popular clubs. On the barricades, "the people" could only mean those who labored, those whose lives depended on the right to work. Little wonder that, as I mentioned earlier, popular societies had if anything a negative impact on rates of insurgent participation.

The second point of caution stems from Mark Traugott's important research on the Garde Nationale Mobile (henceforth Mobile Guard), the security force composed of relatively young Parisian men recruited by the Provisional Government immediately following the February Revolution. Eyewitness accounts generally agreed that the Mobile Guard took the lead in suppressing the June insurrection, demonstrating far more zeal than the regular infantry. Yet a sample of men enrolled in the Mobile Guard reveals that the occupational backgrounds of these young recruits were barely distinguishable from those of arrested insurgents. No theory relating class position to political behavior in a deterministic and unmediated way can survive this empirical challenge; Traugott's counterproposal is that organizational factors (response to rank-and-file demands, insulation from the local population, and the like) account for the different political orientation of the Mobile Guard and Workshop members in June.[42]

Not only is this interpretation entirely consonant with the claim that class

41. For an extended treatment of this incident, see Amann, *Revolution and Mass Democracy*, pp. 264–80.

42. Traugott, *Armies of the Poor*, pp. 182–90.

was the dominant participation identity in the uprising; it lends considerable support to the theory I outlined regarding the connection between collective identities and patterns of social interaction. Nothing in the definition of a participation identity requires that *everyone* falling within its boundaries take part in, or even sympathize with, collective action; after all, most of the people who might join in protest usually stay home, especially when joining carries the risk of imprisonment or death. Any conception of collective identity that required full participation of the group to which the identity corresponded would thus be useless for empirical research, because real-world behavior would never live up to the definition. What matters in deciding if a class-based collective identity dominated the mobilization process is whether the workers who *did* join did so because they were workers. While the presence of wage-earners in the ranks of the repressive forces certainly merits explanation, it does not by itself cast doubt on the claim that the June insurgents viewed what they were doing as inextricably related to their status as workers.

The fact that workers fought on both sides of the June barricades engages the propositional theory I sketched in chapter 1, not the particular conception of collective identity in terms of which the theory is stated. In setting out the theory, I explicitly assumed that people play multiple social roles whose salience can vary with circumstances, and proceeded to make claims about the mechanisms of that variation. It is consequently not merely consistent with the theory, but actually one of its premises, that apparently similar individuals may diverge in the way they view their allegiances during moments of social conflict. In short, the respective political orientations of the Mobile Guard and the National Workshops conform exactly to what one would expect if collective identities depend on patterns of social interaction. Members of the Guard had joined an organization whose public mission was to defend the Republic by maintaining order in the capital; through the determined efforts of the officer corps, Guardsmen were thoroughly isolated from the Parisian population, and above all from the politically suspect National Workshops. Furthermore, their demands for adequate food, clothing, and living quarters were promptly met, giving them every reason to view the government as an ally rather than an adversary and no particular reason to see their destinies as related to their working-class backgrounds.

In contrast, members of the National Workshops enrolled to take the Provisional Government up on its guarantee of the right to work and saw this guarantee undermined with every session of the National Assembly. Even more important was the fact that, unlike Mobile Guardsmen, large numbers of Workshop members (as well as employed workers living in the industrial areas of eastern Paris) met nightly in socialist clubs and workers' societies, and daily in delegations to the Luxembourg Commission, where the issue of the organization of work was a constant topic of debate. The consequence was nearly four months of social contact fostering (1) the elaboration of a view of workers' interests as common to all trades and (2) the mutual recognition that this view was widely shared. These are the two conditions that I pointed to in chapter 1 as essential for a jump in scale in collective identity and that I argued result from the bridging of preexisting group boundaries that formal organizations encourage.

The contrast between the actions of the Mobile Guard and the National Workshops during the June uprising thus constitutes strong support for the argument that organizations exert an enormous influence on the efficacy of collective identities in mobilizing protest. The conservatism of the Mobile Guard can be attributed to the satisfaction of its members' demands and to the successful effort of the officer corps to isolate the rank and file from the general population, as Traugott points out; but it is also essential to acknowledge, on the other side of the barricades, the role of extensive social interaction across trade lines *in the context of a political conflict about the place of work in French society.* This cross-trade interaction was the direct consequence, moreover, of the existence of large-scale formal institutions whose boundaries did not respect those of everyday craft communities. The Workshops and the Luxembourg Commission were uniquely responsible for the plausibility of a minimally inclusive collective identity above the level of the craft group—the level at which artisanal militancy traditionally rested. Ironically, organizations created by political elites to control the behavior of the newly enfranchised turned out to be essential for mass mobilization based on class identity.

This observation in turn provides the key to the third issue I raised above, namely, the overtly spatial dimension of insurgency. The barricade, a central icon of the French revolutionary tradition, is intrinsically a tool for blocking off sections of (urban) space as a challenge to the state—whose solidity is itself, of course, a function of the control it exerts over the physical space within its borders. Thus nothing could be less surprising in nineteenth-century France than the use of a ring of barricades to close off a well-defined area of the French capital as a challenge to state power. The question, though, is whether this simultaneously tactical and symbolic use of urban space necessarily implies the operation of a collective identity associated with the "urban community" rather than one based on class.

The contrast with earlier insurrections in Paris—and, as I shall show in chapter 6, with the Commune of 1871—makes it clear that it does not. To be sure, the June insurgents made a point of sealing off what they now saw as the workers' half of the city, and in that sense laid claim to a sort of community, defined in both spatial and socioeconomic terms, that they perceived to be under attack. But earlier Parisian barricades, for instance those of 1830 and 1832, had been distributed more diffusely or had closed off more limited areas such as the Faubourg Saint-Antoine, the home of the *sans-culottes* of the year II. The June Days were the only moment in the nineteenth century when paving stones and rifles drew with such clarity the boundary between the "bourgeois" Paris of the west and the "proletarian" Paris of the east. If the insurgents were defending a community, it was one that had no place for merchants, bankers, lawyers, or industrialists. This was a major reason for the failure of the neighborhood-based and socially heterogeneous National Guard to act as a significant mobilizing force.

What, then, was the connection between physical space and the collective identity of class? The answer lies in the stark but often unacknowledged contrast between outright insurrection and the more institutionalized forms of militancy typically referred to as the "labor movement." The working-class mobilization that drove events in Paris during the first few months of the 1848 revolution took place, as I pointed out earlier, in the densely populated streets of the capital's eastern districts—the areas where most of the city's industrial activity took place and where most Parisian workers lived. In less turbulent times, this was where everyday life in the workplace spilled over into the corner cabarets and cafés that provided male workers with their midday meals and evening entertainment, facilitating the formation of mutual-aid societies, resistance societies, and strike organizations (see chap. 4). The industrial *arrondissements*, in other words, housed the informal social networks that under the July Monarchy had underpinned most of the artisanal response to developing capitalist enterprise. Ordinarily, however, these informal social networks remained craft-bound, as workers in the same trades clustered in their own centers of sociability. The collective identity governing worker militancy thus remained at the craft level, constrained simultaneously by the workplace focus of the disputes that triggered it and by the patterns of social interaction in terms of which group identities were framed. Although one might call the craft groups at the heart of these disputes "communities," this would only be true in the relational, not the geographical, sense.[43] The

43. Craig Calhoun has proposed a purely relational conception of community in his discussion of English radical activism (see *The Question of Class Struggle*, pp. 174–82). The theory of collective

clearest evidence of this is the degree to which workers' societies, and working-class activism more generally, remained an exclusively male domain in nonrevolutionary times: the dependence of organizational solidarity on social interaction in sex-segregated public spaces contributed to male workers' view of female wage-earners (above all in the needle trades) as unwanted competitors rather than potential allies in the labor movement.[44] The minimally inclusive collective identity in labor protest thus systematically excluded both workers who were female and workers who belonged to different occupational groups from those embroiled in a specific dispute.

But in June 1848, insurgents literally outlined an entire section of the city as the workers' community, embracing wage-earners of both sexes and all trades. This behavior was eminently sensible because for the first time the conflict and its organizational armature encompassed all kinds of workers (including women) and because eastern Paris, in addition to being the city's "workshop," had also become the site of daily interaction across the social boundaries that craft-based militancy had always respected in the past.[45] Moreover, the novelty of the phenomenon was not lost on the people who witnessed it: the vast street assemblages of workers that began to disquiet the police and other Friends of Order in May impressed observers as much with their diversity as with their anger. In short, the spatial inclusiveness that distinguished the insurgent identity of June resulted from these new arenas of social and political interaction—the same factors that underlay the plausibility of class as a collective identity. Space mattered because craft boundaries did not.

---

action under consideration in this book explicitly asserts that mobilization depends in part on constellations of preexisting social relationships—in other words, on the existence of communities defined in relational terms. The issue here, though, is the conditions under which relationally defined communities view their collective identity in specifically spatial terms. Furthermore, I have emphasized that some kinds of social ties may matter more than others in mobilizing collective action, depending on the specific political context. To the extent that most social settings incorporate multiple networks, it may be misleading to say that community *in general* is conducive to radical mobilization.

44. See Joan Wallach Scott, "Work Identities for Men and Women: The Politics of Work and Family in the Parisian Garment Trades in 1848," pp. 93–112, in *Gender and the Politics of History;* Lorraine Coons, *Women Home Workers in the Parisian Garment Industry, 1860–1915* (New York: Garland Publishing, 1987).

45. The failure of the workers' electoral strategy in April doubtless had much to do with this expansion of the insurgent collective identity to include women. It is instructive to note in this context that feminist clubs and newspapers explicitly linked women's political rights to their status as producers, thereby underscoring their similarity to male workers.

❧ Conclusion ❧

The implications of this chapter are threefold. First, the fact that the rights of "working people" so dominated public debate in the first days of the February Revolution was due not merely to the severe bout of unemployment France had undergone for over a year but also to the political circumstances surrounding the inception of the July Monarchy in 1830. The elitist electoral reform of 1830 ensured that calls for a republic in 1848 would be practically synonymous with calls for the enfranchisement of workers; and this merger of republican demands with workers' demands made possible the sudden intuitive appeal of the *république démocratique et sociale*. The events of February 1848 thus highlighted the issue of labor in a way that made widespread commitment to a class-oriented collective identity more likely.

Second, the identification of the February Revolution (at least in popular quarters) with the emancipation of working people made it almost inevitable that workers' societies would mobilize for electoral activity alongside the more middle-class political clubs that sprang up in March. Even before the elections, in other words, working people mobilized for political action in a distinctly class-oriented way. When it became evident that most of France's voters viewed the issue of labor as a decidedly secondary concern in the work of the Constituent Assembly, workers in Paris had all the more reason to see themselves as a collective victim of the elections of April. The critical events of the revolution's first four months set the stage for the world of labor, epitomized in the industrial neighborhoods of eastern Paris, to become the geographical and cognitive locus of political mobilization.

Third, two new organizational entities, the Luxembourg Commission and the National Workshops, created institutional settings in which the problems of falling wages, unemployment, and hunger could for the first time be viewed, discussed, and—many hoped—resolved as issues relevant to all workers simultaneously. By posing the dual questions of "the right to work" and "the organization of labor," the National Workshops and the Luxembourg Commission provided the organizational apparatus through which thousands of workers in Paris could frame and debate social issues that were defined on the level of an entire class rather than keyed to individual craft groups in struggles with employers. And this was in no way a purely abstract transformation. Workers in Paris, through their daily interactions in the Workshops, in delegations to the Luxembourg Commission, and in electoral meetings, saw that the issue of the "organization of labor" constituted them not just conceptually as the collective object of a social problem but concretely as a collective actor with the capacity to assert its interests in the public realm. The bitterness of defeat in June—a bitterness that resulted not just from its violence but from its construal as a defeat *of workers*— was thus possible only because of the profound organizational achievements of the four preceding months.

3

Urban Transformations, 1852–70

THE REPRESSION of the June insurrection put a rapid but grim end, in Paris at least, to the radical social experiment begun in the heady days of February. With eleven thousand suspected insurgents and the leaders of the abortive May 15 coup in custody awaiting trial, the moderates and conservatives in the Assembly quickly began to impose their version of the February Revolution on a discredited left. The Luxembourg Commission was gone, closure of the National Workshops proceeded as planned, and the Assembly passed a law placing severe new restrictions on clubs and workers' associations. At the end of July, the renowned socialist thinker Pierre-Joseph Proudhon demonstrated his political naiveté by presenting to the legislature a radical program for the reorganization of production along socialist lines. He was practically driven from the tribune by laughter. In August, the Assembly reinstated a law dating from the July Monarchy that required newspapers to place a large sum of money on deposit with the government, to be forfeited if the editors violated any of a variety of restrictions on public expression.

To be sure, the movement for radical social change did not simply disappear in France. In fact, the events of June had triggered a wave of political activism in many urban and rural regions whose earlier quiescence had contributed to the center-right majority in the National Assembly; and, thanks in part to concerted "démoc-soc"[1] mobilization throughout the country, the legislative elections of May 1849 were ultimately to turn out much more favorably for the left than those of April 1848. At the same time, however, provincial administrators and police officials sympathetic to the "party of order," and strengthened by the tightening of controls on the freedom of assembly, initiated a broad campaign of harassment and repression against republican societies, the radical press, and workers' associations suspected of a too active interest in politics. As John Merriman has ar-

---

1. This term was an abbreviation of *démocrate-socialiste* and referred broadly to those who supported the idea of the *révolution démocratique et sociale*.

gued, the repressive net began to close even more securely after the election of Louis Napoleon Bonaparte as president in December 1848, and this weakening of the left's organizational apparatus proved a decisive factor in the success of his coup d'état three years later.[2]

But if the forces of reaction and the coming to power of "Napoleon the Little" (as Victor Hugo contemptuously called him) spelled the end of a grand democratic experiment, they also set a more authoritarian one in motion. In the course of twenty-two years (four as president and eighteen as Emperor Napoleon III by plebiscite), Louis Bonaparte strove to complete the task begun by his legendary uncle, Napoleon Bonaparte, half a century earlier: the construction of a modern state bureaucracy in the service of an Empire. In some respects—principally those relating to foreign affairs and colonial conquest—his efforts were ultimately disastrous and indeed contributed directly to the collapse of the Second Empire in 1870. But in other respects he was more successful: in encouraging economic growth, in quelling political dissent, and in transforming Paris into a model city equipped simultaneously to sustain a burgeoning population, stimulate commercial activity, and dazzle the world with its grandeur as an imperial capital. It is with the last of these projects—the accomplishment of which was also intended to facilitate the first two—that Bonaparte, assisted by the irrepressible Baron Haussmann, made his most lasting mark; and it is the impact of this project, above all on social life and political identities in the capital, that forms the focus of this chapter.

Three theoretical perspectives underlie the various interpretations of events in Paris between the coup of 1851 and the Commune. From the liberal standpoint, the Empire was a surprisingly successful attempt at enlightened despotism, a largely benevolent regime whose repressive character derived from the political and economic crises of 1848–1851 and thus gradually diminished in virulence as social stability was restored. Major public works projects in Paris fostered social stability by providing employment and making traditional seats of insurrection accessible to government troops, but their chief purpose was the creation of a model capital city that would glorify the Empire while meeting the needs of the full range of social groups composing its population. If the outcome

2. John M. Merriman, *The Agony of the Republic: The Repression of the Left in Revolutionary France, 1848–1851* (New Haven: Yale University Press, 1978). See also John Merriman, "Radicalisation and Repression: A Study of the Demobilisation of the '*Démoc-Socs*' during the Second French Republic," pp. 210–35, in Price, ed., *Revolution and Reaction*, and Margadant, *French Peasants in Revolt*.

tended to favor property owners and developers more than the laboring poor, it was because the former were better positioned to defend their interests in the complex political environment of the period.[3]

The structural Marxist view, originally articulated by Marx himself and elaborated recently by David Harvey (see chap. 1), sees the Napoleonic regime instead as the result of a compromise between the financial and industrial fractions of the capitalist class.[4] What might appear to have been an autonomous, centralized state under a strong monarch was merely the result of divisions within the capitalist stratum that rendered it incapable of ruling in its own name. By presenting himself as a ruler whose legitimacy depended on the Bonapartist legend and on popular consent secured through state policies favoring economic growth, Napoleon III could paper over the deep social fissures that had produced 1848—but only so long as the bourgeoisie remained internally divided. The extensive urban renewal project in Paris was, on this view, dictated by a "crisis of overaccumulation" which could only be alleviated through public spending designed simultaneously to absorb surpluses of capital and labor and to remake urban space in a manner suitable for modern capitalist production and finance. If the clearing away of slums in the city center and the encouragement of new construction financed by floating debt failed to eliminate overcrowding and even produced new forms of urban blight on the periphery, this was not because of oversight or political corruption; from the structural Marxist viewpoint, the recurrence of old problems and the emergence of new ones reflected the intrinsic logic of a new mode of capital accumulation in an industrial city. The growth of a "communalist" movement in the late 1860s and the violent conflagration of 1871 can therefore be traced directly to the contradictions at the core of this new system for the accumulation and circulation of capital and credit.

The third perspective, which is best described as humanist in the Marxist vein, derives principally from the writings of Henri Lefebvre and from Manuel

3. See, for instance, Alain Plessis, *De la fête impériale au mur des fédérés* (Paris: Editions du Seuil, 1979). In *La population et les tracés de voies à Paris depuis un siècle* (Paris: Presses Universitaires de France, 1928), Maurice Halbwachs argued that the phenomenal period of expropriation and renovation that occurred during this period was a response to "social needs" rather than the product of rapacious profiteering. Although his perspective might be more appropriately regarded as strictly Durkheimian—he was, after all, one of Durkheim's disciples—it seems reasonable to include Halbwachs in the "liberal" category on the ground that he viewed the social process underlying the urban renewal effort as essentially free of class bias.

4. Karl Marx, *The Eighteenth Brumaire of Louis Bonaparte* (New York: International Publishers, 1963); Harvey, *Consciousness and the Urban Experience*.

Castells in his post-Althusserian mode (see, again, my discussion in chap. 1). Because the issue of interest for these scholars is the historically specific production of "urban meaning" through varying practices of land use, architectural innovation and the spatial arrangement of production and consumption, it makes no sense to speak of urban transformations under Napoleon and Haussmann as the products of struggles among well-defined interest groups, whether these are identified in terms of class or some other set of categories. Instead, changes in the experience of city life during the Second Empire are themselves responsible for the coalescence of competing social groups in Paris, each espousing its own vision of urban meaning. In consequence, the humanist approach sees no need to relate the political maneuvering of 1852–70 or the Commune itself to a deeper structure of (presumably material) interests. The theoretically relevant phenomena, for Castells and Lefebvre, are those that exist on the level of "meaning": the urban forms of streets and buildings, and the debates about these forms that took place explicitly in settings like the Paris Municipal Council and symbolically in the street fighting of 1871. According to both authors, if there was a direct link between the Commune and the urban renewal projects of the Second Empire, it lay in the symbolic reclamation by the insurgents of the historic city center, from which they had been driven by soaring rents and wholesale condemnations of tenement streets. And, for Lefebvre, the Commune expressed above all the rejection of an increasingly planned, homogenized, and rationalized urban world in favor of spontaneity and carnival. These clashes over urban form and the divergent visions of urban meaning they expressed are, from the humanist standpoint, the only kind of structure worth talking about.[5]

Unfortunately, much of the distance between these perspectives is unbridgeable through research inasmuch as they take different views of what the relevant theoretical objects are. On the one hand, the humanist Marxism of Castells simply brushes past the materialism of structural Marxist or liberal interpretations in its pure search for meaning; on the other hand, the structuralism of Harvey's

---

5. Lefebvre, *La production de l'espace; La proclamation de la Commune.* Castells, *The City and the Grassroots.* See also Jeanne Gaillard's monumental *Paris: La ville, 1852–1870* (Paris: Editions Honoré Champion, 1977). A less explicitly Marxist version of this argument appears in T. J. Clark, *The Painting of Modern Life: Paris in the Art of Manet and His Followers* (New York: Alfred A. Knopf, 1984). For reasons of discipline and audience, Clark is less concerned than Castells or Lefebvre with the connection between Haussmann's projects and the political upheavals at the end of the Empire, and more concerned with understanding changes in urban form and meaning as such. Even so, he specifically ties the rebuilding of Paris to the emergence of a new form of capitalism and relates both of these processes to various kinds of protest in the late 1860s.

approach discovers contradiction where the liberal sees unintended consequence, systemic exploitation where the liberal sees isolated instances of self-
seeking or corruption. Few scholars dispute the proposition that, at least in the
early years of his reign, Napoleon III served the interests of industrial capital by
repressing the left and adopting an expansionist fiscal policy focusing on development of a national rail system and on public works in the capital. What they
disagree about is whether this demonstrates that imperial administrators were
"prisoners of class forces"[6] or whether it is even important to answer this
question.

There is, however, one major empirical question on whose relevance all three
perspectives agree and whose answer may therefore help to judge their relative
merits. It is also, I argue, one of the keys to explaining the striking dissimilarity
between the events of 1848 and the Commune, which constitutes the central
theme of this book. Phrased in general terms, the question is, In what ways did
the profound transformations of Paris between the 1851 coup and the fall of the
Empire in 1870 shape the terrifying events of 1871? Empirical support for the
structural Marxist view would take the form of evidence that Haussmann's projects—including extensive rebuilding of the city center and annexation to the
city of eighteen suburban towns—systematically rearranged urban life in a way
that facilitated the circulation of capital and the creation of opportunities for
profit; and these changes would in turn have altered the form and depth of exploitation in a way that brought about the municipal revolution at the end of the
Empire. Specifically, Harvey argues that the working class was driven out of the
historic city center by rising rents, creating a ring of distinctly working-class
neighborhoods in the newly annexed suburbs, particularly those in the north and
east such as Montmartre, Belleville, and Charonne. The resulting isolation of
workers from the middle class, *combined with* changes in the nature of work during a period of rapid industrialization, made possible the emergence of a form of
working-class solidarity that was simultaneously understood in communitarian
terms—hence the peculiar mixture of loyalty to class and community that, Harvey claims, uniquely characterized the Commune.

In the humanist view, the frustration of the laboring poor in Paris that was
expressed in 1871 had relatively little to do with changes in the nature of work
and everything to do with the "loss of community" that accompanied the forced
exodus from the center of Paris to outlying districts. The humanist position thus

6. Harvey, *Consciousness and the Urban Experience*, p. 93.

implies two things: first, that Parisians experienced the disruptions associated with "haussmannisation" as a series of social and spatial detachments from the urban life to which they were accustomed; and second, that these detachments formed the core issue in terms of which the insurgents of 1871 understood their actions. Subsequent chapters will address the empirical accuracy of the latter proposition, while the present chapter will focus on the former.

Liberal treatments of the Second Empire, finally, characteristically discount the connection between Haussmann's public works and the violence of 1871, except to note that the ease with which troops and artillery could move through the widened streets and boulevards facilitated the army's recapture of the city from the insurgents (as, indeed, the Emperor had intended). David Pinkney's landmark history of the period does not mention the Commune (except to note its effect on population figures for 1872), while Anthony Sutcliffe's study considers only the setback it posed for the completion of the urban renewal plan.[7] The 1871 revolution, in the liberal perspective, was principally a response to the short-term strictures of war, the Empire's collapse, and the insensitivity of the interim Government of National Defense. Since past history had shown Paris to be a tumultuous city in any case, liberal historians have seen no particular reason to engage in a special inquiry relating the insurrection to details of urban planning under Napoleon III and his ambitious Prefect of the Seine.

A central claim of this study, however, is that the distinctively urban orientation of protest during the Commune is so surprising in light of the intensely class-based conflict of 1848 that it demands explanation. Moreover, any adequate explanation of the difference must refer to changes in the nature of urban life that took place in the intervening twenty-three years (as both the structural Marxist and humanist perspectives attempt to do). This requirement is all the more pressing when one observes the uniqueness of the Paris Commune in relation to France's other major cities in 1870–71: even though a number of other cities joined in the call for municipal liberties when the Empire fell, and in some cases went so far as to proclaim revolutionary Communes of their own, none experienced anything like the mass mobilization that took place in the capital. Contrast this with the contagion—in cities and countryside alike—sparked by the June Days of 1848, and it becomes clear that something very unusual must have taken place in Paris in the interim. The remainder of this chapter will address the ques-

---

7. David H. Pinkney, *Napoleon III and the Rebuilding of Paris* (Princeton: Princeton University Press, 1958); Anthony Sutcliffe, *The Autumn of Central Paris: The Defeat of Town Planning, 1850–1970* (London: Edward Arnold, 1970), pp. 43–47.

tion of just what this something was and how closely it conforms to the claims of the various authors I have just discussed. Following a background discussion of the physical changes wrought in the Parisian landscape under the Second Empire, I shall explore their consequences for patterns of social interaction. Contrary to both the loss-of-community and the class isolation arguments, the evidence indicates that workers pushed to the periphery by urban renovations formed social networks that were relatively *less* class-homogeneous, and actually more neighborly, than those remaining in the center. The distinctive trait of social ties in outlying districts was that they were structured less by the world of work and more by attachments to specific neighborhoods.

⁺✻ The Rebuilding of Paris ✻⁺

The coup d'état with which Louis Napoleon Bonaparte sealed the fate of the Second Republic in December 1851 was unquestionably good for business. Stocks in the publicly traded railway companies instantly posted a healthy gain on the Paris Bourse, and short-term state bonds, which had plummeted in November, finished the year with an increase of 14 percent over the high of February (see fig. 3.1). Long-term state securities rose 7 percent over February's value (14 percent over November), as investors expressed a newfound faith in the regime's stability. Whatever their differences, the propertied interests in France could agree that Bonaparte's seizure of power was welcome news.

There were three reasons for this revival of business confidence. First, by preempting the upcoming elections, the coup ended uncertainty about Bonaparte's successor as President (the Constitution having precluded reelection by permitting only a single term). Second, beyond the mere fact of continuity, the Friends of Order were particularly pleased with the President's uncompromising stance toward left-wing agitation.[8] Armed resistance to the coup provided an opportunity to remove any doubts that might have remained about his commitment to order: following the quick suppression of uprisings in Paris and the provinces, military courts deported over eleven thousand insurgents to penal colonies in Africa. Third, the President's views on economic policy were encouraging to all

---

8. In point of fact, this intolerance of political unrest had come as a surprise to many. Because of his reputation as an adventurer (he had, after all, been imprisoned for his unsuccessful attempt to overthrow Louis-Philippe and while in prison had written a quasi-socialist tract, *L'extinction du paupérisme*), Louis Bonaparte's election to the Assembly in April 1848 had occasioned a considerable controversy on the floor of the legislature. A number of moderate and republican deputies argued vigorously that he be denied the right to take his seat, on the ground that he could not be trusted to uphold the Republic. In that regard, it turned out, they were quite right.

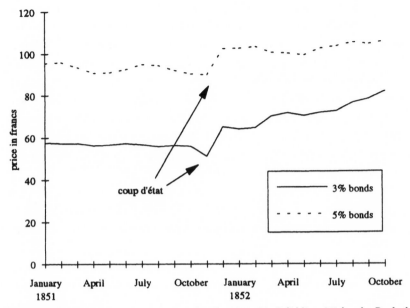

Figure 3.1 Value of French government bonds, 1851–52. *Solid line,* 3% bonds. *Dashed line,* 5% bonds.

but the most fiscally conservative of France's political and financial elite. Heavily influenced by followers of Claude Henri de Saint-Simon, Bonaparte had frequently committed himself, in writing (in his *Idées napoléoniennes,* for example) and in public addresses, to an expansionist fiscal policy aimed at stimulating economic development through state spending on public works. The advantages would be twofold: improvement of infrastructure (in particular the national rail network and urban thoroughfares) would facilitate flows of raw materials and merchandise, and the provision of useful employment on a large scale would eliminate a major source of the discontent that underlay the "troubles" of 1848. As President of the republic, he had already attempted to put this policy to work in the capital, authorizing two major projects in the city center: the extension of the rue de Rivoli eastward to the place de la Bastille and the replacement of the aging Halles Centrales (the historic wholesale food market) with a new, enlarged structure capable of accommodating the food supply of 1 million Parisians.

Urban engineers had already drawn up plans for these very renovations under the July Monarchy and in the early years of the Second Republic (in fact, they were originally proposed by Napoleon I), but had repeatedly run into a familiar obstacle: lack of funds. The municipal council and the Prefect of the Department of the Seine, Berger, reluctantly agreed to issue securities to pay for the first two projects but insisted that expenses for any further work be covered in advance by new taxes. It was therefore only the seizure of absolute power that enabled Bonaparte to indulge his fantasy of rebuilding Paris. With control over nominations to the municipal council (the city had no elected mayor) and the right to replace Berger with a Prefect whose fiscal proclivities were more expansive, the "Prince-President," as he now styled himself, initiated a program of town planning unprecedented in French history—both in its scale and in the nature of its financing.

The ambitious but fiercely loyal Georges Haussmann, a civil servant from an Alsatian family with ties to the first Emperor, proved to be the ideal candidate for the job of executing Louis-Napoleon's bold plans. As Prefect of the Var and then the Yonne, he had already attracted the attention of the President and the Interior Minister, Persigny, with his able administration of the campaign of repression against the left. Rewarded with the prefecture of the Gironde in November 1851, he engineered that region's relatively passive acceptance of the December coup and, one year later, organized the mammoth celebration in Bordeaux at which the Prince-President proclaimed himself Emperor Napoleon III.[9] Persigny, who chose him as Berger's replacement in June 1853, wrote later that, more than his intelligence and energy, it was Haussmann's character flaws— intense stubbornness, egotism, and ruthlessness—that recommended him for the position.[10]

Armed with expanded powers, including the title of Baron and a seat in the Senate, Haussmann immediately set to work on the enormous street improvement plan Louis-Napoleon had presented to him at their first meeting. Over the next seventeen years, the Emperor's most faithful servant oversaw the annexation and integration into the city of eighteen suburban communes (see map 1); the opening to the public of two vast parks, the Bois de Boulogne and the Bois de Vincennes; and the creation of three systems of wide boulevards, each designed to enhance the beauty and imperial majesty of the capital while easing the burden of ever-expanding commercial traffic between the city's rail stations, docks, and marketplaces. Between 1853 and 1870 the "haussmannisation" of Paris added 85 miles of new streets to the 450 that already existed and, more importantly, doubled the

9. Pinkney, Napoleon III and the Rebuilding of Paris, pp. 40–44.

10. Victor Fialin Persigny, Mémoires du duc de Persigny (Paris: Plon, 1896), p. 253.

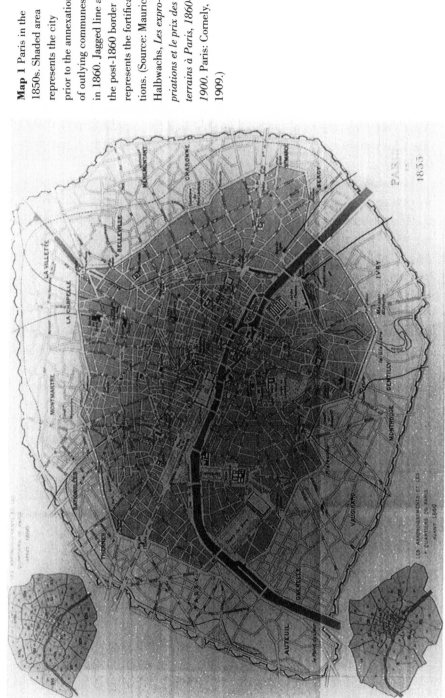

Map 1 Paris in the 1850s. Shaded area represents the city prior to the annexation of outlying communes in 1860. Jagged line at the post-1860 border represents the fortifications. (Source: Maurice Halbwachs, *Les expropriations et le prix des terrains à Paris, 1860–1900*. Paris: Cornely, 1909.)

average width of the city's thoroughfares. Most of the celebrated avenues in Paris today—the boulevard Saint Germain, the boulevard Saint Michel, the avenue de l'Opéra, the ring of streets converging on the Arc de Triomphe, and so on—owe their existence, or in a few cases their present aspect, to the rough sketch Bonaparte handed his eager Prefect in June 1853. In many cases, the plazas and public buildings (such as the Opera itself and a number of *mairies,* or district town halls) lying on the axes of the new boulevards were also built during this period, satisfying Haussmann's predilection for streets with a monumental terminus. Less visible, but equally important to the modernization of the city (and the achievement of which Haussmann was most proud), was the ingenious new system of storm drains to carry away waste water as well as the rainfall that flooded the streets annually. In addition to making the streets more passable during the rainy season, the collector sewers were intended to help prevent outbreaks of cholera, which had twice ravaged the population of Paris since 1830.[11]

Most remarkable of all, the entire enterprise depended on financial resources that did not exist—not, at least, in the minds of financiers and civil servants with traditional ideas about fiscal restraint. But Haussmann, encouraged by Persigny and supported by a coterie of progressive financiers associated with Isaac and Emile Pereire, boldly embraced the Saint-Simonian idea of deficit-financed public investment. In his funding requests to the Corps Législatif (the legislative body created by the imperial constitution), Haussmann made an argument whose outlines would become familiar in the twentieth century but which at the time was nothing short of revolutionary: because the improvements of the city center would stimulate economic activity and enhance property values by clearing away slums, future increases in tax revenues would pay for current loans.[12] Moreover, property confiscated by the city to make way for new streets would (so the argument ran) be resold after the streets were completed, with the difference between

11. Donald Reid has recently argued that much of the appeal of the new sewers stemmed not just from a straightforward concern with hygiene but also from the association of the disorder and disease of the underground channels with the specter of social unrest. Mastering the chaos of the sewers through the application of modern science and bureaucratic administration was symbolically linked, in other words, to the project of rationalizing the troubled social order. *Paris Sewers and Sewermen: Realities and Representations* (Cambridge, MA: Harvard University Press, 1991).

12. Most of the city's revenue derived from taxes on property and on the *octroi,* a municipal customs duty imposed on merchandise entering the city limits. The extension of those limits in 1860, resulting from Haussmann's annexation of eighteen suburban towns, produced a one-time surge in the *octroi*—at the expense of commercial enterprises in the annexed areas. I will discuss later the implications of this fact for structural Marxist interpretations of the Haussmann period.

the resale value and the original reimbursement price going into municipal coffers.[13] In short, public works were to be financed by long-term debt, serviced with funds furnished by the state. The scheme persuaded the municipal council and the legislative body twice, once in 1855 and again in 1858, for a total of 110 million francs in loans and 103 million francs in state subsidies.[14] The Pereires profited handsomely in this new fiscal environment by founding the Société Générale du Crédit Mobilier, an innovative brokerage concern that consolidated capital from small investors and furnished it to the rail companies, municipalities, public works contractors, and builders (including the Pereires' own Compagnie Immobilière de Paris, founded in 1858). Needless to say, members of the conservative financial community, epitomized by the Rothschilds, were horrified.

As plans for the second and third networks took shape in the 1860s, Haussmann managed to obtain two more loan authorizations, but by this time soaring costs far outpaced the willingness of the increasingly skeptical councillors and legislators to take on new obligations. Completed improvements inevitably enhanced the value of neighboring lands, making new right-of-way purchases more expensive; and property owners in the city center had in any case learned to hold out for higher expropriation indemnities, cutting into the city's resale profits. In addition, an 1858 ruling by the Conseil d'Etat, France's high court, limited the city's right to expropriate land lying on either side of projected streets, with the result that improvement values went directly to landlords. Finally, after 1860, tenants too were entitled to an indemnity, even if their leases were allowed to run out before they were evicted.[15]

Faced with spiraling costs, Haussmann was forced to resort to ever more unorthodox methods of financing. He discovered that it was possible to negotiate agreements with public works contractors in which the latter would make the capital outlays, including the enormous expenditures for expropriations, and in which the city would begin payments only after the project's completion. The contractors in turn could borrow the needed capital from third-party banks, by transferring to the lender delegation bonds representing the city's promises to pay in future installments. The arrangement thus amounted to a short-term loan

13. Louis Girard, *La politique des travaux publics du Second Empire* (Paris: Armand Colin, 1952), pp. 116–21. Siegfried Giedion, *Space, Time, and Architecture: The Growth of a New Tradition* (Cambridge, MA: Harvard University Press, 1977), pp. 765–66.

14. Pinkney, *Napoleon III and the Rebuilding of Paris*, pp. 182–84; Girard, *La politique des travaux publics*, p. 166.

15. Sutcliffe, *The Autumn of Central Paris*, p. 41.

to the city—with the important difference that, on paper at least, it was only the contractor who was borrowing cash. By the late 1860s, Haussmann had secured 500 million francs in this way and the city's total indebtedness came to 2.5 billion francs.

In 1868, Jules Ferry, a republican legislator and future Third Republic luminary, made a name for himself by publishing *Comptes fantastiques d'Haussmann*, a scathing attack on the Prefect's recently acquired habit of contracting debt in ways that circumvented the normal political process.[16] As public inquiries revealed the scale of the abuses, the management of urban renewal in the capital became a key symbol of the authoritarian style of the imperial regime. The next two years saw dramatic growth in republican opposition in the legislature and in public discourse, and Napoleon III, whose legitimacy depended more than ever on plebiscitary approval, gradually withdrew the crucial support on which his embattled protégé had relied for seventeen years.[17] Finally, in January 1870, the Emperor announced Haussmann's dismissal on the heels of a set of reforms designed to give France a genuinely parliamentary government. The Second Empire itself was to collapse nine months later; but Bonaparte and Haussmann had already effected such historic and irreversible changes on the face of Paris that their successors in the Third Republic had no choice but to finish what remained of their work.

❧ The Impact on City Life ❧

If there is one proposition on which scholars of this period can agree, it is that the rebuilding of the Paris city center pushed thousands of less affluent women and men outward toward the periphery, often into the new *arrondissements* formed by the annexed communes of Grenelle, Vaugirard, Belleville, Montmartre, and so on. Even though new construction in the central districts ultimately provided more housing units than had been demolished, the emphasis on luxury construction and the consequent increase in rents ensured that the working poor would

16. Jules Ferry, *Comptes fantastiques d'Haussmann: Lettre adressée à MM. les membres de la commission du Corps Législatif chargés d'examiner le nouveau projet d'emprunt de la ville de Paris* (Paris: Le Chevalier, 1868). The title was a pun on the French edition of E. T. A. Hoffmann's fairy tales, *Contes fantastiques d'Hoffmann*.

17. I shall investigate the contours and determinants of this growing opposition in the next two chapters.

have to seek lodging elsewhere.[18] Between 1861 and 1872, the total population in the first through the fourth *arrondissements* (corresponding to the historic center) decreased by roughly 12 percent, while the number of inhabitants in the twelfth through twentieth increased nearly 30 percent (though this rise also included many new migrants from the provinces, drawn in part by the heavy demand for construction and excavation workers).[19] That these shifts disproportionately involved the poorer segments of the capital's population is indicated by the fact that the pattern was even more pronounced among those receiving public assistance (see fig. 3.2). Vocal critics of urban renewal, like the journalist Louis Lazare, declared that Paris was being transformed into a city segregated by wealth, as affluent inhabitants clustered in the west and in the center and the poor migrated to the north, east, and south.[20]

From the structural Marxist standpoint, the effects on ordinary people of this vast reshaping of the city cannot be detached theoretically from the changes in the nature of production and the flow of credit that Haussmann's innovations provoked. In Harvey's view, the unleashing of a powerful new system of money and credit allocation, and the real-estate speculation to which it led, produced a spatial arrangement of land use dominated by the imperatives of capital accumulation. Dramatic shifts in the rent surface thus engendered a twofold segregation, separating working-class from bourgeois residential areas, on one hand, and areas of unsightly industrial production from high-rent districts dedicated to finance and middle-class consumption (as in the new department stores, or *grands magasins*), on the other.[21]

What this meant, according to Harvey, was that two kinds of community

18. Gaillard, *Paris: La ville, 1852–1870*, pp. 75–77 and 171n; Adéline Daumard, *Maisons de Paris et propriétaires parisiennes au XIXe siècle, 1809–1880* (Paris: Editions Cujas, 1965), p. 203.

19. Département de la Seine, *Résultats statistiques du dénombrement de 1881 pour la ville de Paris* (Paris: Masson, 1882); Toussaint Loua, *Atlas statistique de la population de Paris* (Paris: J. Dejey, 1873). Population figures for the fifth, sixth, and seventh *arrondissements*, also located in the center but on the left bank of the Seine, exhibited comparatively little change of this kind. In part this resulted from the fact that considerably less construction activity occurred in these districts than in their neighboring areas across the river and on the completely rebuilt Ile de la Cité. As a result, rents grew less quickly on the left bank and existing housing stock absorbed some of the population driven from the right bank (though this influx eventually drove up rents here as well). See Gaillard, *Paris: La ville, 1852–1870*, pp. 85–90.

20. See, e.g., Louis Lazare, *Les quartiers pauvres de Paris* (Paris: Bureau de la Bibliothèque Municipale, 1869), and *Les quartiers de l'est de Paris* (Paris: Bureau de la Bibliothèque Municipale, 1870); Alcide Dusolier, *Les spéculateurs et la mutilation du Luxembourg* (Paris: Librairie du Luxembourg, 1866).

21. Harvey, *Consciousness and the Urban Experience*, pp. 94–95.

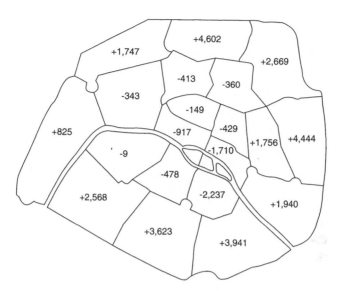

Figure 3.2 Net change in number of indigent residents of Paris districts, 1861–69.

emerged in Second Empire Paris. The most visible was Haussmann's official, modern version, "in which the power of money was celebrated as spectacle and display on the *grands boulevards,* in the *grands magasins,* in the cafés and at the races."[22] But in the outlying districts, beyond the old borders of the city, there emerged another kind of community, in which the men and women of the working class forged a response to the bourgeois control of space in the center:

> The space over which community was defined altered as the scale of urbanization changed and spatial barriers were reduced. But it also shifted in response to new class configurations and struggles in which the participants learned that control over space and spatial networks was a source of social power.
>
> . . . Zones and wedges, centers and peripheries, and even the fine mesh of quarters were much more clearly class-determined or occupationally defined in 1870 than they had been in 1848. Though this had much to do with the spatial scale of the process that Haussmann had unleashed, it was also a reflection of fundamental transformations of the labor process, the industrial structure, and class relations. The consolidation of commercial and financial power, the

22. Ibid., p. 163.

growing separation of workers and masters, and increasing special-
ization in the division of labor were all registered in the production
of new communities of class.[23]

These new communities of class, Harvey argues, were the key element in the
fusion of labor struggles to the movement for municipal autonomy in 1868–71,
"that volatile mix that gave the Commune so much of its force."[24]

In contrast, most authors writing from the humanist point of view have insisted that the work of Napoleon III and Haussmann simply eradicated the sense
of urban community that had tied many Parisians to their city. Jeanne Gaillard,
for example, argues that the workers and small-shop owners forced by rising rents
toward the periphery experienced the transformations as a permanent dispossession from neighborhoods where they had lived and worked their whole lives—a
dispossession made all the more poignant by the fact that many continued to
work in the artisanal center, descending on foot each morning from the heights
of Montmartre, Ménilmontant, and Les Buttes-Chaumont. It was this ravaged
feeling of attachment to the community, she claims, that the insurgents sought to
regain in 1871:

> In effect, haussmannisation deprived the city-dwellers of their mi-
> lieu, took away a culture that was all the more necessary to the extent
> that school and church were, in the Paris of the Second Empire, al-
> most supplementary institutions, less significant than the workshop,
> the street, the meeting-hall, the wine-shop. The disruption and the
> nostalgia that resulted were such that, just as soon as the Empire
> had fallen, the Parisians of the periphery descended on the Hôtel de
> Ville. The reconquest of the center from which they had been driven
> by the public works was not in itself their most important goal; it
> seems incontestable that they were searching beyond this for the re-
> conquest of a *personality* denied by the Empire, of which the old
> quarters of Paris were at once the place and the symbol.[25]

Henri Lefebvre has gone even further, claiming that the tearing up of the capital's
crooked central streets and their replacement with rectilinear boulevards ne-
gated not simply the personality of Paris but the very humanity of urban life.
Throughout western history, he asserts, the city—not Paris in particular but the

23. Ibid., pp. 167–68.
24. Ibid., p. 167.
25. Gaillard, *Paris: La ville, 1852–1870*, p. 3.

city in general—had been an expression of human reason, a haven of sanity and freedom in a chaotic world. But modern capitalism and the peculiarly abstract form of rationality it imposed on daily life turned urban civilization into an oppressive caricature of itself. Once a medium for the representation of meaning, the modern industrial city, aided by a centralizing imperial state, came to force its own meaning on its inhabitants: "Industrialization and the State dominated the City, threw it into a state of confusion, threatened its core and exploded it out toward its periphery . . . The City ceased to be the measure of human existence, the embodiment of majestic reason."[26] The Commune, then, was a movement of an urban population—or of the city itself—desperate to re-create Paris as it was meant to be: "The Parisian insurrection of 1871 was the city's grand and supreme attempt to construct itself as the measure and norm of human reality."[27] Despite its tendency toward mysticism, Lefebvre's argument shares with those of Gaillard, Castells, and Clark (see note 5) a simple, basic claim: the large-scale renovations of 1852–70 took away Parisians' sense of belonging to an urban community, and it was this profound loss that ultimately determined what the Commune was about.

The questions of whether and to what extent the fury of 1871 can be distilled into conflicts over class, community, and state centralization will occupy the next three chapters; my task for the remainder of this chapter is to determine whether either of the interpretations just discussed—one describing a loss of community, the other the formation of "communities of class"—adequately describes the changes in social life in Paris under the Second Empire.[28] To adumbrate the findings, neither perspective is very consistent with observable patterns: the humanist view underestimates the degree to which outlying areas were communities in their own right, while the structural view is wrong to portray social life in these neighborhoods as class-homogeneous.

Community in Center and Periphery

There is a cliché, formulated by paternalist bourgeois reformers during the Second Empire and often repeated since, that the migrations of the working poor

26. Lefebvre, *La proclamation de la Commune*, p. 32.

27. Ibid.

28. The reader will have observed that I have left off discussing the liberal perspective on the changes wrought by Haussmann's projects. The reason is that, as I noted earlier, liberal historians of the Second Empire have tacitly assumed no connection between these changes and the insurrection of 1871. Consequently, demonstrating that such a connection did exist, irrespective of its nature, will imply that the liberal view is inadequate in this regard.

from center to periphery broke their ties to the middle class. Where the poor had previously lived in the same buildings as the wealthy (apartments on higher floors renting at lower rates), they were now cloistered in their own areas, leaving the center free for the bourgeoisie to lead the good life but simultaneously depriving the working class of the former's "civilizing influence."[29] Less condescending versions of this argument, according to which workers were liberated from elite surveillance and thus able to develop an independent (or "counterhegemonic") social and cultural environment, have appeared more recently—Harvey's account being one example.

It is true that the populations of peripheral areas like Montmartre, Belleville, Charonne, La Villette, Grenelle, and Vaugirard were heavily composed of male and female laborers and their dependents. Contrary to the refrain of Haussmann's critics, however, the predominance of workers in these areas was scarcely higher in 1870 than it had been prior to the Second Empire. Take, for example, the case of Belleville, the area most frequently cited as the quintessential working-class section of Paris in the postannexation period. Although boundary changes that occurred at the time of annexation make exact comparisons impossible, census figures for 1851 and 1872 show minimal differences in terms of class composition between the commune of Belleville and the two *arrondissements* (the nineteenth and twentieth) that shared its surface area after 1860 (see table 3.1). In particular, the proportions of people listed as employers (*patrons*) and as laborers (*ouvriers* and *journaliers*) remained practically constant. The central *arrondissements* may have become wealthier, but the residents they lost appear to have made little difference to the socioeconomic composition of districts on the periphery.[30]

Nonetheless, it remains true that workers who migrated to the periphery now found themselves in sections of the city where the population was more uniformly working class than in the center (see fig. 3.3). Accordingly, the key question in evaluating the "community of class" hypothesis is whether these working-class areas now housed families of workers whose social interactions with employers, rentiers, and merchants—in short, with the middle class—had evaporated. Was it really the case that the outlying districts so feared by bourgeois reformers (and

29. Lazare, *Les quartiers pauvres de Paris*.

30. This should hardly be surprising: since the populations of the suburbs already consisted mainly of working people, even the arrival of several thousand more workers would have relatively little impact on the character of these areas. Much more significant would have been an exodus of the middle-class residents who lived in the periphery.

Table 3.1 Occupational Composition of Belleville (1851) and 20th *Arrondissement* (1872)

Occupational Category	Belleville (1851)	20th *Arrondissement* (1872)
Employers	10.0	10.2
Liberal professions	2.3	1.4
White-collar employees	3.9	5.1
Workers	76.4	81.6
Domestic servants	7.4	1.7
TOTAL	100.0	100.0

NOTE: Figures refer to total population, i.e., members of the labor force and their dependents.
SOURCE: Gérard Jacquemet, *Belleville au XIXe siècle: Du faubourg à la ville* (Paris: Éditions de l'École des Hautes Études en Sciences Sociales, 1984).

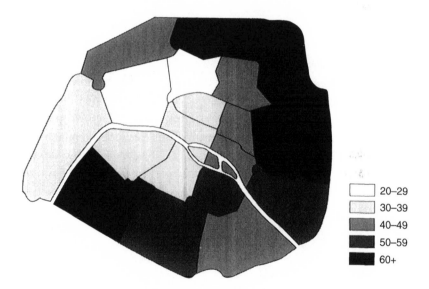

☐	20–29
☐	30–39
▨	40–49
■	50–59
■	60+

Figure 3.3 Percentage of population with working-class occupations, by district (1872 census).

even, it appears, by the police) had forged a working population that was self-contained with respect to its social contacts?

Civil marriage records (*actes de mariage*) from the municipal archives of Paris afford a rare glimpse into this issue. Marrying couples were required by law to sign a marriage certificate at the *mairie* of the bride's district of residence, in the presence of four witnesses. Because all parties to the marriage ceremony gave their names, addresses, ages, and occupations, the *actes de mariage* record basic attributes of the close personal associates of brides and grooms—subject to the unfortunate constraint that witnesses had to be adult men.[31] Tables 3.2–3.5 reproduce residential and occupational information for the witnesses to 153 randomly selected marriages that took place in four adjacent *arrondissements* in 1869. A little more than half of the marriages occurred in the third and tenth districts (Arts et Métiers and Enclos-St. Laurent, located in the eastern half of the old city), while the remainder took place in the nineteenth and twentieth (comprising the three former communes of La Villette, Belleville, and Charonne).[32] The four areas were chosen so as to provide a contrast between the densely populated, artisanal core of the city and the newly annexed, heavily working-class sections of the northeast.

One more detail requires mention: it is well known that artisanal occupational titles like "mason" or "shoemaker" could refer to either employers or wage-workers unless accompanied by a modifier (as in *ouvrier imprimeur* or *maître boulanger*). To avoid incorrect characterizations of employers as workers, I searched the commercial directories of 1869 and 1870 for every name that appeared in the marriage records (918 names in all), coding an individual as an employer if the name was listed in the directory at the appropriate address.[33] This procedure minimized erroneous assignment of witnesses, brides, and grooms to class categories based on omitted modifiers. In addition, individuals listing their occupation as "manufacturer" or "merchant" (for example, *fabricant de boutons* or *marchand de vins*) were coded as middle class.[34] (See appendix A for a list of

31. Another difficulty that occasionally arises in the use of marriage records is that city clerks or merchants located near the *mairie* might occasionally fill in for missing witnesses, with the result that their repeated appearances could distort the occupational composition of witness groups. This does not appear to be a problem here: only 2 witnesses out of 612 appear more than once in the sample, and then only because two sets of relatives were married in the same year.

32. The official names of the nineteenth and twentieth *arrondissements* were, respectively, Buttes-Chaumont and Ménilmontant. Residents continued to use the commune names well past the end of the century, however; I shall adhere to the informal usage in my discussion.

33. The directory in question was the *Annuaire du commerce et de l'industrie pour la ville de Paris* (Paris: Société Didot-Bottin, 1869 and 1870).

34. In the tables presented here, individuals listing a white-collar occupation (*employé de commerce, garçon de bureau, comptable,* and so on) are coded as middle class, as there is considerable evidence that many people in these jobs came from bourgeois families. This occupational category was diverse, however, creating a potential source of distortion in the data—particularly if poorer white-collar employees tended to live on the periphery. I therefore performed the same analysis with all white-collar employees (witnesses, brides, and grooms) coded as workers rather than middle class.

occupations and their assignment to class categories; the same classification scheme is used for arrested insurgents in chap. 6).

Table 3.2 reports the socioeconomic composition of witness groups for the four districts, separating middle-class from working-class couples and central from peripheral neighborhoods.[35] Not surprisingly, middle-class couples overall had more middle-class people in their witness groups; and witnesses to marriages in peripheral neighborhoods were more likely to have working-class occupations than those in central neighborhoods. The former pattern indicates a noticeable but hardly overwhelming level of class homogeneity in friendship networks, while the latter reflects the smaller number of middle-class people residing in outlying areas. (Note that *both* working-class and middle-class couples in these areas invited fewer middle-class people to witness their marriages.)

What is striking, however, is that middle-class witnesses appear with surprising frequency for all worker couples, even those in peripheral neighborhoods. Three-fourths of working-class marriages in the two outlying districts included at least one middle-class witness; the average number of middle-class witnesses at such marriages was 1.19 out of 4. Overall, then, nearly one-third of the witnesses to marriages among workers had middle-class occupations—despite the fact that the population of this part of the city was nearly 80 percent working class. In other words, the middle class was systematically overrepresented in the immediate personal networks of these couples. In contrast, workers in the third and tenth *arrondissements* invited middle-class people to their marriages at rates *below* what one would expect if the selections had been made at random from the surrounding area:[36] 43 percent of their witnesses were listed as having middle-

---

This procedure yielded essentially the same findings as those reported here; in fact, the overrepresentation of middle-class witnesses on the periphery actually increased. For a good discussion of white-collar workers in the capital, see Lenard Berlanstein, *The Working People of Paris, 1871–1914* (Baltimore: Johns Hopkins University Press, 1984), pp. 30–35.

35. The occupations of the bride and groom were almost always class-consistent; in particular, it was extremely rare for a middle-class woman to marry a man whose occupation identified him as a laborer. On the other hand, most middle-class men married women who reported having "no occupation." When one member of a couple reported a middle-class occupation, the couple was treated as middle class.

36. This assumption represents an admittedly unrealistic "null model," insofar as it ignores the fact that Parisian social networks spanned district boundaries. In addition, the extent to which witness groups crossed neighborhood lines varied across geographical areas. But, as I shall demonstrate presently, witness groups in peripheral *arrondissements* were more likely to be neighbors than those in the center, making the overrepresentation of middle-class witnesses in the nineteenth and twentieth *arrondissements* even more noteworthy.

Table 3.2 Class Makeup of Witnesses to Parisian Marriages, 1869

Number of Middle-Class Witnesses per Marriage	Central Districts		Peripheral Districts	
	%	N	%	N
All couples				
0	8.2	7	23.5	16
1	27.1	23	30.9	21
2	22.4	19	35.3	24
3	30.6	26	10.3	7
4	11.8	10	0.0	0
TOTAL	100.1	85	100.0	68
MEAN	2.11		1.32	
Working-class couples only				
0	8.9	4	27.6	16
1	40.0	18	32.8	19
2	22.2	10	32.8	19
3	26.7	12	6.9	4
4	2.2	1	0.0	0
TOTAL	100.0	45	100.0	58
MEAN	1.73		1.19	

NOTE: "Middle-class" includes employers, proprietors, merchants, and white-collar employees; see appendix A for full list with French-language terms.

class occupations, even though the middle-class outnumbered the working-class population in these two districts (employers, proprietors, and white-collar employees made up 56 percent of the population in the third *arrondissement*, and 52 percent in the tenth). Thus, even though the absolute frequency of bourgeois witnesses at working-class marriages was higher in the center of Paris, in relative terms it was decidedly lower than in the periphery. Whatever the workers of La Villette, Belleville, and Charonne were doing in their personal lives, they were not sealing themselves off from the bourgeoisie.[37]

As for the argument that urban renovations created craft-specific neighborhoods on the periphery, marriage documents suggest that the contrary took place.

37. Part of the difference could be interpreted in the contrary sense, as showing that middle-class people in the center were more likely to demur when invited to witness workers' marriages. But this would not account for the overrepresentation of middle-class witnesses in outlying districts; nor, in any case, would it change the conclusion, which is that class boundaries were more permeable on the periphery.

Table 3.3 Number of Marriage Witnesses in Same Craft as Bride or Groom
(couples with at least one craft worker)

Number of Witnesses in Same Craft	Central Districts		Peripheral Districts	
	%	N	%	N
0	32.6	14	38.8	19
1	27.9	12	42.9	21
2	25.6	11	12.2	6
3	11.6	5	6.1	3
4	2.3	1	0.0	0
TOTAL	100.0	43	100.0	49
MEAN[a]	1.23		0.86	

[a]Difference between means is significant at the .10 level.

In the center, witness groups for craft-worker marriages frequently included two or more individuals who listed the same occupation (or a closely related one) as either the bride or groom (see table 3.3).[38] In Belleville, La Villette, and Charonne, on the other hand, shared occupational categories appeared with significantly less frequency: the proportion of marriages in which the bride's or groom's occupation matched that of two or more witnesses was less than half the corresponding figure for the central districts (for the third and tenth, 39.5 percent; for the nineteenth and twentieth, 18.6 percent). As I shall show in the next chapter, a number of craft communities survived in the artisanal center of the city, a fact that was critical for the reemergence of a labor movement in Paris in the 1860s. But toward the periphery, contrary to Harvey's assertion, there is little evidence of the existence of craft enclaves; instead, laborers in these neighborhoods appear to have drawn on a wider variety of occupational groups, including nonworkers, in forming their first-order personal networks. Social networks on the periphery do not appear to have respected the boundaries of either class or craft.

In another sense, though, the former suburbs did form enclaves—defined in spatial rather than occupational terms. In contrast to what one might predict on the basis of the humanist claim concerning the "loss of community," Parisians residing on the fringe of the enlarged city exhibited a distinct pattern of neighborhood solidarity. This was especially true for workers. To begin with, 85 percent

38. For example, if the bride gave her occupation as "wood gilder" (*doreuse sur bois*) and a witness was listed as a frame-maker (*ouvrier en cadres*), they were coded as having a related occupation—since almost all frame-making shops employed gilders.

Table 3.4 Number of Marriage Witnesses Living in District where Marriage Occurred

Number of Witnesses Living in Same District	Central Districts		Peripheral Districts	
	%	N	%	N
All couples				
0	21.2	18	19.1	13
1	41.2	35	11.8	8
2	24.7	21	41.2	28
3	9.4	8	14.7	10
4	3.5	3	13.2	9
TOTAL	100.0	85	100.0	68
MEAN[a]	1.33		1.91	
Working-class couples only				
0	15.6	7	12.1	7
1	44.4	20	8.6	5
2	20.0	9	48.3	28
3	17.8	8	15.5	9
4	2.2	1	15.5	9
TOTAL	100.0	45	100.0	58
MEAN[a]	1.47		2.14	

[a]Difference between means (center vs. periphery) is significant at the .01 level.

of couples marrying in the nineteenth and twentieth *arrondissements* lived in the same district at the time of the ceremony, compared with 65 percent for marriages in the central districts; often, in fact, the bride and groom lived in neighboring buildings.[39] Moreover, witness groups on the periphery included significantly larger numbers of residents of the district where the marriage took place, as table 3.4 demonstrates: more than twice as many working-class marriages in the nineteenth and twentieth *arrondissements* were witnessed by two or more people from the same *arrondissement* as in the third and tenth (average number of "neighbor" witnesses for the center, 1.47; for the periphery, 2.14). To ensure that the pattern observed in table 3.4 is not merely an artifact of the placement of official boundaries, table 3.5 defines a witness as a "neighbor" if his residence was located

39. It was not uncommon for working-class couples to live together before marrying, and they occasionally legitimized one or more children as part of the marriage ceremony. However, the frequency of such marriages did not differ between center and periphery, and so cannot account for the pattern observed in table 3.4.

Table 3.5 Number of Marriage Witnesses Living within 100 Meters of Bride or Groom

Number of Witnesses Living < 100 m Away	Central Districts		Peripheral Districts	
	%	N	%	N
All couples				
0	29.4	25	16.2	11
1	45.9	39	29.4	20
2	15.3	13	27.9	19
3	9.4	8	19.1	13
4	0.0	0	7.4	5
TOTAL	100.0	85	100.0	68
MEAN[a]	1.02		1.74	
Working-class couples only				
0	24.4	11	12.1	7
1	46.7	21	29.3	17
2	15.6	7	29.3	17
3	13.3	6	20.7	12
4	0.0	0	8.6	5
TOTAL	100.1	45	100.0	58
MEAN[a]	1.18		1.84	

[a]Difference between means (center vs. periphery) is significant at the .01 level.

within 100 meters of either the bride's or the groom's residence. Even with this rather restrictive definition of neighborhood—particularly so given the lower population density of the peripheral districts—the pattern remains. If the notion of "urban community" is taken to refer to groups whose shared social identification draws in part on a common spatial location—that is, on a sense of place—it appears that Parisians in the annexed suburbs of the northeast were more clearly attached to an urban community than were those in the city center. Social groupings in the center, in contrast, revolved around communities of craft and were more homogeneous in class terms.

Given the industrial geography of Second Empire Paris, this contrast makes considerable sense. Even though large numbers of wage-earners moved to the annexed communes, industrial establishments did not. Artisanal manufacture, much of it occurring in workshops with fewer than ten employees, remained fixed in the *arrondissements* of the center, while large industrial enterprises situated their factories outside the city's extended borders so as to avoid the city's tax on supplies. In between, the former suburbs remained heavily residential in charac-

0.5–1.49
1.5–2.49
2.5–3.49
3.5–4.49

Figure 3.4 Ratio of industrial establishments to residential buildings, 1872.

ter, organized more by the logic of collective consumption than by the imperatives of industrial production (see fig. 3.4 and plates 1 and 2). Social life reflected
this difference: where wineshops and cabarets in the center catered to clienteles
from specific crafts employed in nearby workshops, filling up with groups of coworkers during lunch breaks and after working hours, those on the periphery
served constituencies defined by place. In the absence of trade-specific enclaves,
like the wood-working district of the Faubourg Saint Antoine, they drew on the
full range of local residents, thereby becoming neighborhood institutions rather
than extensions of the workplace. Life on the periphery was not characterized by
a loss of community but by a substitution of neighborhood bonds for communities
based on the world of work.

Conclusion

The transformations that Paris and its inhabitants experienced during the Second
Empire were monumental in every sense of the word. Just as Louis Bonaparte
and Haussmann had intended, the capital became a model of urban planning for
architects, engineers, and monarchs throughout Europe.[40] And despite the tur-

40. Giedion, *Space, Time, and Architecture*, p. 755; Hervé Maneglier, *Paris Impérial: La vie quotidienne sous le Second Empire* (Paris: Armand Colin, 1990), p. 263.

Plate 1 A commercial-industrial street in the center of Paris: rue du faubourg Saint Denis, near the intersection of the second, third, and tenth *arrondissements*. (Source: Bibliothèque Historique de la Ville de Paris.)

Plate 2 Neighbors (*at rear*) conversing in a residential street on the Paris periphery: intersection of the rue des Saules and the rue Saint Vincent, in Montmartre, 1860s. Note the cabaret (Au lapin agile) at left. (Source: Bibliothèque Historique de la Ville de Paris.)

moil that enveloped the Prefect's final years, the boulevards he created and the new construction that sprang up around them contributed to a sixteen-year period of unparalleled growth in the French economy.

The dark side of this experiment with urban splendor was the disruption it caused for the mass of the city's population, those whose bearing and attire did not suit them for the genteel existence of the Opera, the boulevards, and the cafés. Indeed, it was already clear to critics in the 1860s that most of the investment in the new Paris had been concentrated in the historic center, where returns were likely to be higher. Comparatively little construction occurred outside the first ring of boulevards, and the quality of the housing stock that did appear in outlying areas was largely unregulated—in contrast to building on the large boulevards, where Haussmann specified everything from the kind of quarry stone to be used to the height and design of windows.[41] To the extent that Haussmann concerned himself with poorer neighborhoods, whether on the periphery or closer to the center (such as the celebrated Faubourg Saint Antoine), it was primarily to ensure that they were pierced with streets wide enough to accommodate troops and artillery.

But the result of this general neglect was not the loss of community lamented by Gaillard, Castells, and Lefebvre; nor was it the creation of a second Paris beyond the reach of the forces of order. Viewing the transformations of Paris from a standpoint in the historic center, scholarly treatments of the period have all too easily lost sight of the fact that the annexed suburbs were communities too—with their own laborers, merchants, markets, and wineshops—for centuries before Haussmann's surveyors incorporated them into the urban grid.[42] The arrival of thousands of new residents, chased from the center by rising rents or drawn from the provinces by rising wages, was hardly sufficient to destroy these vibrant communities; on the contrary, the marriage records I have examined suggest that the new arrivals found themselves in, and ultimately joined, something akin to an urban village.[43]

To say that neighborhoods on the urban periphery matched commonsense

41. Gaillard, *Paris: La ville, 1852–1870*, pp. 78–80; on the demanding specifications for boulevard façades, see Pierre Lavedan, *Histoire de l'urbanisme à Paris* (Paris: Hachette, 1975).

42. For a vivid account of life in these areas, see David Garrioch, *Community and Neighborhood in Paris, 1740–90* (New York: Oxford University Press, 1986).

43. It is generally impossible to distinguish in the marriage records between recent arrivals from central Paris and long-time residents of the suburban communes. To my knowledge, however, there is no evidence that migrants from the provinces or from inside the first ring of boulevards were systematically excluded from neighborhood life in the peripheral districts.

Plate 3 One of Haussmann's boulevards: boulevard Ornano, in Montmartre. (Source: Bibliothèque Historique de la Ville de Paris.)

notions of "community" is not to romanticize everyday life in the areas that eventually became known as the *faubourgs*.[44] Belleville, Montmartre, La Villette, Vaugirard, and Grenelle contained areas of crushing poverty, unsanitary living conditions, vagrancy, and crime. But they also provided innumerable places of sociability, such as the *marchands de vins* or *bals populaires;* narrow, winding streets on which one could not but acknowledge the people in one's path; and patterns of close personal association that bridged social strata and trade boundaries but consistently favored residents of the immediate neighborhood.

In one sense, in fact, Haussmann's street renovations may have enhanced the experience of neighborhood for many Parisians by impressing upon them a new

44. The term was not new, just its application to the areas that had been suburban communes until 1860. The idea that the *faubourgs* were marginal areas (in both the social and spatial sense) that harbored the "dangerous classes" dated at least to the previous century and probably earlier. See Louis Chevalier, *Classes laborieuses et classes dangereuses pendant la première moitié du dix-neuvième siècle* (Paris: Plon, 1958); John Merriman, *On the Margins of City Life: Explorations on the Urban Frontier, 1815–1851* (New York: Oxford University Press, 1991), pp. 59–64.

and inescapable contrast. The cutting of wide boulevards through dense areas to accommodate the growing volume of commercial and private vehicles simultaneously siphoned through-traffic away from residential areas and drew stark boundaries around them (see plate 3). In place of a largely seamless, citywide web of intersecting streets, there emerged a series of enclaves, dominated internally by foot traffic and punctuated by wide, tree-lined thoroughfares with monumental vistas. If the groups promenading on these boulevards and relaxing in the cafés heralded a new era of capitalism, "the power of money," and upscale consumption, the streets themselves—not to mention the endless rows of uniform facades mandated by Haussmann's strict specifications—announced the presence of an assertive and centralizing state authority. Community in Paris had not been eliminated, nor had it been redefined along strict class lines; but it had been visibly set apart from, and thus thrown into relief by, the urban imprint of the imperial state.

That contrast, initially inscribed in mortar and stone, soon found its way into political activity once the Empire liberalized in the 1860s. Moreover, it furnished the conceptual basis for a neighborhood collective identity reinforced by the networks of social relations described in the last few pages. This neighborhood identity ultimately crystallized in militant form in the popular club meetings of 1868–1870, a protest movement contemporaneous with and related to, but nonetheless quite distinct from, the revitalized Parisian labor movement. These parallel movements, and their differences, form the subject of the next two chapters.

4

Labor Protest in Paris in the 1860s

I N T H E class-formation narrative I described in chapter 1, workers fought their century-long struggle against capital on many fronts at once. On this view, each of the numerous forms of working-class militancy was part of an elaborate and increasingly self-conscious challenge to the growth of industrial capitalism and the resulting erosion of the status, autonomy, and economic well-being of manual laborers. Responding to the novel threats posed by capitalist production in the decades following 1830, French craft workers organized strikes and blacklists (*interdictions*) against unpopular employers, published radical newspapers attacking capitalism and market society, and founded producers' cooperatives often associated with clandestine unions (usually called *sociétés de résistance*). This diverse collection of protest tactics and the vision of social emancipation that emerged with it have become known as "the labor movement"—and in France, even more tellingly, as *le mouvement social*.

As I noted earlier, students of nineteenth-century France consistently apply the analytical frame furnished by the class-formation narrative to the great upheavals of 1830, 1848, and 1871. This theoretical tactic has highlighted those aspects of French urban insurrections that can be mapped comfortably into the schematic story of emerging class activism—in particular, the spread of socialist rhetoric and the creation of organizational forms through which workers were able to confront employers collectively and on a large scale. Katznelson, for instance, views these revolutionary upheavals as watershed moments in the French labor movement, above all because they simultaneously expressed and solidified class consciousness:

> Utilizing a radical republican discourse fused to the language of socialism, workers resisted at the microlevel of the village and, in the 1830s but especially in 1848, in a national workers' movement that was underpinned organizationally by workers' corporate associations. At these moments there was a remarkable unity to the targets

of working-class mobilization—both employers and the state—and
to the rhetoric of the working-class movement.[1]

A major virtue of this perspective is its analytical power: it resolves half a century
of immensely differentiated and complex events into a persuasive account of
working-class mobilization against the rise of capitalism. Moreover, it accom-
plishes this task in a nondogmatic way, insofar as thirty years of social history
have led to deep revisions of the proletarianization thesis advanced by Marx.
While scholars continue to differ on the basic causes of working-class protest
(mechanization, deskilling, and paternalistic cultural hegemony are among the
candidates), most now agree that skilled artisanal workers rather than unskilled
industrial proletarians formed the dedicated core of the French labor movement.[2]
It was not because they had nothing to lose but their chains that handicraft workers were able to mount a fierce struggle against capitalist production; on the contrary, studies of labor protest in France and elsewhere in Europe usually account
for the distinctive ability of artisanal workers to mobilize effectively by pointing
to their extensive social organization and strong corporate traditions.

Despite its success in making sense of protest in industrializing France, the
class-formation narrative necessarily—even deliberately—understates the extent to which social conflict in this period drew on participation identities other
than class. In chapter 2, I showed that the striking clarity of the working-class
solidarity that crystallized in the first six months of 1848 could be traced to a
highly specific and transient set of political and organizational circumstances:
the fact that extension of the suffrage to the laboring poor coincided with an
employment crisis that made the "right to work" a matter of life and death, and
the creation of two major institutions—the National Workshops and the Luxembourg Commission—whose constituents were identified explicitly and exclusively in terms of their status as workers. The corollary of this argument is obvious: when these exceptional circumstances ceased to obtain, social protest

1. Katznelson, "Working-Class Formation: Constructing Cases and Comparisons," p. 25.

2. See Sewell, *Work and Revolution in France;* Jacques Rougerie, "Composition d'une population insurgée: L'exemple de la Commune," *Le mouvement social,* no. 45 (July–September 1964), pp.
31–47; Shorter and Tilly, *Strikes in France, 1830–1968;* Michael Hanagan, *The Logic of Solidarity:
Artisans and Industrial Workers in Three French Towns, 1871–1914* (Urbana: University of Illinois
Press, 1980); Joan Wallach Scott, *The Glassworkers of Carmaux: French Craftsmen and Political Action in a Nineteenth-Century City* (Cambridge, MA: Harvard University Press, 1974); Bernard Moss,
The Origins of the French Labor Movement, 1830–1914: The Socialism of Skilled Workers (Berkeley:
University of California Press, 1976); Ronald A. Aminzade, *Class, Politics, and Early Industrial Cap-
italism.*

reverted to a reliance on collective identities linked to more durable forms of social organization.

One form that offered a powerful alternative to class mobilization was the craft group. Indeed, a principal lesson of recent historical scholarship on French labor protest has been the recognition that occupational loyalties continually interfered with radical attempts to forge a universal class solidarity consistent with socialist ideas (recall Louis Blanc's admonition to Parisian workers, cited in chap. 2). Workers' organizations such as mutual-aid societies and cooperative associations routinely restricted membership to those exercising a specific trade, and street brawls between rival sects of *compagnonnage* far outnumbered instances of cross-trade cooperation until the 1880s. Throughout the nineteenth century, and on into the twentieth, working-class militants mobilized industrial protest in ways that were dominated by what many have termed "trade consciousness." To the degree that this term refers to an articulated ideology, it means that the overarching program guiding these activists was that of cooperative socialism: they envisioned a future in which producers' associations would eventually supplant market competition and private ownership of capital, and society would be governed by a federation of trades.[3] But to the degree that "trade consciousness" concerns the kind of solidarity that enabled workers to mobilize for collective action, it means that membership in a specific occupation (shoemaker, mason, tailor, etc.) formed the minimally inclusive collective identity for most artisanal participants in labor struggles.

This chapter will be devoted to the task of explaining why craft identities remained so central to labor protest in Paris even after the class-oriented upheavals of 1848. A major factor in this persistence, I contend, was the survival of several craft enclaves—occupational groups in which informal social ties coincided with professional ties—in the industrial city center. In contrast, trades whose practitioners gradually spread across the expanded city were significantly more passive in the labor movement, partly because of transformations in the organization of work but also because their dispersion produced patterns of social interaction that cut across trade boundaries, linking them to neighborhoods rather than occupational groups.

The next chapter will show that the urban transformations of the Second Em-

3. Moss, *The Origins of the French Labor Movement;* Sewell, *Work and Revolution in France;* Gossez, *Les ouvriers de Paris;* Duveau, *La vie ouvrière en France sous le Second Empire;* Jeanne Gaillard, "Les associations de production et la pensée politique en France (1852–1870)," *Le mouvement social,* no. 52 (July–September 1965), pp. 59–84.

pire contributed to the reemergence of another kind of activism: the public meeting. These tumultuous assemblies were thoroughly detached from shop-floor conflict and, I shall argue, relied on the participation identity of neighborhood rather than that of craft. Moreover, unlike their revolutionary forerunners (the "sections" of 1792 and the democratic clubs of 1848), these meetings were recorded by police stenographers and supervised by police officials with the authority to dissolve them at any moment. This conspicuous and often repressive intrusion of state authority into neighborhood gatherings created a galling echo of the state/community opposition I described in chapter 3—an opposition that was expressed in Haussmann's imperial boulevards and reinforced by the emergence of residential areas where social ties were structured more by neighborhood than by craft. The major failing of the class-formation narrative has been to obscure the deep influence of this opposition, and the participation identity it implied, on the character of the 1871 insurrection.

✺ Craft Communities and Labor Militancy in the 1860s ✺

The law of May 25, 1864, granting French workers a restricted "right to strike"[4] was intended to give the laboring classes a means to express their grievances while at the same time integrating them into a "workers' movement" subject to the paternalistic guidance of the state. To this end, the new law permitted strikes but at the same time forbade workers to form associations whose purpose was to enforce strikes or otherwise interfere with the "freedom to work." The only formal organizations permitted under the law were producers' cooperatives and mutual-aid societies, which were required to register with the government and even submit the names of their elected officers to the Ministry of the Interior for approval.

Despite these precautions, however, and to the dismay of public officials all over France, the new law unleashed a rash of strikes that seemed to many observers to pose a serious threat to the economy, if not to the entire social order. By November of 1864, the Paris Prefect of Police was already able to report serious citywide strikes on the part of bookbinders, armchair makers, copper founders, bronze workers, zinc workers, iron founders, and others.[5]

One of the more troubling features of these strikes, from the point of view of employers, was the increasing tendency of participants to add calls for greater shop-floor control to their wage demands. Even when wages were the central is-

---

4. Though widely used, this phrase is something of a misnomer since the law made no mention of a "right" to anything. Rather, it simply repealed the statute of 1791, which made strikes illegal.

5. Archives Nationales (henceforth A.N.) F[12] 4651—Ministère du Commerce.

sue, the strikers' typical strategy was to propose a *tarif*, or uniform wage scale, to which all local employers in the industry were expected to adhere. More often, workers simultaneously demanded a wage increase and a variety of new regulations involving the length of the work day, management practices, and the like. In an 1864 strike that attracted the police prefect's attention, fourteen copper molders submitted to their employer a collective letter demanding

> Elimination of piece-work;
> Dismissal of the present foreman;
> Reduction of the work day from 11 to 10 hours;
> Limitation of the number of apprentices to four.[6]

The scope and character of these demands show clearly that workers struck not simply to augment their daily earnings but to combat tangible encroachments on their autonomy in the workplace. The attempt to regulate the number of apprentices, which was a common tactic among older trades with strong roots in the corporate traditions of the old regime, is particularly revealing: workers were acutely aware of the connection between their bargaining power and the process by which their skills were imparted to new practitioners of the trade. If workers relinquished control over the training of apprentices, employers would have the power not only to increase the supply of new labor when they saw fit but also to tinker with the production process itself in ways that could further weaken workers' monopoly on skills.

This erosion of workers' shop-floor autonomy was already quite advanced in certain Parisian trades in the 1860s, most notably in the shoe and clothing industries: thousands of tailors and shoemakers, many of whom had once been employed in—or owned—small *ateliers* with three or four coworkers, now worked at home or in large factories assembling shoes and garments from prefabricated pieces. The expansion of this form of production, known generally as *confection*, was accompanied not only by an intensification of the division of labor but also by a substantial increase in the number of women employed in the industry.[7] The proportion of women workers in the clothing and shoe trades, which had already

---

6. A. N. F^{12} 4651.

7. Gérard Noiriel, *Les ouvriers dans la société française, XIXe–XXe siècles* (Paris: Editions du Seuil, 1986); Roger Price, *A Social History of Nineteenth-Century France* (London: Hutchinson, 1987); Lorraine Coons, *Women Home Workers in the Parisian Garment Industry, 1860–1915*. For a discussion of the reactions of workers and employers to the growth of the female labor force in the Parisian garment industry, see Joan W. Scott, *Gender and the Politics of History*, chap. 5.

reached 64 percent in 1848, was over 73 percent at the time of the 1866 census.[8] At the same time, the dilution of skills which *confection* entailed was expressed in the language: more and more workers were identified as "shoe cutters" (*coupeurs en chaussures*) or "stitchers" (*brocheurs*) in place of the more general "shoemaker" (*cordonnier*), reflecting the gradual disappearance of the true artisan whose skills encompassed the entire production process, from the design stage to the finishing touches. Although these changes occurred over decades, they did not pass unnoticed in Paris: workers in numerous trades frequently included among their strike demands the dismissal of women workers and the elimination of domestic outwork.[9]

The opposition to the hiring of women demonstrates that workers frequently responded to the changes they observed by attacking symptoms rather than causes. Nevertheless, some workers—most often those affiliated with the socialist International Workingmen's Association—explicitly interpreted these transformations as aspects of the proliferation of capitalist enterprise: during the tailors' strike of April 1867, a worker at one meeting began his remarks by identifying as the twin enemies "that monstrous octopus, known as *confection*, which we must exterminate, and the squalid, greedy hand of capital which uses it to enslave all workers."[10]

The same worker concluded with the declaration that "the future of the labor movement depends on the decision that this assembly will make." Both of these statements are striking because of their deliberate identification of the struggle of a single occupational group—the tailors—with a movement of the working class as a whole. The increasingly common use of this kind of language over the course of the nineteenth century has, naturally, led some scholars to argue that French workers were gradually developing "class consciousness" in the standard sense: an awareness that they shared a common interest, regardless of their trade, by virtue of their economic position vis-à-vis capitalist employers. For example, in his study of Toulouse, Ronald Aminzade argues that trade loyalties began to yield to a more universal class identification in the decades preceding 1871:

8. Chambre de Commerce de Paris, *Statistique de l'industrie à Paris, résultant de l'enquête faite par la Chambre de Commerce pour les années 1847–1848* (Paris: Guillaumin, 1851); Statistique générale de la France, *Résultats généraux du dénombrement de 1866* (Paris: Imprimerie Nationale, 1869).

9. See, for example, the police records on the typographers' strikes in 1862 and 1865, both of which were staged in response to the hiring of women workers—A.N. BB[18] 1645, dossier 6292, and BB[18] 1719, dossier 3421—Police Générale.

10. AN BB[18] 1747, dossier 6427—Police Générale.

Changes took place in the nature of the solidarities to which strikers appealed, as well as in the composition of strike participants and demands. Class solidarities came to play a more important role in strikes which, even when centered around the defense of trade interests, increasingly displayed a more general class character and a growing cooperation among workers of different trades. The threat and experience of proletarianization fostered the growth of class solidarities among workers, generating an acknowledgement of their common plight as propertyless wage laborers. This acknowledgement was reflected in the increasing exchange of strike support across occupational and city boundaries and even across the traditional barrier between skilled and unskilled workers . . . Strike activities, and the support they generated among workers from other trades and other cities, fostered direct personal ties to the symbols, history and culture of the working class rather than to those of any single occupational group.[11]

Whether or not it is valid in the case of Toulouse, such an assertion would be difficult to support in the Parisian context, as I shall now show.

It is certainly true that, like the tailor quoted above, some workers viewed strikes as trade-oriented actions which nevertheless contributed to a more broadly defined working-class movement. This viewpoint manifested itself in the Parisian bronze-workers' strike, which preceded the tailors' strike by a few months and received considerable public support from the First International. (Henri Tolain, a bronze chaser who had helped found the Paris chapter of the International in 1865, was instrumental in mobilizing outside support for the strike; Zéphirin Camélinat, a bronze mounter and another early member of the International, was one of the strike's principal leaders.) In the course of this conflict, representatives from a variety of trade unions circulated an appeal to workers from all trades, proclaiming,

> Workers, we are all under attack! Let us all rise as one and prove that, through our unity, right may triumph over injustice . . .
>
> But words are not enough: we ask, our interests demand, generous assistance.
>
> Let us join together and give strong support to our fellows—sup-

11. Aminzade, *Class, Politics, and Early Industrial Capitalism*, pp. 81–82.

port which they will return later—so that abundant good may come from this temporary evil.[12]

Clearly, some labor activists in Paris were adopting the class struggle language of 1848 in an effort to forge alliances across trade lines. On the other hand, these workers continually mixed this new language with terms that underscored the very divisions they were trying to bridge. The circular just quoted, despite its emphasis on the common plight of all workers, bore the title "Appeal to the Corporations" (*Appel aux corporations*)—employing a term dating from the old regime which in the 1860s could refer either to a formal workers' organization or simply to the entire body of workers practicing a particular trade in one city.[13] Whichever interpretation we assign to the word, its use in this context demonstrates that even the most universalistic appeals to working-class solidarity continued to recognize the framework of trade loyalties that shaped labor conflicts. As far as language was concerned, the labor movement in Paris in the 1860s was still substantially under the influence of the "corporate idiom."

The identification of workers first as members of a *corporation* and only secondarily as part of a broader population of "workers" or "laborers" was closely linked to the dominant pattern in the French labor movement and in French—particularly Proudhonist—socialism throughout the second half of the nineteenth century. Beginning in the 1830s, the central theme in French socialist thinking as well as in the popular worker's press was the idea of association: by pooling their resources to form cooperative producers' associations, workers

12. A. N. BB[18] 1747, dossier 6427.

13. In the flurry of organizational activity that followed the fall of the Empire in September 1870, the term "corporation" was used almost constantly in newspaper announcements of workers' meetings. Thus, in the popular journal *Le mot d'ordre* on February 18, 1871, a notice appeared stating, "The members of the upholstery workers' union wish to make known to the entire corporation that our public meetings will resume beginning the 20th of this month." Similarly, on February 20, "The corporation of tailors is summoned . . . " and on May 22 in *Paris libre*, "A call to the entire corporation of butcher workers to form a union." Workers in the first half of the nineteenth century used the term "corporation" to refer to their formally constituted associations, which in this earlier period usually consisted of all of the workers in one trade living in the same city. See the extensive discussion of the term "corporation" and other related terms, such as "corps d'etat" and "corps de métier" in Sewell, *Work and Revolution in France*, pp. 187–93. In the 1860s, trade associations frequently included only a fraction of their constituents as actual members; the fact that the term "corporation" continued to refer to all the workers practicing a given trade suggests that workers retained a sense that their professions defined a community regardless of whether they belonged to a formally constituted association.

would gradually and peacefully replace competitive capitalist production, leading to a just and egalitarian society in which labor, not capital, would be supreme. A necessary feature of this program, then, was that the basic unit of the labor movement, the association, would be confined to workers in a single trade. During the national strike wave of 1833, especially in Lyon, and again in the revolution of 1848, this utopian vision developed a further dimension with the emergence of the concept of an association of associations—that is, a federation made up of worker-representatives from every trade which would ultimately preside over the social order.

From the standpoint of this discussion, the most significant aspect of this vision is how little it changed in the decades following its first appearance in 1833. Indeed, Bernard Moss has argued that substantially the same program—which he terms "federative trade socialism"—underlay both the cooperative socialist movement of the 1850s and 1860s and the emergence of working-class political parties in the twenty years preceding the First World War.[14] The Paris branch of the First International helped set up in 1869 a federation of workers' organizations (Chambre Fédérale des Sociétés Ouvrières), with the explicit purpose of preparing workers for the day when "the government is replaced by a union of trade councils [les conseils des corps de métiers réunis] and by a committee of their respective delegates, regulating labor relations which will take the place of politics."[15] In other words, the organization most dedicated to promoting working-class solidarity across trade boundaries (many of the signers of the *Appel aux corporations* I quoted earlier were members of the International) was equally dedicated to the notion that workers should unite *as members of their respective trades.* In this respect, the French socialists of the 1860s hardly differed from the workers of Lyon in 1833, who hoped that cooperation among different trades would eventually lead to the establishment of a grand association of trades or "confraternity of proletarians."[16]

To sum up briefly, claims about the emergence of a "more general class character" in labor activism would be misleading if applied to Paris, since they would obscure the continued primacy of trade as a participation identity in the Parisian labor movement.[17] Insofar as a general working-class consciousness can be said

14. Moss, *The Origins of the French Labor Movement,* p. 12.

15. J. Freymond, *La Première Internationale* (Geneva: Droz, 1962), vol. 2, pp. 108–9.

16. Sewell, *Work and Revolution in France,* p. 213.

17. Of course, since this discussion is confined to Parisian workers, the evidence presented here does not necessarily militate against Aminzade's conclusions, which concern Toulouse. On the other

to have developed in this period, it did so by building upon—not by replacing—preexisting solidarities based on occupational groups. As a result, socialist activists and thinkers, in their language as in their programs, continued to assume the integrity of trade groups even as they explored the idea of building an alliance among all workers.

Although I have focused on the language in which calls to action were couched as evidence of the continued importance of trade loyalties in the French labor movement, the reader should not infer that conceptual and linguistic developments determined the shape of labor conflicts between 1830 and 1871. On the contrary, it was only because the realities of working-class life reinforced the laborer's self-identification as the member of a specific profession that the trade-oriented conceptualization of the labor movement continued to have relevance for strikers and activists. To see why this is so, it is necessary to explore the ways in which patterns of social relations in Paris held some craft groups together long after capitalist production began to erode their economic basis.

It is well known that, under the old regime, masters' guilds (*métiers jurés*) and confraternities were not simply economic units organized to enforce legal monopolies on trade but also deeply spiritual communities with patron saints, sacred rituals, and often strictly enforced discipline. Initiations were elaborate ceremonies which usually required the new member to swear a solemn oath of loyalty to the patron saint and to the *corporation;* likewise, the confraternity generally paid for—and attended en masse—the funerals of deceased members. The clandestine organizations of journeymen, which ultimately gave rise to the still extant institution of *compagnonnage,* modeled themselves in many respects after the royally authorized corporations of their masters. Moreover, as William Sewell has shown, workers' organizations continued to exhibit many of these features in the nineteenth century, despite the abolition of *compagnonnage* and other forms of workers' corporations in 1791. Mutual-aid societies (*sociétés de secours mutuels*), which became a common type of working-class organization following the Bourbon Restoration in 1815, usually provided their members with

---

hand, while it is conceivable that the labor movement in Toulouse—and more particularly the development of proletarian class consciousness—followed a different path from that in Paris, this seems unlikely: the evidence Aminzade gives for the growth of class solidarity in Toulouse is limited to six instances of cooperation among striking workers in different trades between 1830 and 1870. Given that, during this same period, Aminzade identifies forty-eight strikes that took place in the city, it would seem that appeals to class rather than trade solidarities were the exception rather than the rule. It is therefore possible that workers in Toulouse remained as wedded to their traditional craft identities as Parisian workers.

health insurance, retirement pensions, and, finally, funeral expenses, much as the confraternities had done before 1789. While these societies varied with respect to their criteria for membership, most were organized within a single trade and were often named after patron saints. This practice continued late into the nineteenth century: in May of 1871, for example, the Commune's Commission of Labor and Exchange received a letter from the Mutual-Aid Society of the Bakery Workers of the Seine. Founded in 1865, the organization was also known as the "Saint Honoré" and described its purpose as the "supply of medical care to sick members, the payment of a pension to infirm or elderly members, and provision for the funeral of members who are deceased."[18] Although they were far more secular than their old-regime predecessors and generally eschewed elaborate rituals, mutual-aid societies played a significant role in perpetuating their members' sense of the trade as a solidary group.

Many occupational groups were communities in a more mundane sense as well. A map of practically any city in France will reveal dozens of small streets with occupational names such as passage des Charpentiers, rue des Boulangers, or rue des Tanneurs. Not surprisingly, these names derive from the fact that medieval artisans with a common trade tended to live and work near each other, frequently taking over an entire street. In many cases, occupational inheritance and a propensity toward endogamy combined to link a neighborhood with a particular trade for centuries.

Urbanization, population growth, and increased demographic mobility began to disrupt this pattern in the eighteenth and nineteenth centuries, but many neighborhoods continued to be associated, both in the minds of residents and in reality, with individual trades. To cite just a few examples, Paris in 1791 had a goldsmith's quarter on the Île de la Cité, a tanner's neighborhood near what is now the Panthéon, and a large community of cabinet-makers and other furniture workers—still in evidence today—in the Faubourg Saint Antoine.[19]

Despite the massive dislocations provoked by Haussmann's projects in the 1850s and 1860s, a number of tightly knit artisanal communities persisted. In 1871, over half of the leather workers in Paris lived in the fifth and thirteenth *arrondissements*—precisely where they had been concentrated since the seventeenth century. Similarly, 31 percent of luxury goods workers (manufacturers of

18. Archives Historiques de l'Armée de Terre, series Ly, carton 11.

19. George Rudé, *The Crowd in the French Revolution* (Oxford: Oxford University Press, 1959), pp. 15–16.

artificial flowers, fans, umbrellas, and the like) lived in the third *arrondissement*, with another 20 percent in the neighboring second district. Other notable enclaves included that of the jewelers, in the third and fourth districts, and the bronze workers in the third and eleventh.[20] Moreover, as I demonstrated in chapter 3, workers who stubbornly remained in the industrial center—the third, fourth, tenth, and eleventh *arrondissements*—were considerably more likely than residents of the periphery to associate with members of the same trade.

The tendency of workers in some occupations to cluster in residential enclaves was more than a vestige of a defunct artisanal tradition; rather, it was a critical factor in maintaining craft as a participation identity in the face of capitalist development. Because data on French strikes before 1871 are scarce, it is difficult to provide a rigorous demonstration of the connection between the cohesiveness of craft groups and their level of strike activity in Paris in the 1860s. Nevertheless, the facts that are available make it possible to conclude with confidence that the labor movement established a more secure footing in those Parisian trades with more tightly knit artisanal communities.

The most dramatic evidence of this relationship comes from the famous bronze-workers' strike, by all accounts one of the most bitterly contested of the 1860s. The strike began in mid-February 1867 with a wage dispute at the Maison Barbedienne, one of the capital's larger bronze manufacturing firms; workers walked out to enforce their demand for a new *tarif,* and the strike quickly spread throughout the city. One day after the employers' association announced an agreement to lock their doors until the *interdiction* or blacklist[21] was lifted, workers responded with a formal list of demands that had been drawn up at a meeting of approximately three thousand bronze workers, or roughly half of the workers in the trade.[22] In an apparent attempt to undermine this show of solidarity, the employers announced that they would reopen their workshops to anyone willing to work at the current wage. According to a police report filed with the Ministry of Commerce, their offer was not warmly received: "In the third *arrondissement,*

20. Residential patterns were tabulated from 1871 electoral registers (*listes électorales*) in the Archives de Paris.

21. *Interdiction* was the usual tactic for dealing with employers who refused to abide by a *tarif:* the local workers' organization would declare the establishment in question *interdit* (literally, "forbidden"), which meant that workers were prohibited from accepting employment there until the owner agreed to the terms of the *tarif.*

22. A. N. F[12] 4652—Ministère du Commerce. The Lyon newspaper *Le progrès* reported on February 27 that the meeting was attended by four to five thousand workers.

the principal seat of the industry, sixty-two employers reopened their doors; but of the more than 1,850 workers they had employed before the strike, only 251 appeared."[23] With some modest financial help from the London branch of the International, the strike ended in victory for the workers about one month later, when employers agreed to a new *tarif* providing for a 25-percent wage increase.

The success of the bronze-workers' strike was due in large measure to their organizational resources, which were substantial. The formal leadership of the strike was in the hands of a mutual-aid society founded in 1864, during an earlier citywide strike; this organization, though officially called the Mutual Credit Society of Bronze Workers, clearly doubled illegally as a trade union and was occasionally referred to as a "resistance society" (*société de résistance*). A pamphlet that appeared shortly after the strike claimed that the society comprised five thousand members; even if one assumes that the true membership was closer to the three thousand reported at the meeting of February 24, the organization was quite large for Paris, both in absolute terms and proportionally to the number of workers in the industry.[24] A further indicator of the bronze-workers' solidarity was the remarkable consensus they displayed throughout the strike. In a second mass meeting on March 3, four thousand bronze workers reacted to the news that the society's funds were dwindling by unanimously approving an increase in their weekly dues from one franc to five francs, along with a reduction in strike pay from twenty francs per week to fifteen. Three weeks into the strike, with no conciliatory offers from employers, the bronze workers showed no signs of weakening resolve.

The mere existence of the mutual-aid society cannot explain this kind of tenacity: since the society had never before held a meeting of its entire membership, it had never had the opportunity to build such consensus. Rather, the strength of the bronze-workers' strike must be traced to the underlying bases of solidarity that made their formal organization possible in the first place. To begin

23. Ibid.

24. Membership sizes for unions and mutual-aid societies are almost impossible to determine for Paris in this period. Daniel Willbach has attempted to estimate enrollments in Paris between 1864 and 1870; the results are somewhat informative, though in many cases extremely doubtful. Willbach estimates the rate of union membership for bronze-workers to be 89 percent, which is nearly three times as great as the estimated rate for any other occupational group in the study. Thus, even if we take into account the inevitable imprecision of these estimates, it is fairly clear that bronze-workers were the most heavily unionized group in the city. See Daniel Willbach, "Work and Its Satisfactions: Origins of the French Labor Movement, 1864–70," Ph.D. dissertation, University of Michigan, 1977.

with, workers in the bronze trade occupied an elite position among the already privileged Parisian labor force. They were employed primarily in the production of sculpture and decorative fixtures for fine-quality furniture, and were consequently "artisans" in the traditional sense of the word: the trained bronze turner, mounter, chaser, or sculptor was in part a worker with technical skills, but also in part an artist. The appearance of large, factory-like establishments like that of Barbedienne signaled the decline of the small *atelier* and the independent craftsman, but did not yet entail mechanization or the dilution of skills usually associated with the rise of capitalist industry—as in, for example, the textile trades, shoe manufacture, and chemical processing. Especially in Paris, bronze workers were proud and jealous guardians of their skills, which were responsible for the ornate exteriors of many Second Empire buildings.[25] This meant that wages in the industry were very high, which in turn made it easier for bronze workers to pay their monthly dues to their mutual-aid society.[26] In addition, it meant that employers could not easily replace strikers, since training new workers would take months.

In the course of preserving their craft identity, the bronze workers had also maintained a strong craft community: they were more densely concentrated in residential terms than any other occupational group in Paris. Nearly two-thirds of the city's bronze workers lived in just two adjoining districts: 37.5 percent in the eleventh *arrondissement* and 25 percent in the third. Combined with the fact that most employers maintained their workshops in the same area, this meant that bronze workers spent most of their waking hours together: walking to work in the morning, going home in the evening, and relaxing in the local wine shop or café, the typical bronze worker saw few people who were not either family members or coworkers, or both.

If the professional and the personal tended to merge in the routines of everyday life for these workers, they were no less thoroughly linked in times of crisis. While the large assembly of February 24 was held in a rented ballroom, the strike's leaders normally met in a more familiar setting: the Prefect of Police observed that "the Commission [of the Mutual Credit Society] . . . meets regularly at the establishment of the *marchand de vins* Pomey, 11 rue de l'Oseille, or that

25. The strike leader Camélinat, for instance, worked for five years on the sculpture adorning the Paris Opera, considered one of the masterpieces of Second Empire style.

26. Legally, mutual-aid societies were not allowed to give their members monetary assistance when they were out of work, since this kind of insurance could easily be used as a strike fund. Nonetheless, the bronze-workers' society apparently ignored this restriction without repercussions.

of Mogenier, *marchand de vins* at 5 rue St. Claude." (The first of these was, in fact, the official address of the society.) Both wineshops were located a few steps from the border between the third and eleventh *arrondissements*. In other words, the strikers held their organizational meetings precisely where they would have been spending many of their evenings in any case: at a neighborhood bar.

It has become commonplace in discussions of nineteenth-century militancy to call attention to the important role "informal centers of sociability" played in nineteenth-century working-class activism. In fact, contemporary observers were themselves well aware of the link between the working-class wineshops and the labor movement, although they generally interpreted it as evidence that labor strife was the result of workers' excessive consumption of alcohol. The Schneider brothers, owners of the enormous ironworks at Le Creusot, sought to close all the cafés in the vicinity of their plant. Public officials and the press alike continually warned that the proliferation of cabarets, wineshops, and bars in France would lead to a general breakdown in "morality," of which the labor movement was thought to be an early stage.[27] More recent inquiries suggest that these institutions provided an element of social organization in workers' lives, even if the presence of alcohol did lead to an occasional brawl:[28]

> The cabaret was much more to urban workers than a place to go have a drink. They would read the newspaper there, borrow writing materials, play cards. Some employers would even go there to pay their workers; conversely, the *marchand de vin* might act as a banker, keeping deposits and performing simple transactions . . . And this is where they would go to talk, about everything—which is what the Schneiders feared, like all the employers in mining and metallurgy. And, logically, this is where the *chambres syndicales* had their headquarters . . . continuing the tradition strike committees had always followed.[29]

In short, in linking the organization of their strike to their institutions of leisure, the bronze workers were adhering to a now-familiar pattern. But by empha-

27. See, for example, the quarterly reports of the Paris Imperial Prosecutor to the Minister of Justice for 1861–68, which evince a virtual obsession with the problem of cabarets—in A. N. BB[30] 384.

28. More often, judging from police records, drunken workers got into trouble with the law not by engaging in fist fights but by making off-color remarks about Napoleon III or the Empress Eugénie.

29. Maurice Agulhon, Françoise Choay, Maurice Crubelhier, Yves Lequin, and Marcel Roncayolo, *Histoire de la France urbaine.* Vol. 4, *La ville et l'âge industriel* (Paris: Editions du Seuil, 1983), p. 528.

sizing the influence of the wineshop on working-class activism in general, most scholars have obscured the extent to which these informal settings contributed to a narrow, strictly trade-oriented solidarity. The *marchand de vin* at 11 rue de l'Oseille was located in the heart of the bronze-workers' neighborhood; while many workers from different trades lived here as well, they almost certainly frequented other establishments.[30] Thus in many cases—most of all in Paris, where small handicraft industry was still the dominant pattern in the 1860s—the role of the wineshop or cabaret was to reinforce trade boundaries rather than blur them. For workers in residentially clustered occupations, the dense overlap of informal and professional ties made the participation identity of trade an enduring and powerful engine of collective action.

While few strikes from this period are documented as thoroughly as that of the bronze workers, the overall pattern of strike activity in Second Empire Paris is instructive. Most of the strikes that reached a sufficient size to attract attention occurred within industries still characterized by small workshops and skilled artisanal labor, such as coppersmithing, leather manufacture, and printing.[31] Strikes also occurred in the clothing, construction, and metal industries, all of which were increasingly dominated by capitalist production; but in general, the workers who mounted the most successful strikes in these industries constituted a small elite group who possessed a strong craft identity and who maintained a monopoly on skills. In the clothing industry, for instance, the only major strike was that of the tailors, who remained a more cohesive group than shoemakers, dyers, shirt-makers, or launderers. Similarly, the most significant conflict in the construction trades before 1871 was the strike of the marble cutters, who contin-

30. Although many *marchands de vin* were immigrants from the provinces, particularly from wine-growing areas, some were former craftsmen who had saved enough money to start a business. There was consequently a natural tendency for certain cafés to become identified with a specific trade. Coworkers (perhaps former colleagues of the shopkeeper), retired workers, and apprentices would gather after work or in the evenings, boast of their past or recent achievements, tell stories related to their trade, or exchange job information. The fact that many of them were related to each other and shared a specialized language associated with their profession further accentuated the differences between regulars and casual visitors. See Hanagan, *The Logic of Solidarity;* Aminzade, *Class, Politics, and Early Industrial Capitalism;* Louis Chevalier, *La formation de la population parisienne au XIXe siècle* (Paris: Presses Universitaires de France, 1950).

31. The leather industry was actually changing fairly rapidly in this period, with the construction of several large factories in the suburbs and the increasing use of steam-driven machinery. Nonetheless, tanners, curriers, and tawers belonged to one of the oldest Parisian crafts, and they retained a close-knit community in the southeast corner of the city well past the 1880s.

ued to work in small shops and lived in a highly circumscribed area: over 45 percent of the city's marble cutters lived in the eleventh *arrondissement.*

Perhaps the most revealing case of militancy in an industrializing trade was the strike of the iron founders in 1870. Of all the trades practiced in the capital, metal working was the one that had changed the most as a result of industrial capitalism. The development of railroads, the increasing use of iron in construction, and the growing demand for steam-driven machinery in industries like textiles and sugar refining gave rise to a dramatic expansion in metal working under the Second Empire; the most visible sign of this process was the growth in size of metallurgical plants, particularly in France's industrial regions. Though by no means the center of heavy industry in France, Paris too was home to numerous foundries and machine-building factories, some of them employing hundreds of workers. Following a pattern similar to that of the shoe and leather industries, many of the larger factories were built in the suburbs; nonetheless, the two largest machine-building enterprises were located inside Paris (though outside the city's pre-1860 borders): the Gouin locomotive factory, in the seventeenth *arrondissement,* employed a thousand workers, while the Cail metal works, in the fifteenth, numbered two thousand.[32] It was in the Cail plant that the founders' strike began.

The most informative feature of this strike was the way in which it spread. The foundry workers at the Cail factory were joined, not by workers in other crafts employed at the same establishment, but by other founders in large and small shops throughout Paris. Since Cail and Company produced locomotives, steam engines, iron rails, and other industrial machinery, its personnel included not just founders and molders but also machinists (*mécaniciens*), forgers, turners, and other workers specializing in the manufacture of finished products rather than raw material.[33] The workers in this latter group supported the founders and in some cases tried to raise money for their strike fund, but did not go on strike themselves. Indeed, the machinists failed to organize a single large-scale strike during the entire period under study: none of the three machinists' strikes that occurred between 1864 and 1871 involved more than one employer.[34]

32. Duveau, *La vie ouvrière en France,* p. 203; Jeanne Gaillard, "Les usines Cail et les ouvriers métallurgistes de Grenelle," *Le mouvement social,* no. 33 (October–March 1960), pp. 35–63.

33. Émile Turgan, *Les grandes usines: Études industrielles en France et à l'étranger* (Paris: Michel Lévy Frères, 1871), vol. 2.

34. The city-wide strike by a single craft was the more traditional form of labor protest; strikes by workers from diverse trades at a particular firm became more common in the late nineteenth century, as semiskilled work replaced craft work at an accelerating rate. The contrast between

As with the previous examples, this difference in activism between occupational groups in the same industry can be traced to differences in patterns of social relations within trades, which in turn were shaped by changes in the organization of work itself. Iron founders were among the first occupational groups to go on strike in 1864, and the association that emerged during this earlier strike remained active and outspoken throughout the 1860s. Foundry work was relatively unaffected by the managerial and technological developments that were transforming other metal trades, and the practitioners of this craft maintained a close-knit community in the traditional metal-working districts of eastern Paris: 58 percent of the founders lived in the adjoining tenth, eleventh, and twelfth *arrondissements.* Parisian machine builders, on the other hand, began to experience major encroachments on their workplace autonomy and control over skills at mid-century: by the 1860s, professional engineers working separately in a *bureau d'études* dominated the design phase of machine construction. The increasing demand for standardized equipment in the client industries (railroads, textiles, and distilling) pushed managers to eliminate discretion on the shop floor: experienced workers who had previously made innovative design changes as the situation demanded were now forbidden to modify their product without securing approval from management.[35]

Another factor contributing to quiescence among machine builders was the fact that the increasing scale of production in the machine industry led entrepreneurs to move their establishments from the densely populated, high-rent areas of the center into large factories located in the suburbs and in peripheral districts. By the end of the Second Empire, workers employed in this industry were consequently highly dispersed: the eleventh and eighteenth *arrondissements* together accounted for only 31.5 percent of the city's *mécaniciens,* with the fifteenth adding only another 10 percent. Even though many of these workers lived near their places of employment, the trade group as a whole was highly fragmented. The main implication of this change for shop-floor protest was that machinists'

---

foundry workers and machine builders, therefore, reflects the unevenness in the rate at which modern capitalist enterprise transformed various crafts.

35. For a more detailed discussion of this process, see Roger V. Gould, "Trade Cohesion, Class Unity, and Urban Insurrection: Artisanal Activism in the Paris Commune," *American Journal of Sociology* 98 (January 1993): 735–38. See also James Edmondson, *From Mécanicien to Ingénieur: Technical Education and the Machine Building Industry in Nineteenth-Century France* (New York: Garland, 1987).

strikes remained isolated within individual establishments. Overall, trades whose practitioners remained clustered in the artisanal districts were better able to organize effective protest against employers than trades whose practitioners were spread across the city. Some of the difference resulted from erosion in control over skills, but this erosion went hand in hand with changes in industrial geography that broke up craft communities and thereby rendered some occupational groups even less able to organize for collective action.

⁺≈ Formal Organizations ≈⁺

The strongest evidence pointing to the significance of informal social relations for labor protest was the relative unimportance of formal workers' associations.[36] Nearly every occupational group in Paris had a trade union of some kind by 1865, and many had organized producers' cooperatives and mutual-aid societies as well.[37] While it is probably the case that strikes were more successful in trades with high rates of union membership, it is probable that in this period a high membership rate was more a reflection of cohesive social organization than an independent source of solidarity. Recruitment to mutual-aid societies and *chambres syndicales* was invariably an informal process, and was consequently dependent on the extent of social integration within a trade group. Indeed, the formal statutes of workers' organizations usually stipulated that prospective members had to be personally sponsored by one or more established members, thus ensuring that recruitment depended heavily on informal social relations.[38]

In addition, workers' organizations varied considerably in the extent to which workers viewed them specifically as instruments of protest. For example, when the tawers (*mégissiers*) formed a mutual-aid society in 1865, the Prefect of Police was disturbed by the fact that the members openly refused to accept employer control over the organization:

36. As I have argued in earlier chapters, formal organizations are significant to the extent that they provide network bridges among similarly situated informal groups—in other words, they matter enormously for expansions in the scale of collective identities. This examination of strikes indicates that organizations matter a good deal less for the mobilization of groups whose patterns of informal association already underpin a plausible collective identity.

37. A fairly comprehensive list of these workers' societies appears in the *Dictionnaire biographique du mouvement ouvrier français.* Vol. 2, *1864–1871,* ed. Jean Maitron (Paris: Editions Ouvrières, 1968).

38. This was true, for example, of the tailors' union, whose statutes are reproduced in *L'ouvrier de l'avenir,* March 16, 1871, and of the St. Honoré mutual-aid society described earlier.

Mr. Rullière, one of the candidates for president, has stated on behalf of the tawers' commission that the workers feel perfectly capable
of managing their affairs by themselves, that they will happily admit
employers into the society, but only as honorary members; and that
they formally insist that the president be chosen exclusively from
among the workers.[39]

In contrast, the Fraternal Society of Carpenters was thoroughly coopted from
its birth in 1857. Although some sources have identified the organization as a
sect of *compagnonnage*, it emerged among workers who remained deliberately
aloof from the two dominant carpenters' sects:[40] in formulating their initial request for government authorization, the carpenters took care to point out that one
of their goals was to

> maintain the order so often disturbed by certain men who, frustrated
> by the distaste younger workers have for their sects of *compagnon-
> nage*—mystical sects that lurk in the shadows, impeding the march
> of progress—resort to violent means and try to take work away from
> those who will not adopt their ways.
>
> The founders of this society have no interest either in speculation
> or in conspiracy: its prosperity will benefit all its members equally,
> and the society undertakes not to involve itself in any matter foreign
> to its statutes.[41]

Because *compagnonnage* was widely viewed as a secretive, ritualistic, and often
subversive workers' organization, this statement had the double effect of affirming the carpenters' preference for modern institutions while at the same time
reassuring the authorities that they did not plan to use the society to antagonize
employers. From its inception until its demise in 1876, most of the society's officers were employers and foremen, not wage-earning carpenters; the first of its
three presidents was a former carpenter turned café owner, and the last was a
shop foreman. (The occupation of the second president, who held the office from

---

39. A. N. F¹² 5391—Ministère de l'Intèrieur.

40. *Compagnonnage* was actually divided into three sects (*rites*), each with its own special customs and origin myths: the *Enfants du Maître Jacques,* the *Enfants de Salomon,* and the *Enfants du
Père Soubise.* However, there was no carpenter's *compagnonnage* affiliated with the first sect. See
Ministère du Commerce, de l'Industrie, des Postes et des Télégraphes—Office du Travail, *Les associations professionnelles ouvrières,* 4 vols. (Paris: Imprimerie Nationale, 1904).

41. A. N. F¹² 5390—Ministère de l'Intèrieur.

1865 to 1868, does not appear in the Interior Ministry's dossier.) The carpenters' society did not involve itself with strikes or other labor struggles during its nineteen-year existence, and the competition between this organization and the two rival groups of *compagnons* seems to have prevented Parisian carpenters from mobilizing effectively against employers. In fact, a group of workers organized a carpenters' trade union in 1868 with the express purpose of "reducing, even destroying, the privileges which the carpenter *compagnons* enjoy, notably in the area of hiring."[42]

The carpenters' experience was fairly typical of workers in construction. Earlier in the century, the building trades had been extensively organized by *compagnonnage*, the three sects of which maintained chapters in cities and towns all over France. Masons, joiners, carpenters, and other artisans in construction or related crafts typically developed their skills by means of the Tour de France, a practice which involved traveling throughout the country over a period of several years to acquire a thorough knowledge of regional specialties and trade secrets. Upon arriving in a new town, the *compagnon* would go to the *mère*, or local headquarters, of his sect, where fellow members would house him until they could find him employment. All three sects had chapters in Paris in the nineteenth century (but see note 40); consequently, itinerant construction workers had an elaborate system of social support available to them when they worked in the capital. This arrangement offset the more transient character of construction work itself, which relied much more on subcontracting and brief work assignments than other trades.

Even when *compagnonnage* began to decline in importance toward the middle of the century, these workers were able to avoid an isolated existence during their annual migrations to Paris. In the first half of the nineteenth century, building workers would come to Paris only for the warm months, returning to their families during the off-season.[43] While in the capital, they would remain together, working at the same construction sites and lodging in the same transient hotels (*hôtels garnis*).[44]

After the 1840s, however, this pattern began to change, as construction workers started moving to Paris permanently with their families. At one time most

42. Ministère du Commerce, *Les associations professionnelles ouvrières*, vol. 3, p. 31.

43. One of the classic figures in French labor history is the *maçon Creusois:* the mason from the Creuse or Haute-Vienne in the Limousin region of central France. A remarkable number of masonry workers in Paris came from this region, and other trades had similar regional ties. See Chevalier, *La formation de la population parisienne.*

44. Gaillard, *Paris: La ville, 1852–1870*, p. 201.

masons stayed in hotels in the fourth or fifth *arrondissements,* in the neighborhood surrounding the place de Grève, where contractors traditionally gathered to put together work teams. But the dramatic expansion of construction work during the Second Empire resulted in the proliferation of such gathering places as well as the establishment of subcontracting enterprises throughout the city. Combined with the increasing number of workers taking up permanent residence in Paris, this trend helped to disperse the seasonal enclave around the place de Grève. Electoral registers show that, by 1871, only 28 percent of the masons in Paris lived in the fourth and fifth districts, with the remainder distributed more or less evenly throughout the city. The growing population of building workers not affiliated with *compagnonnage* and the division of *compagnonnage* itself into three rival sects—a rivalry that frequently led to violent street fights—only served to fragment construction workers further.

Ironically, then, it was their growing integration into the life of the city that broke down the craft community construction workers once had. No longer bound by strong regional allegiances, dispersed throughout the city's neighborhoods, and increasingly uninterested in the anachronistic organizational life *compagnonnage* seemed to offer, carpenters, masons, and joiners were far more likely than workers in other industries to experience their craft simply as an occupational category rather than as a community. The presence in Paris of multiple and competing construction workers' associations both resulted from and reinforced this perception.

These changes had important implications for construction workers' efforts to win concessions from employers through collective protest. The most common type of workers' organization to emerge in the building trades in the 1860s was the cooperative production association; although they were the cornerstone of the Proudhonist socialist vision, these associations rarely comprised more than a few dozen members and never became the focus of resistance to capitalist employers. In fact, one of the largest and most successful cooperatives of the period, the Fraternal Association of Masonry Workers and Stonecutters, sided with other employers during the 1865 stonecutters' strike, thereby contributing to the strike's failure. Although some trades had established mutual-aid societies—the organizational form that lent itself most readily to mobilizing and sustaining strikes, as the case of the bronze workers illustrates—they were comparatively weak. At its peak, the painters' mutual-aid society included less than one-fifth of the workforce among its members; the stonecutters' society, on the other hand, began admitting workers from other professions soon after it was founded and within a few years had completely lost its trade character. Generally speaking, despite the existence of various formal associations, workers in the construction industry were relatively inactive in the labor movement of the 1860s: their strikes were rarer, smaller in scale, and on the whole far less successful than those of more close-knit trades.[45]

❧ Conclusion ❧

What differentiated militant occupational groups from others during the 1860s was not the existence of workers' organizations but, rather, the patterns of informal social relations that dictated the role these organizations would play in the emerging labor movement. For the bronze workers, tailors, and tawers, mutual-aid societies and unions quickly and naturally became instruments of labor militancy because they built on the highly cohesive social organization these groups already possessed. On the other hand, carpenters, joiners, machinists, and shoemakers were unsuccessful in this regard because their trade communities had been eroded by both economic and demographic developments. As a result, as individuals and as members of organizations they relied more heavily on the cooperation and munificence of employers. In some cases, this meant that their organizations encompassed the whole trade but were dominated by employers or foremen; in other cases, particularly in the metal trades, employers would create company-specific mutual-aid societies whose membership included both workers and management. Some of these trades also suffered from internal divisions that resulted either from rivalries between sects of *compagnonnage* or from elitism associated with differences in skill: garment workers employed in *confection*, for example, were shunned by tailors, and construction workers typically refused to admit unskilled excavators (*terrassiers*) into their organizations.[46]

Overall, then, trades with spatially localized worker enclaves and small workshops exhibited an impressive ability to organize strikes and other forms of resistance to capitalist development. In contrast, workers employed by industries in which much of the production took place through short-term subcontracting, in

45. Michelle Perrot's exhaustive study of strike data shows that, in France as a whole, workers in the construction trades were fairly militant between 1864 and 1871. Their quiescence in the capital, then, does not represent a national pattern but, rather, reflects the special circumstances of Parisian construction workers and their industry during this period. Michelle Perrot, *Les ouvriers en grève, 1871–90* (Paris: Mouton, 1974).

46. Roger Price, *A Social History of Nineteenth Century France* (London: Hutchinson, 1987), p. 245.

large factories, or in the home—industries such as construction, machine building, chemical refining, shoemaking, and dress manufacture—were largely unable to stave off encroachments on their wages and job autonomy that went beyond what had already taken place. Some of this relative weakness derived from uneven development in capitalist production, leading to varying rates of skill erosion and mechanization; the remainder resulted from the differential impact of haussmanisation on the location and organization of work sites. Lower-paid workers were pushed out of the city center and into the peripheral *arrondissements* by rising rents, even as large industrial establishments sprang up in the suburbs to take advantage of the available space. Between the artisanal center and the industrial suburbs, then, lay a zone in which a heterogeneous set of workers shared a considerable degree of geographical separation from their places of work and a corresponding detachment from social lives structured by craft loyalties.

Although they are inflected by a unique coincidence of urban renovation with capitalist development, these observations on the relationship between cohesive social organization and labor militancy correspond closely to the work of other scholars on strike activity in nineteenth-century France, as well as studies of other Western societies during industrialization. The most important lesson to draw from this discussion, however, concerns the somewhat neglected issue of "trade consciousness" and what it implies for the link between patterns of social ties and collective identities.[47] It was precisely because labor protest relied on the social organization of narrowly defined trade communities that craft boundaries remained an essential feature of the labor movement throughout the nineteenth century. As this chapter has shown, even though public declarations and appeals for support increasingly used the language of class, collective action continued to find its social base in these trade communities; and even when workers answered appeals to a broader solidarity based on class, they invariably did so in ways that reaffirmed the trade boundaries they were crossing. Cooperation among workers in different occupations most often took the form of loans from one mutual-aid society to another, not sympathy strikes. When these loans were

47. The two notable exceptions to this neglect are the previously cited works of Moss and Sewell. However, both of these books focus on the ideological dimension of craft loyalties: Sewell concentrates on the corporate nature of the "idiom" in which workers expressed their grievances and demands, while Moss focuses on the ideas and programs of socialist political leaders. As a result, the social foundations of trade consciousness and its effect on the mobilization of working-class activism have received comparatively little attention.

not repaid (as, for example, when the iron founders failed to return the money lent to them by the Parisian copper founders), trade cleavages only deepened.

It is true that public appeals to solidarity among all workers became more common as socialist ideas spread; but the real world of the labor movement, the collective protests with which workers fought against the threat of capitalism, fulfilled the utopian socialist vision rather poorly. By failing to take this fact fully into account, the class-formation narrative exaggerates the extent to which "class consciousness" replaced trade loyalties in nineteenth-century France.

The validity of the central argument presented in this chapter does not depend upon a decision about whether there is such a thing as objectively correct class consciousness. The critical point is that, regardless of whether Parisian workers understood their socioeconomic position "correctly" or "incorrectly," this understanding was conditioned by the patterns of social relations in which they were embedded and by the kinds of activism this social structure encouraged. In the absence of a specific organizational context that might have brought large numbers of workers from a variety of trades together in a regular way (a context that 1848 had fleetingly provided and which the International later tried to re-create, with limited results, in the form of the Chambre Fédérale), working-class militancy both adhered to and reinforced a predominantly trade-oriented framework. That this was so despite the tireless efforts of socialist militants in the 1860s underscores the historical uniqueness of the organizational circumstances of 1848 that had made possible the cognitive leap to genuine class mobilization.

5

Public Meetings and Popular Clubs, 1868–70

MY EXAMINATION of the documentary record on industrial militancy in Second Empire Paris has established that the labor movement relied on the persistence in the city center of craft-specific networks of social relations—networks, that is, in which collegial ties forged in workshops largely coincided with the friendships maintained in centers of sociability close to work. But what of the growing population residing in the districts of the periphery and working in establishments often quite distant from home? Chapter 3 has already shown that the inhabitants of these more residential areas associated less frequently with people employed in the same trade and more frequently with neighbors of varying backgrounds. The task of this chapter is to show that the detachment of these Parisians from the networks of social relations underlying industrial conflict simultaneously made them available for a different kind of radical activity—more precisely, a kind of radical mobilization framed by a different collective identity.

It is not a serious oversimplification to say that the rebuilding of central Paris, the geographical dispersion of workers in a number of industrializing trades, and the significant expansion of the population in the new peripheral *arrondissements* created the conditions for a mode of social protest in which the collective identity of community was largely divorced from the work-based identities of craft and its more elusive cousin, class. Spatially separated from the traditional sites of industrial production in the city center, residents of the annexed zone experienced urban life in a way that was less thoroughly structured by craft labor. Even though many continued to commute—usually on foot—to work in the center, laborers living in the peripheral districts no longer spent their leisure time in occupationally exclusive wineshops and cabarets, for the simple reason that they were now too spread out: in the annexed zone, neighborhoods did not contain enough workers in any one trade to sustain a critical mass of craft solidarity. Unlike workers in such trades as tailoring, leather processing, cabinetmaking, bronze working, and iron founding—trades which remained highly cohesive in terms of both organized protest and residential clustering near centrally located places of employment—many Parisians now led social lives that disregarded craft in the double sense that informal social relations were physically distant from the workplace and increasingly likely to bridge craft lines.

At the same time, the dramatic alteration of the urban landscape occasioned by Haussmann's renovation projects literally drew stark boundaries around neighborhoods, accentuating the contrast between everyday life in an urban community and the monumental pretensions of the imperial state. The liberal reforms of the late 1860s facilitated the crystallization of this contrast into a politically significant collective identity by permitting public meetings under the conspicuous and repressive surveillance of a state official. The consequence was that, by the end of 1870, as Paris fell victim to the war with Prussia, vocal protest founded on the collective identity of the urban community had developed into a full-fledged social movement distinct from the labor militancy on which historians and other social scientists have focused so much of their attention. The direct link between the urban transformations of the Empire and this new form of activism manifested itself most succinctly in the latter's geographical locus: whereas labor protest remained concentrated in the city's traditional artisanal center, the most contentious public meetings routinely occurred in the peripheral zone, above all in the northeastern sections of Montmartre, La Villette, Belleville, and Charonne.

Well before the proclamation of the Commune in March 1871, the organizational and cognitive basis for neighborhood protest, anchored by new patterns of informal interaction in the urban environment and independent of work-based relationships, was firmly in place. But the emergence of neighborhood as an overtly political collective identity required the creation of an organizational context within which inhabitants of the capital could recognize it as such. This context was provided initially by the public meetings of 1868–70 and later, just prior to the Commune itself, by their reincarnation as "clubs" during the Prussian siege. As I shall demonstrate in chapter 6, it was this recently forged collective identity, rather than the work-oriented identities of 1848 or the resurgent labor movement of the 1860s, that was to make the Commune such an explosive uprising.

✺ The Meeting Movement ✺

In 1868, attempting to make good on his promise to liberalize the Empire, Napoleon III pushed through the legislature a law granting general authorization of electoral assemblies and public meetings of a nonpolitical nature.[1] Organizers of such meetings were now required only to inform the Prefect of Police in advance; they no longer needed to obtain official permission. The response in Paris was immediate: the first meeting was held on June 18, less than two weeks after the law's passage, and thirteen meetings took place in July. Before long, the meetings, with announced topics ranging from "women's work" and "children born out of wedlock" to "the influence of monopolies on production," were a nightly occurrence. In the larger meeting halls, many of them theaters and public ballrooms, the number of attendants frequently reached one or two thousand.

Early meetings, held for the most part in upscale establishments in the center of Paris, tended to be sedate and heavily male affairs, with a considerable contingent of liberal bourgeois notables—lawyers, economists, and other public figures. But the rougher-edged denizens of the outlying *faubourgs*—both women and men—soon developed a taste for public meetings as well, and by the beginning of 1869 the frequency of meetings in peripheral *arrondissements* (the eleventh through the twentieth) outstripped that of the center by a factor of three (see fig. 5.1). In all, 776 meetings took place between June 1868 and April 1870—not counting the many electoral assemblies of May–June 1869. (Also excluded from this count are the numerous public lectures delivered by various prominent Parisians—moderates and radicals alike—who considered that the democratic format of the public meetings accorded less time to their own opinions than they deserved.)

For most historians, the principal significance of these meetings lay in the inchoate revolutionary ideas that gradually took shape over two years of impassioned debate. It was here, scholars like Jacques Rougerie and Alain Faure have argued, that the "idea of the Commune," a coherent revolutionary ideology merging socialism with the movement for municipal liberties, was born and nurtured. Indeed, for Faure and his collaborators, the insurrection of March 1871 was at bottom an opportunity for Parisian militants to put into practice the plan they had worked out breathlessly in the smoky, tumultuous, crowded spaces of the Salle Molière, the Grand Pavillon, and the Folies-Belleville. Moreover, in their

1. In the same year, also at the Emperor's behest, the legislature relaxed restrictions on the press and the Minister of the Interior made it known that trade unions (*chambres syndicales*) would be informally tolerated. However, clandestine unions already played a significant role in the labor movement, and numerous journalists—including the future Communard general, Charles Delescluze—had made their reputations by flouting the press laws. It was, consequently, the decree on public meetings that made the greatest impact.

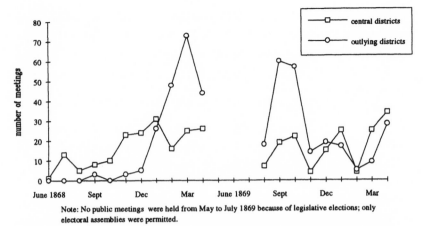

Note: No public meetings were held from May to July 1869 because of legislative elections; only electoral assemblies were permitted.

Figure 5.1 Public meetings in Paris, 1868–70. (No public meetings were held from May to July 1869 because of legislative elections; only electoral assemblies were permitted.)

view, the murderous reprisals against priests, policemen, and the military that the Friends of Order made notorious as the "crimes of the Commune" resulted directly from the class-based analysis of the state elaborated in these meetings:

> Far from seeing in these massacres a "regrettable wartime episode," we maintain that they were the logical conclusion of an act of accusation that the public meetings had drawn up over a two-year period. We have, we think, sufficiently demonstrated that speakers continually affirmed that, once they were in power, their class enemies would have to disappear. Is it surprising, then, that their avenging hand struck down those who formed the most solid ramparts of the dominant class and its power: priests, generals, police officers and judges?
>
> The last two years of the Empire witnessed the development of a vast strategy of attacks on the State. It is in these attacks that one must search for the originality of the Commune. If in 1871 the Communards smashed the state apparatus, thereby showing the way to the true proletarian revolution, it was thanks to the reflection that took place in the public meetings.[2]

2. Alain Dalotel, Alain Faure, and Jean-Claude Freiermuth, *Aux origines de la Commune: Le mouvement des réunions publiques à Paris, 1868–1870* (Paris: Maspero, 1980), pp. 208–9. See also Jacques Rougerie, *Paris libre, 1871* (Paris: Editions du Seuil, 1971), chap. 2.

I will address in the next chapter the issue of how reasonable it is to characterize the Commune as a model of "proletarian revolution"; for the moment, I wish merely to show that the antagonism against the state that Parisians expressed in the public meetings owed at least as much to the institution of the meetings themselves, and in particular their direct relationship to the agents of the state, as to any coherent analyses expressed there.

Of analyses there were plenty (their coherence being another matter), as an entire generation of radicals, revolutionaries, and socialists sought to take advantage of this sudden opportunity to rally supporters to their cause. Police records and newspaper accounts show that virtually every militant of note made regular and vocal appearances at the meeting halls of Paris—some playing the entire circuit, others confining their visits to one or two favored sites. The list of prominent participants is studded with names made familiar by the Commune: Émile Duval, Gustave Flourens, Napoléon Gaillard, Prosper Lissagaray, Raoul Rigault, and so on. Only Auguste Blanqui, incarcerated as usual, was missing—though his devoted followers, including Rigault, Théophile Ferré, and Alphonse Humbert, figured often as speakers.

The most radical participants, moreover, rarely bothered to cloak their revolutionary ideas in subtleties, most of which would in any case have been lost amid the vociferous cries of support or derision emanating from the crowd. For example, Ferré, who was to become one of the few Communards sentenced to death by the military courts, made the following remarks at a January 1869 meeting on unemployment: "The primary cause of unemployment is the power employers have over the laborers. They say to the worker, 'Save some of your wages if you can, but if you make demands with your voice raised, if you attack us, look out: there is a legal system to defend us, the owners.'"[3] In the same meeting hall a week later, a young man named Chauvière ("a boy of 17, perfect example of a young thug," the police report noted) sketched the revolutionary socialist's history of the nineteenth century:

> The bourgeoisie, our enemies! In '93, they let in a young, ambitious
> sort who, receiving France in its great Revolutionary glory, returned
> it to us shrunken and bent under the lance of the Cossack. Here is
> what our enemies did. In 1830, they stretched out their hands for us
> to save them; in 1848, in February, they did the same; in June, when

3. Archives de la Préfecture de Police (hereafter APP), series BA 1520 ("Observations sur la pratique de la loi du 6 juin 1868"), transcript for meeting of January 6, 1869.

you wanted to have your turn, they answered you with lead. Today, what have we done? For 86 years revolution has been the watchword and today we are talking about unemployment! The workers will only save themselves by the same means that were used in '93.[4]

For those interested in listening, the public meetings were filled with calls to violent action on behalf of the working class. The bitter fighting of June 1848 was for some—even those who, like Chauvière, had not been there—a defining experience that resolved thousands of individual antagonisms into a single struggle between classes. Anyone attuned to this conceptual framework could not miss it in the rhetoric of these events.

The language of class struggle was not, however, the only one spoken in Paris in this period, and—as I showed in chapter 4—it cannot be said to have played the dominant role in determining the shape of Parisian protest, even when that protest focused on the workplace. I do not mean by this that militant leaders failed to argue forcefully for their view of France under the Second Empire as a society controlled by capital; on the contrary, a detailed reading of the sources—transcripts of the public meetings and records from the widely publicized trials of the International—leaves no doubt on this matter.[5] My point, rather, is that there is little evidence that this focus on class conflict by socialist activists exerted much of an influence on the way Parisians experienced either the meetings themselves or the various conflicts that ultimately led to the mass mobilization of 1871.

To see what this means, it is necessary to examine more closely just what took place in the meetings of 1868–70. In the first place, despite the continual verbal assaults on the bourgeoisie launched by radical speakers (often warmly encouraged by the crowd), not one incident appears in the police transcripts in which a middle-class person was openly denounced as such in the course of a meeting (and it is hardly conceivable that the police would have disregarded such an incident). Nor was this the result of any established pattern of respect for participants, as the following police report shows:

The meeting of 6 October [1868] on "marriage and divorce" was one of the most tumultuous to take place in the Pré aux Clercs. Peyrouton

4. APP, BA 1520, transcript for January 13, 1869.
5. For instance, Dalotel, Faure, and Freiermuth, *Aux origines de la Commune*, demonstrate convincingly that radical leaders consistently used the capital/labor opposition as the analytical basis for their critique of French society.

rose first to denounce the transcripts of meetings printed in certain newspapers. His words, he said, "had been strangely distorted." He then spoke of women who drag their husbands into dishonor and who attend mass.

"What! We're not free to go to mass?" someone shouted.

"No! No!" the entire room responded.

M. Lenormant, librarian at the Institut, spoke in favor of religion and recommended to the attendants that they read a "small, extremely inexpensive volume, the catechism." He was booed and his remarks created a large commotion. In vain, Peyrouton called out, "Let the man speak! Catechism—this is very amusing." Lenormant threatened Peyrouton with his fist, but faced with the attitude of the crowd, he stepped down from the tribune.[6]

As the months wore on, some eyewitness accounts indicated that middle-class people attended the meetings in smaller numbers and workers mounted the tribune with greater frequency.[7] But neither the police report nor the various journalistic treatments of the meeting movement attest to any effort on the part of speakers to identify the audience as a collection of workers, and the lists of speakers reveal that a middle-class (and centrist) contingent continued to appear throughout the two-year life of the public meetings.[8] The changing composition of the crowd seems to have had more to do with the distaste some middle-class moderates felt for the radical views expressed than with any open harassment they experienced because of their social standing.

One figure, though, quickly earned the enmity of the public and became a routine target of abuse and ridicule: the local *commissaire de police*, enjoined by the June 6 law to attend meetings in his *quartier* and to keep order. (Later, the police prefecture decided to send a stenographer along as well, the better to collect evidence for the prosecution of speakers charged with violating sedition laws.) Order, in this context, meant not only calm but also respect for the Emperor and the Church, and strict adherence to the declared topic of the meeting. If a Police Commissioner felt that a speaker had ventured too far afield and if his warnings to this effect were not heeded, he had the right to declare the meeting

6. APP, BA 1520, meeting of October 6, 1868.

7. Dalotel et al., *Aux origines de la Commune*, p. 127.

8. APP, BA 1520; Gustave de Molinari, *Le mouvement socialiste et les réunions publiques avant la révolution du 4 septembre 1870* (Paris: Garnier Frères, 1872). Molinari complains that left-wing speakers merely repeated the same socialist formulae month after month and claims that audiences in general, not just their bourgeois members, were eventually rather bored with the tired rhetoric.

dissolved. The first dissolution occurred in February 1869, at a meeting in the fourteenth *arrondissement* on "salaries and property"; they became increasingly frequent thereafter, as speakers and police engaged in an escalating battle of provocation and repression. This development lent an increasingly theatrical aspect to the nightly events, and the various meeting halls competed for audiences on the basis of the intensity of the verbal confrontations they could promise. With regard to the Salle Molière, for instance, the police noted a falling rate of attendance for the early months of 1869; but this trend was temporarily reversed as "the two successive dissolutions of March 9 and 23 attracted attention to this series of meetings, and the Salle Molière was for a while able to cover its costs."[9] Similarly, Gustave de Molinari argued that these confrontations were the main point of interest for many of those attending the meetings:

> Is it necessary to abolish the right to hold public meetings or to regulate it more strictly? I think not . . . For those, like me, who have witnessed the public meetings, is it not evident that the dangers come more from an excess than from a lack of restrictions? As I have already remarked, obliging police commissioners to attend socialist meetings imposes on them a burdensome chore that drains resources from their other duties, and with what result? To lend these meetings their principal, if not their only, attraction, the prospect of a conflict between the tribune and the representative of authority, clad in his official sash. How many times have we seen a speaker bogged down in his own rhetoric extricate himself by addressing to the commissioner a provocative remark designed to elicit a warning? The audience, three-quarters of them asleep, suddenly awakens; the speaker, taking care to adopt a proud and ironic attitude, as befits a man who takes on the agents of tyranny, is applauded wildly, and the applause is followed by cheers when he "improvises" (has he not had a day to prepare?) some crushing response to the official. Perhaps he risks a sojourn in Pélagie [one of the Paris prisons]; but that is of little consequence, as he has had his moment of popularity, and as he descends from the tribune with a firm step and his head held high, he leaves a wake of flattering murmurs. The meeting is dissolved, but what of it? *La France démocratique et sociale* has one more speaker, and the next meeting's ticket sales are assured.[10]

9. BA 1520, report for March 1869.
10. Molinari, *Le mouvement socialiste et les réunions publiques*, pp. 94–96.

The direct, tangible, and ongoing conflict between meeting participants and the Police Commissioners soon became more important than the nominal topic announced for each meeting. At the March 25 meeting on "rights and duties" at the Folies-Belleville, the socialist Pellerin congratulated Parisians on their actions of the night before at the Salle Robert, where the crowd had refused to heed the dissolution order:

> "In 1789, the Third Estate, feeling the force of its rights, challenged the monarchy by meeting in the Jeu de Paume [the tennis court that housed the first National Assembly]. We too felt the force of our rights yesterday evening, when we continued our discussion despite the dissolution imposed by the authority."

> These words [the police report states], greeted by the frenetic applause of the 3,000 persons present, provoked the intervention of the Police Commissioner and a warning to the bureau. Flourens [the presider] responded, "Since the speaker has not deviated from the question, the bureau does not accept the intervention and declares the warning completely illegal."

> Pellerin continued, "I recognize only one authority, that of the people. When the people tell me not to speak, I will be silent . . . Every man recognizes one master, himself; at present, we have other masters, but we wish to recognize them no more."

> The Police Commissioner rose to deliver a reading of the law [signaling his intention to dissolve the meeting]. The level of shouts and insults increased to the point of complete disorder. Flourens and Ferré intervened so as to allow the Commissioner to read the law and issue the dissolution order, producing even more tumult than during the meeting. Flourens spoke: "The text of the law just read by the citizen Commissioner—"

> Loud protests erupted against the use of the term "citizen" to refer to the Commissioner.

> "If you please," replied Flourens, "personally, one is always a citizen. The meeting was not disorderly in the sense of the law. The speaker did not stray from the subject. Now, we are men and no one has the right to mock us. We shall not accept this dissolution, we shall remain within the bounds of the law . . . The meeting must continue and the citizen Police Commissioner is free to leave."[11]

11. Ibid., meeting of March 25, 1869.

As the tension between the crowd and the police became an institutionalized aspect of the meetings, speakers learned to mix pointed satire with their frontal attacks on the representative of state authority. In so doing, they emphasized that what was actually said was less significant than the fact of public resistance to state-sponsored repression of popular politics. At an April meeting in Belleville, the future Communard Gustave Lefrançais prompted laughter and applause by announcing that

> the meetings at the Pré aux Clercs have been dissolved twice as a result of the topic of discussion, "rights and duties of society regarding the education of children." As this subject clearly can be discussed no longer, on Tuesday we will talk about "the art of raising rabbits and deriving an annual income of 3,000 *livres* therefrom."[12]

The Aesopian language that characterized the meeting in question was such that even the putatively obtuse Commissioner could not fail to grasp its meaning. One speaker, for instance, asserted that "human beings have created artificial warrens where, under the illusion of liberty, the unhappy rabbit is actually at the mercy of his master." A week later, at the Salle de la Fraternité, the police officer present found the superficially anodyne discussion of "French crinoline" sufficiently objectionable to dissolve the meeting. For participants, the point of the absurd topics was obvious: since the police had already made a mockery of the right of assembly, no purpose was served by holding meetings to discuss serious issues.

Eventually, of course, the cycle of provocation led to violence. By October 1869, some Police Commissioners had reached the point of dissolving meetings at the slightest hint of impropriety. The meeting at the Folies-Belleville on the 10th of that month, the police report notes, "brought to its peak the overexcitement of spirits and made for an eye-opening lesson on the dangers resulting from the law of 6 June 1868."[13] The officer present gave the following account of the meeting, at which the prominent journalist Lissagaray presided:

> Loud applause repeatedly greeted the speaker's remarks [a denunciation of arbitrary arrests], provoking immediate dissolution of a

12. APP, BA 1520, report of April 25, 1869.

13. As the report makes clear, police officials strongly supported repeal of the law, as its enforcement strained their resources, not to mention its impact on their dignity. But the imperial government refused to reverse its decree, fearing the consequences such an action would have on popular perceptions of the sincerity of the liberalization effort.

meeting that had barely begun . . . People began to incite one another to resist; a number of these seized benches and chairs to use
as weapons. During this time the Commissioner had managed to
reach the door, and returned a few moments later accompanied by
an Officer of the Peace and several *sergents de ville* [constables]. The
crowd tried unsuccessfully to barricade the door, and the police, now
more numerous, burst into the hall. In reaction to the violent attack
of the crowd, several of the *sergents de ville* drew their swords. They
occupied and cleared the bureau. The disorder was total, with people
screaming and shouting insults. The officers, at the center of the hall,
were unable to expel the crowd, which refused to leave. The *sergents
de ville* were struck with benches, and a number of fights ensued.
Napoléon Gaillard was wounded; one member of the audience was
thrown off the tribune, and another was allegedly injured by a sword
blow. The fleeing crowd—including women and children—was
packed solid at the exit, preventing evacuation.

The most vivid lesson Parisians learned from these encounters was not, then,
that the capitalist order was inherently exploitative but, rather, that their prime
adversary was the state and its armed servants. There was only one epithet routinely hurled at unpopular speakers or disruptive audience members: *mouchard,*
or "police spy." The accusation was the same regardless of whether a participant
voiced opinions that were inconsistent with the dominant mood, made remarks
that might provoke a dissolution, or simply behaved in an unruly fashion.[14]

But if the pattern of contention in public meetings cast the state as the enemy,
what collective actor emerged in opposition to the state? The theoretical perspective I outlined in chapter 1 holds that collective identities frame social conflict
by depicting the social world in terms of relations among distinct groups and
plausibly identifying potential participants as members of one such group or another. This proposition poses the question of the collective identity in terms of
which participants in the public meetings of 1868–70 came to understand their
nightly jousts with the police. Who were "the people" whom Pellerin was com-
mending for their defiance of the authorities?

14. Numerous examples of this phenomenon appear in Dalotel, Faure, and Freiermuth, *Aux
origines de la Commune,* pp. 139–44. Consistent with their view that the meetings were a locus of
class struggle, Dalotel et al. argue that "the struggle against authority of which the police and their
informants were the embodiment was the occasion for the people to learn to demonize the power of
the Empire and of property-owners." Yet there is no evidence that the police commissioners or those
accused of being police spies were ever depicted explicitly as the defenders of the propertied class.

It was not until the 1870 siege of Paris, to be described in the next section, that the collective identity governing participation in public meetings emerged explicitly and unambiguously as that of the neighborhood. But three circumstances that already obtained during the meeting movement of 1868–70 made it highly probable that the collective self-understanding established in these gatherings would eventually focus on the idea of the urban community, and more particularly the *arrondissement*. In the first place, there is some evidence that meetings drew largely on the immediate vicinity for their crowds: the same people who frequented the local *bal populaire* returned for the more serious proceedings that took place there on off nights.[15] For example, the signers of a petition protesting the dissolution of an August 1869 meeting at the Belle-Moissonneuse predominantly listed addresses in neighboring areas. Of 122 signers, 71 lived in the thirteenth *arrondissement* (where the ballroom was situated), and 31 more lived in the adjacent fifth and sixth.[16] Because the gatherings in question were meetings rather than clubs, there are no membership rolls with which to determine the overall residential distribution of audiences; nonetheless, this instance suggests that Parisians generally attended the meetings taking place near their homes. This meant, of course, that the average participant would find that his or her neighbors typically made up a significant portion of those present.

Second, the demographic makeup of the crowds at most meetings precluded other available participation identities from mapping plausibly onto the relation between the police and the audience. Apart from the fifteen meetings dedicated explicitly to the founding of a *chambre syndicale* or mutual-aid society, all of the meetings were heterogeneous with respect to craft, class, and gender.[17] In the

15. The public ball, by all accounts an enormously popular form of entertainment in Second Empire Paris, was considered a quintessentially Parisian spectacle. As one Paris guidebook for English-speaking tourists remarked, "When full, the ballroom presents a scene of extraordinary animation, and here may be seen rare specimens of Parisian dancing." Another oft-noted feature was the diversity of social strata in the crowd, which was thought to pose a difficulty for the more "delicate" of visitors: "As a general observation, we may remark that the character of the French population is nowhere to be seen to more advantage than at places of this description. They cannot, however, properly be recommended as fitting places for an English lady to visit, unless well attended and incognito." *Galignani's Paris Guide* (Paris: Galignani, 1867), pp. 478–81.

16. Dalotel et al., p. 71.

17. It bears remarking, though, that even the discussions of women's work and political rights were dominated by men, despite the vocal participation of such feminists as Paule Minck and Elisa Gagneur. Moreover, most of the male speakers at such meetings, socialists as well as republicans, openly denounced the idea of political and economic equality between women and men.

overwhelming majority of cases, therefore, conflicts erupting between the police functionary and the crowd could not reasonably be interpreted as confrontations pitting "workers"—either in general or in specific craft groups—against the authorities. In contrast to the numerous instances in 1848 in which political meetings were officially and popularly designated as gatherings of *travailleurs* or *ouvriers*, I have found no examples of meeting participants being collectively described in the press or in the meetings themselves as "workers."[18]

Third, the Paris Police Commissioners were organized geographically, with one *commissaire de police* stationed to each *quartier*. Accordingly, a major reason for the insults regularly hurled at the police both from the tribune and from the rank and file was that the officer present was also generally the man responsible for arrests of local residents for public drunkenness, petty theft, and disorderly conduct—the full range of minor transgressions that afforded Parisians their occasional contact with state authority. At one meeting, an Internationalist bronze worker named Louis Chalain, after being subjected to repeated interruptions, recognized among those responsible for the noise a police spy with whom he had had a run-in some months previously. When Chalain exposed his antagonist, the latter and a number of other "moustachioed men" left the meeting hall in embarrassed haste.[19] In short, the organization of the repressive effort paralleled, and consequently highlighted, the neighborhood basis of the meetings.

For anyone attending a meeting near his or her home, then, the demographic heterogeneity of the crowd prevented any locally significant collective identity other than the neighborhood—for example, trade or class—from furnishing an adequate summary description of the group present; and at the same time, because even the representatives of authority were tied to the locality, no collective identity defined on a more general level (such as "the French people") could improve upon that defined by the neighborhood. The neighborhood constituted the least upper bound for a collective identity in the sense that it included nearly everyone present at the nightly spectacle of social conflict while minimizing the number of absent people who were also included.[20]

18. This generalization is based on a comprehensive examination of the police reports and of published accounts of the meetings. See APP, BA 1520; Molinari, *Le mouvement socialiste et les réunions publiques;* Dalotel, Faure, and Freiermuth, *Aux origines de la Commune;* Auguste Vitu, *Les réunions publiques à Paris, 1868–1869* (Paris: E. Dentu, 1869).

19. Incident recounted in Dalotel et al., p. 144.

20. Given the size of the crowds, in fact, it is very likely that most inhabitants of any given district attended at least a few local meetings over the course of the movement. Integrating over time, then, the collective representation of neighborhood probably embraced very few nonparticipants.

The fact that the urban neighborhood could serve as a basis for collective action that was independent of struggles over work was inseparable from the changes in Parisian social life wrought by the transformations of the 1850s and 1860s: the most contentious meetings tended to occur in the residential outlying areas, not in the industrial core of the city. This contrast can be observed most vividly in the pattern of dissolutions, which indicates that the area with the most intense conflict was the ring of suburbs annexed to Paris in 1860. Of 341 meetings in the central districts (first through tenth *arrondissements*), 32 (9.4 percent) were dissolved by the police; in contrast, 89 of 435 meetings (20 percent) held in the outlying districts ended in dissolution. Forcible closure was thus twice as likely in the outer ring than in the city center, and highest of all in Belleville, La Villette, and Charonne—the areas identified in chapter 3 as exhibiting comparatively high levels of neighborhood cohesion. While the greater likelihood of confrontation probably owed as much to police apprehension about the peripheral *faubourgs* as it did to genuine differences in behavior at the meetings, it also undoubtedly amplified the sense of opposition between the urban community and imperial authority in these neighborhoods. Either way, this observation offers persuasive evidence that the expansion of the Parisian population into areas of the city more easily characterized as residential than industrial literally paved the way for mass mobilization predicated on identification with the urban community rather than with craft or class.

❦ The Prussian Siege and the Club Movement ❧

The right to hold public meetings was finally suspended, following isolated riots on the occasion of the Emperor's May 1870 plebiscite. But four months later, the Empire had fallen in the wake of a military debacle (which included the capture of Napoleon III) and Parisians had a new set of enemies to arouse their ire: the troops of Prussia's Iron Chancellor and a group of republican leaders secretly negotiating an armistice while the foreign army starved and bombarded the capital. It was the aftermath of the Franco-Prussian war that triggered the communal insurrection of March 1871, a fact that has underpinned the traditional liberal interpretation of the Commune for much of the past century: according to the liberal view, the hardship imposed by the siege together with the humiliation of defeat provoked sufficient anger to spark a patriotic uprising in the capital.[21]

Not surprisingly, the more recent influence of the class-formation narrative

21. The chief example of this view is to be found in Alistair Horne, *The Fall of Paris: The Siege and the Commune, 1870–71* (London: Macmillan, 1965).

has inspired historians to relegate the Franco-Prussian war to the status of a triggering event, and to trace the uprising to the underlying struggle between capital and the (emerging) working class. Where the siege of Paris had been understood as the principal grievance, it is now usually seen as part of a breach in the political order that permitted the rapid mobilization of workers' forces by temporarily weakening the state's control over the urban population. Rather than causing the Commune, in other words, the collapse of the Empire and the ensuing military defeat provided the opening for a profound social and political struggle that the imperial regime had merely suppressed by force.

Contrary to both of these interpretations, I suggest that the Commune did reflect a genuine social conflict that pre-dated the events of 1871 but that it was founded on a mapping of people into collective actors other than social classes. The collective actors in question were neighborhoods, and their adversary was the state—initially in its imperial guise and later, after the Emperor's abdication, in the form of the conservative Government of National Defense. The previous section detailed the ways in which the organizational context of the public meetings, in particular the recurrent confrontations with local representatives of the state, contributed to the plausibility of neighborhood as the basis for a collective identity that had little to do with the world of labor. In the remainder of this chapter, I shall describe the process by which activity in the clubs of September 1870–January 1871 pushed the conceptual opposition between neighborhoods and the state to the point of revolutionary collective action.

⁓❧⁓

Despite the widespread social protest that erupted in France during the Empire's last few years, internal strife was not the ultimate cause of Louis Napoleon's fall. In fact, by 1870 domestic affairs were looking better for the government: the Emperor had responded to the embarrassing 1869 election results by proposing a set of constitutional reforms that finally granted real political power to the legislature, and the plebiscite of May 1870 demonstrated general approval of the Emperor's liberal reforms (and, by extension, of the Empire itself). Had France not blundered into a war for which it was pathetically ill prepared, the regime of Napoleon III might have lasted quite a bit longer.

The Franco-Prussian war of 1870–71 began as a conflict over the succession to the Spanish throne, though many historians ultimately attribute the entire affair to the imperialist designs of the Prussian Chancellor, Otto von Bismarck. When, with Bismarck's encouragement, the Spanish offered the monarchy to

Prince Leopold von Hohenzollern-Sigmaringen, a relative of Prussia's King Wilhelm I, the French government immediately denounced the arrangement as an insult to French honor and a threat to the European balance of power. The Prince's candidacy was withdrawn, but France's Foreign Ministry pushed its luck by demanding guarantees that it would not be renewed; when Wilhelm politely declined, Bismarck published the king's message (known as the Ems dispatch) in an abbreviated manner that made the refusal appear insulting. Emile Ollivier, the Prime Minister, could not accept another humiliation at the hands of Prussia, and so had no choice but to declare war.

After an initial burst of patriotic optimism, the French quickly discovered that they were no match for Prussia's numerically superior, better equipped, and better trained army. The summer of 1870 brought little but the news of embarrassing defeats. In August, one army under Marshal Bazaine was encircled at Metz; on September 2, a second army at Sedan was forced to surrender and the Emperor himself was taken prisoner.

When the news of Napoleon's capture reached the capital on September 4, the Second Empire simply vanished. Following Paris's standard ritual, crowds invaded the legislature at the Palais Bourbon to demand the Third Republic, then descended on the Hôtel de Ville, where revolutionary regimes were traditionally proclaimed. A predominantly republican group of legislators formed a provisional Government of National Defense, with promises to hold elections for a Constituent Assembly and to field new armies for the war effort. In preparation for the impending Prussian siege of the capital, the newly appointed Interior Minister Léon Gambetta began to rearm the Paris National Guard, the popular militia that Louis Napoleon had disbanded following the coup of 1851. The siege began on September 9, and General von Moltke's armies completed their blockade of the city on September 20.

Rather than staging a direct assault on the fortifications surrounding Paris, which were formidable, von Moltke decided to starve the city into submission. For its part, the Government of National Defense, under the leadership of the conservative General Jules Trochu, was unwilling to rely on the untrained, partially armed, and insufficiently loyal National Guard to launch a full-scale counterattack. Despite initial approval of this defensive posture, Parisians ultimately began to agitate against Trochu's inaction when they learned in October that the government had made overtures to Bismarck in the hope of negotiating an armistice. On October 31, this revelation, combined with reports of new military disasters, brought crowds into the streets for the second time that fall; and a number of Paris's professional revolutionaries, most of them followers of Auguste Blanqui, took advantage of the situation by occupying the Hôtel de Ville and setting up a revolutionary government. Only a few hours later, Trochu succeeded in recapturing the Hôtel de Ville along with most of its occupants, counterbalancing his use of force by releasing his prisoners—although most were rearrested the next day—and promising to schedule elections for a municipal council. This pledge, on which the government also reneged the next day (ultimately holding elections for *arrondissement* mayors only), was a response to demands for municipal self-government that the populations of several French cities had begun to voice almost immediately after Bonaparte's abdication. This demand had already become the heart of a nationwide movement for municipal autonomy, to be discussed presently.

Following the collapse of the Empire on September 4, it had not taken long for crowds to fill the meeting halls of Paris once again. With the proclamation of the Republic, there was no more police presence (though the epithet *mouchard* was still routinely hurled at disruptive individuals) and topics of discussion were no longer restricted. As the siege dragged on into the winter, however, the clubs (as they were now called) again became the crucible for resentment against the authorities, who were held responsible for (among other things) the continued military setbacks and the inadequate supply of provisions to the capital. Speakers gave voice to profound frustration at the apparent inaction of the Government of National Defense and concocted wild plans for breaking the Prussian blockade. Rumors of armies marching to the rescue under the command of Gambetta or the Italian patriot Giuseppe Garibaldi repeatedly came to nothing, ultimately reinforcing the belief that a reversal of fortune could only come from within the city walls. A common element of the popular plans was, for some reason, the imaginative employment of Greek fire, as the following eyewitness account of a December 9 meeting of the Club Démocratique des Batignolles shows:

> The question of "Greek fire" has a special ability to inspire the assembly. The reason is that the club recently opened a subscription to bestow upon France a supply of this infernal engine, and that doubts have arisen concerning its efficacy. According to one speaker, the citizen Delescluze [a republican veteran of 1848 and a future martyr of the Commune], whose expertise in the matter of explosives is beyond doubt, announced this morning that Greek fire has a dramatic effect in the water but is less destructive on dry mate-

rial. (*Signs of disappointment in the audience.*) It will first be necessary, therefore, to direct high-caliber fire-pumps at the Prussians to get them wet.[22]

The sensational rumors and flights of fancy in which club participants indulged certainly indicated a lack of political sophistication, but more importantly they gauged the depths of desperation which life in the besieged city had reached. As deaths from starvation and disease mounted, residents of Paris worked out an often contradictory but nevertheless pointed analysis of their plight, an analysis whose main themes were that the Government of National Defense was deliberately holding back in the war effort (which was eventually true, given the movement toward capitulation), that "reactionaries" secretly hoped for a Prussian victory and the restoration of the monarchy in France, and that the only way to save Paris (and by implication the Republic itself) was through the proclamation of the Commune, to be followed by a revolutionary *levée en masse* in the tradition of 1793.

In the ensuing months, political agitation in the capital intensified as the misery of the Parisian populace deepened. The government's penchant for liberal political economy meant that food and firewood were not initially rationed, with the result that social inequalities became even more pronounced than usual: while the wealthiest segments of the population continued to eat full, if unorthodox, meals (elephants, zebras, and other exotic animals from the zoo soon became delicacies served in Paris's finest restaurants and most affluent homes), those with fewer resources literally began first to freeze and then to starve to death. Club speeches increasingly contained denunciations of wealthier Parisians—not because of their role in the exploitation of workers (a detail about which I will say more presently) but because they were widely suspected of hoarding comestibles in their cellars:

> Last night [January 15, 1871], the club Favié resembled a buzzing hive. People participated in an animated discussion concerning the bread rationing that had begun that morning in the [twentieth] *arrondissement* and the women in particular distinguished themselves with the vehemence of their complaints. In some groups it was said

22. Gustave de Molinari, *Les clubs rouges pendant le siège de Paris* (Paris: Garnier Frères, 1874), p. 141. The term "Greek fire" (*feu grégeois*) referred to an incendiary substance used by the Byzantine Greeks to attack naval vessels. It was reputed to ignite on contact with water.

that the people at the Hôtel de Ville are indulging themselves freely; they eat as much meat as they please, they and the rich folk who support them; they keep hams in their cellars and have wild parties in the restaurants, accompanied by young ladies. Since they are not subject to rationing, they comfortably make patriotic speeches about "fighting to the end" [*la guerre à outrance*] at the expense of our stomachs. But we, we who have nothing left but bread, can we live on a pound or even 100 grams of bread a day? They want us to die of hunger so they can be rid of Belleville, which threatens them even more than the Prussians do.[23]

The inequitable distribution of privation during the siege had, in short, heightened class resentment to its highest pitch since 1848. Moreover, the horrific vividness of hardship—club meetings were occasionally interrupted by announcements that someone had collapsed from hunger or disease in the street outside—meant that the terms in which this resentment was expressed left little to the imagination. Later the same evening at the club Favié, the man presiding over the meeting vowed that bourgeois Parisians would perish with everyone else:

"Look at the death toll for this week, and that is only the beginning. One hears more and more coughing in Belleville; we are falling ill waiting in line for bread, for meat, and for firewood. How are we to care for ourselves? We shall be dead by spring. Better to end it now; but before we do that, we must nonetheless settle our score with the bourgeoisie. We must not be the only ones to suffer the torments of hunger. We are being rationed, we who live on bread; we have to requisition the others, those who live on conserves and fine foods. Before we die, we will pay a visit to their cellars, and we shall have a few words to say to their hams (*applause and laughter*). After that, we will all die together, and since they have not wanted to make a community with us in life, we shall have it in death." Another citizen declares that it is not for the people to hold out a hand to the bourgeois. "The victim does not give his hand to the executioner; the executioner must first make amends."[24]

Two months before the actual insurrection, then, the collective identity of class resonated grimly but persuasively with poorer Parisians' experience of the siege. When words like "we" and "the people" cropped up in speeches of the sort just

23. Ibid., pp. 246–47.
24. Ibid., pp. 254–55.

quoted, they clearly referred, at least some of the time, to the Parisian poor, including (though not necessarily limited to) manual laborers. The popular discourse that characterized the siege thus seems at various moments to have achieved the same telescoping of "the people" into "the workers" that had occurred in June 1848.

But despite this apparent reprise of 1848, several features of the political activism of September 1870 to January 1871 reveal that the set of collective self-understandings embraced by victims of the siege was rather more complex. In the first place, given the minuscule number of people not profoundly affected by the blockade, the "bourgeois" parasites demonized in the popular clubs were a largely imaginary group; for the most part, the numerous shop owners and small employers who would normally have been the targets of working-class antagonism were subject to the same travails as everyone else. Because it was, for the moment, framed primarily in terms of access to food and fuel rather than in terms of production relations, the conceptual opposition of "the people" and "the bourgeois" had the unusual property of mapping a considerable number of middle-class Parisians into the former category. The most visible members of the latter group were, in point of fact, officials of the Government of National Defense.[25]

Despite the surface plausibility of class as the dimension in terms of which the conflict was understood, then, it makes little sense to liken the collective identity invoked by the appeals cited here to that which pervaded the mobilization of 1848. What the victims of the siege shared was not working for a wage but cold, famine, and Prussian shrapnel; and the people whom they held responsible for this brutal existence were the holders of political and military power, not the property owners and employers. The perceived mechanism of oppression was the political economy of war rationing rather than the institutions of private property and wage-labor. This was a struggle of the people against the state, not of workers against capital.

A more telling indicator of the existence of alternatives to a class-based identity was the intense neighborhood localism that characterized political agitation during the siege, most apparent in denunciations of the government's war effort and calls for a massive popular assault on the blockading army. As the speeches

25. In addition, a considerable number of wealthier Parisians (it is impossible to know precisely how many) had been able to escape to second homes in the provinces before the blockade closed all ports of exit. This fact in itself does not appear to have caused any popular resentment, but it surely made it more difficult to find actual examples of bourgeois families living the good life while their poorer neighbors starved.

just quoted indicate, club speakers regularly denounced the government's policies on behalf of the "people of Belleville," or of whichever district they inhab-
ited, rather than "the people" as a whole. In addition, popular efforts to deal with
the practical problems of the siege were invariably organized on the district level.
As early as September 7, republican activists in each *arrondissement* of Paris
had set up local "committees of vigilance" with the dual purpose of safeguarding
the republic and organizing the defense of the capital against the Prussian army.
Although members of the International instigated the formation of several such
committees and encouraged their federation into a citywide Central Republican
Committee of the Twenty Arrondissements, the political and practical activities
of these committees remained thoroughly parochial in orientation: most concerned themselves with the arming of National Guard battalions in their own
districts, with the selection of *arrondissement* mayors, and with local rationing
of provisions. Indeed, many of their proposals, such as the demand that Police
Commissioners be democratically elected by *quartier*, constituted explicit attempts to decentralize state authority.[26] In announcing its formation in a Paris
newspaper, the vigilance committee for the eighteenth *arrondissement* asserted
that "the *quartiers* are the fundamental base of the democratic republic."[27]

Popular agitation of this sort took its cue not from debates over the organization of labor or even the question of equitable rationing but from the decentralist
impulse that swept across France's major cities in the aftermath of the Empire's
fall. A hallmark of Louis Bonaparte's regime had been an impressive centralization of political and administrative power, and one of the most versatile tools
wielded by his departmental prefects had been the repeated dissolution of the
municipal councils they considered troublesome until weary voters chose councillors who would be cooperative.[28] The largest cities, Paris and Lyon, had been
completely stripped of the right to elect their own councils, which were instead
appointed by the Minister of the Interior, and voters in other cities justifiably
feared a similar fate. (Marseille, for example, had barely escaped the abolition of
its municipal elections in 1859.) Given that republicanism had in any case found
a stronger base of support in cities than in rural areas since at least the 1840s,
the reinstatement of municipal liberties had become a standard plank in the re-

26. Edwards, *The Paris Commune, 1871*, pp. 67–69; Jacques Rougerie, *Paris libre, 1871*, pp.
34–38; Lefebvre, *La proclamation de la Commune*, pp. 183–85.

27. *Le combat*, September 21, 1870, quoted in Edwards, *The Communards of Paris*, p. 73.

28. Merriman, *The Agony of the Republic*, pp. 110–15; Howard Payne, *The Police State of Louis
Bonaparte* (Seattle: University of Washington Press, 1966), pp. 108–14.

publican opposition's platform. Thus one of the first acts of the Central Republican Committee of the Twenty Arrondissements, even before the Prussian blockade of Paris was complete, was to publish an appeal to the Government of National Defense (conventionally referred to as the first *affiche rouge*, or "red poster") that explicitly tied the stability of the Republic to local administrative autonomy:

> Citizens:
>
> On September 5, just after the proclamation of the Republic, a large number of citizens proposed the constitution of a Central Republican Committee formed by the twenty *arrondissements* of Paris and taking as its objectives the security of the fatherland and the definitive founding of a truly republican regime, by means of enduring individual initiative and popular solidarity.
>
> Since that day, public meetings have elected "committees of defense and vigilance" in each *arrondissement*. As soon as most of the districts were represented, each by four delegates, the Central Republican Committee began its operations. It has presented to the Government of National Defense a proposal for the following measures, acclaimed in the popular meetings:
>
> I. Measures concerning public safety
> —Suppression of the police as it has been constituted under all monarchical governments, as a means to subjugate the citizens rather than defend them.
> —Placement of police functions under the control of elected municipal councils.
> —Nomination by *quartier*, in large cities, of magistrates invested with the personal responsibility of overseeing public safety.
> —Dissolution of all special corps of the former centralized police, such as *sergents de ville*, so-called agents of public security, *gardes de Paris* . . .
> —Abrogation of all repressive, restrictive, or fiscal laws against freedom of the press, of speech, of public assembly, and of association.
>
> II. Subsistence and lodging
> —Expropriation in the public interest of all edible and other essential goods currently warehoused in Paris, guaranteeing their owners payment for said goods after the war.
> —Election in each street or at least in each *quartier* of a commission

to inventory all consumable goods and to declare their holders personally responsible to the municipal administration . . .

III. Defense of Paris

—Delivery to all citizens of long-range weapons with sufficient ammunition to defend against possible attack.

—Preparation through the activities of the twenty *arrondissement* committees of the material and organizational means necessary for the defense of each *quartier* . . .

In presenting these emergency proposals, the undersigned are convinced that the Government of National Defense will transform them in all haste into official decrees for the good of the fatherland and the Republic.[29]

The forty-eight signers, many of them radicals who made frequent appearances in popular clubs, left implicit a detail that they hoped would be abundantly clear: that the proposals' undeniable legitimacy derived not merely from their manifestly republican content but also from the committee's adherence to the principle of popular (and local) sovereignty in constituting itself. A week and a half later, on September 24, they issued a manifesto that made the point explicit with the use of the term "Commune":

The welfare of France and the triumph of the European Revolution depend on Paris. The government might be forced to relocate to the provinces [it had already done so, just prior to the blockade]; the Commune must live or die with the capital.

Never, therefore, have municipal elections, set for the 28th of this month, had the importance given to them by the present grave circumstances. [The government was to postpone them indefinitely on the 26th.] Never has universal suffrage been faced with such an immense duty, which it must fulfill on pain of death.

The Central Republican Committee, in the various messages it has published since September 4, has proposed the following measures, essential to the safety of Paris and the fatherland as well as to the future of the Republic:

[the proposals quoted earlier are repeated here, followed by a new one:]

29. Reproduced in *Les murailles politiques françaises* (Paris: Lechevalier, 1874), vol. 2, pp. 90–91.

The establishment of the sovereign Commune, which will mobilize a
revolutionary defeat of the enemy and facilitate the harmony of interests and direct government of the citizens by themselves . . .

We cannot repeat too often, citizens, that upon the constitution of the
Commune of Paris, formed of resolute republicans, depends the life
or death of the fatherland, and the success or the ruin of the political
and social principles of the Revolution.[30]

Formal demands for the Commune, like this one, referred primarily to the creation of a popularly elected municipal council. The more impassioned and radical club speakers tended to associate it as well with the French Revolution—in
particular with the Commune of the Year II, the democratic council of local delegates in Paris that had spearheaded the street massacres of September 1793 and
pushed the revolution into its radical phase under Robespierre. One orator in
Belleville announced to the public, "What we need is '93! Well, '93 will return,
and you can be sure that we will find our Robespierres and our Marats!"[31] Nevertheless, the ambivalence this association aroused in the minds of many Parisians
pushed many club speakers calling for the Commune to distance themselves from
the Jacobin version, insisting that the Commune of Paris would ally itself with
France's other cities—some of which had already begun to demand Communes
of their own—rather than imposing its revolutionary authority on them as in
1793.

Like most symbols, the Commune derived some of its appeal from the multiplicity of meanings it could evoke in the minds of besieged Parisians: municipal
liberty, equal distribution of rations, mass mobilization against the Prussians,
republican solidarity, or simply "the only way to bring back beans and lentils."[32]
But there was no mistaking the common thread that ran through the hundreds of
leaflets and speeches that strove for the definitive account of what the Commune
would be ("the Commune, in sum—is the Commune!" shouted one speaker
whose enthusiasm outran his command of the subject).[33] Whether the interpreter

30. *Le rappel*, 24 September 1870, p. 1.

31. Molinari, *Les clubs rouges*, p. 91. André Découflé has pointed out that the war with Prussia
in itself made the references to 1793 relevant as a reminder of the connection between popular
mobilization and patriotic war against foreign tyrants and domestic counterrevolutionaries: "Ninety-
three was first of all the flame of the armed resistance of the people against the foreign invader and
the *chouans.*" *La Commune de Paris (1871): Révolution populaire et pouvoir révolutionnaire* (Paris:
Editions Cujas, 1969), p. 46.

32. Molinari, *Les clubs rouges*, p. 195.

33. Ibid., p. 213.

was an Internationalist inspired by Proudhon's vision of a society of independent towns, a republican devoted to popular sovereignty, or a Jacobin dedicated to the destruction of European monarchy, the idea of municipal self-government always made an appearance. Whatever their disagreements, and there is no denying that there were many, everyone clamoring for the Commune in Paris knew that, at a minimum, this meant the election by universal male suffrage of a city council in which each *arrondissement* would be represented by at least four delegates. On the other hand, existing accounts of club speeches contain no instances of the Commune being equated with the emancipation of labor or the right to work.[34]

The movement for local autonomy had no parallel in the political mobilization of 1848. To be sure, public pronouncements following the February Revolution consistently talked of safeguarding the Republic and of the sovereignty of the people. But, as I demonstrated in chapter 2, the expansion of the suffrage and the debate over the right to work made "the people" interchangeable with "the workers," and popular political activity surrounding the elections concentrated on the theme that working for a wage was the surest guarantee of a candidate's commitment to the Republic. In the fall of 1870, "the people" referred to the diverse multitudes crowding into the clubs in their neighborhoods—and the guarantee of the Republic was local self-government, not political representation by wage-earners. Universal male suffrage in national elections was already established, and in any case was obviously an insufficient guardian of the Republic, having helped to shore up the plebiscitary Empire for the past two decades. Attention therefore fell on a social unit whose political independence had been crushed in the aftermath of the 1851 coup and which the meeting movement of 1868-70 had revived as a plausible challenger to central state authority: the local community.

The current political situation and the experience of centralization under the Empire thus made it highly likely that republican activists would tie the time-

---

34. Molinari, *Les clubs rouges*, passim; Rougerie, *Paris libre, 1871*, pp. 33–66. Some socialist members of local vigilance committees called for "workers" (*ouvriers*) or "laborers" (*travailleurs*, or those, including small-scale employers, who performed manual work) to serve on the hypothetical Commune. It was very rare for activists to call publicly for an exclusively working-class Commune—in fact, the principal example was a proposal submitted anonymously to the Central Republican Committee. Most often, the justification for ensuring a working-class presence was their greater familiarity with "the needs of the people." See the extensive collection of Central Republican Committee documents in Jean Dautry and Lucien Scheler, *Le Comité Central Républicain des vingt arrondissements de Paris* (Paris: Editions Sociales, 1960).

honored rhetoric of popular sovereignty to the notion of local self-government. There was no ideological reason, however, for "local" to mean the *quartier* or *arrondissement:* the term "commune" applied formally to whole towns, and the general understanding, even in Paris, was that the elected council would govern Paris as a whole. So it was by no means established in advance that Parisians would owe primary allegiance to the *arrondissement* and only secondary allegiance to the city taken in its entirety. Indeed, in the absence of the idea of the Commune, "local" sovereignty could have been defined on a variety of scales: individual buildings, streets, neighborhoods, or the city as a whole.

But daily patterns of political interaction occurred on the scale of neighborhoods: until January, clubs across the city remained the essential organizational locus for the assertion and solidification of the residential community as a politically relevant collective identity. (The National Guard, which became the basis of mobilization during the Commune, will be discussed in detail in the next chapter.) The most plausible scale on which to conceive of the collectivities formed by these nightly gatherings, therefore, was defined by the area in which most of the people attending lived (as it had been during the meeting movement).[35] And this is just what club participants did: following the October 31 affair, in response to which the government had acceded to Parisians' demand to elect the mayors of each *arrondissement,* it even became customary for speakers to refer to the "citizens" of Montmartre, of La Villette, and so on. Political conflict was increasingly represented in terms of struggles between specific neighborhoods and the Government of National Defense, as this November meeting in the twentieth *arrondissement* illustrates:

> The meeting passes to the order of the day, to wit, "the government's nomination, contrary to the principles of justice and popular sovereignty, of a municipal commission to replace the captive mayor of Belleville and his adjuncts." [The men in question, Gabriel Ranvier, Jean-Baptiste Millière, and Gustave Lefrançais, were in custody for their participation in the October 31 seizure of the Hôtel de Ville.] A formal letter has been drafted protesting this unjustifiable and infamous act; all citizens are invited to sign it. The committee of vigilance wished to have it printed in the form of a poster, but no printer has dared to take on the job, such is the nature of the despotism to

35. As winter drew near and fuel grew scarce, the clubs most likely became ever more local in character: with people dying every day from pneumonia, Parisians could hardly be expected to stray farther than the nearest meeting place.

which we have lately been subjected. The citizen Gaillard *fils* appeals nonetheless to the citizens of Belleville to refuse to let themselves be defeated: the letter shall be covered with signatures, and a deputation will carry it to the Hôtel de Ville, as is done in England, to demand the liberation of the prisoners. If the government refuses, that will demonstrate that it has declared war on Belleville, and we will know what to do. (*Thunderous applause.*)[36]

The inhabitants of Belleville were unmatched in the fierceness with which they expressed their local pride; two weeks later, at the Salle du Grand-Pavillon, one man actually shouted, "It is Belleville that will save Europe!" (From what, precisely, he neglected to say.) Yet people in other neighborhoods, principally those on the periphery, demonstrated a similarly profound sense of the *arrondissement* as the basic unit of collective action and solidarity during the siege. At the Club de l'Élysée Montmartre on December 23, the recent and unanticipated return from the city ramparts of a Montmartre National Guard battalion was the focus of concern: "It seems that the sudden return of the 32d battalion caused a considerable stir in the neighborhood. The women of the boulevard Ornano remonstrated with the arrivals in the manner of the women of Sparta, accusing them of having conducted themselves less than heroically on the field of battle."[37] It was a matter of general agreement, it seems, that the comportment of a Guard battalion in the defense of Paris reflected primarily upon the residents of the neighborhood in which it was recruited and only secondarily on the city as a whole. At the very least, it was an essential part of a Parisian's patriotic duty to express support (or scorn, depending on the circumstances) for the battalions in his or her district. Indeed, club participants explicitly spoke of the *arrondissement* as the fundamental collective actor in the defense of Paris and drew comparisons across districts in the effort to stir up enthusiasm:

> There are other *quartiers* where they have more energy than in Belleville ("It's true! We are soft!"), where they are determined, this very evening, to march on the Hôtel de Ville. Are we going to let ourselves be outdone by La Villette or Montmartre? ("No! No!") You shout, "No!" but when the moment to act arrives, you won't find 500 men in Belleville. ("Yes! Yes!" The women jump to their feet, shout-

36. Molinari, *Les clubs rouges* (meeting of November 10), p. 80.
37. Ibid., p. 173.

ing, "We shall be the first to go! We shall march to demand that they give us bread!" *Extreme agitation.*)[38]

During the rare moments of contact between residents of different districts, rivalry usually took over from the spirit of fraternity that presumably motivated the encounters. For example, at a meeting in the Folies-Bergère in the ninth *arrondissement*, a delegate from a Belleville club who was touting his fellow Bellevillois's "patriotism and courage" was interrupted by a local who shouted, "They're not the only ones!" A second local drew laughter and applause when he reported that a friend of his had stopped attending the Club Favié in Belleville "because he was afraid of turning into a reactionary."[39] At a meeting of the Club de la Marseillaise in La Villette, a visitor from the third *arrondissement* ("unknown to the assembly, but claiming to live in the rue Chapon") made clear just how unused he was to venturing outside his own neighborhood by repeatedly forgetting whom he was addressing:

> The citizen from the rue Chapon . . . says he has heard from a "neighbor" of Trochu's that everything is ready for the capitulation, and he expects very soon to be able to communicate to the club another piece of information that will be even more decisive; but in the meantime, he implores "the energetic citizens of Belleville (*exclamations, objections:* 'You're not in Belleville here!')—pardon, the citizens of La Villette and the other republican faubourgs to watch the government's every move. We must not count on the *quartiers* of the center, particularly the rue Chapon, which I know well: they are completely weak. It is Belleville (*expressions of greater impatience*)—no! It is La Villette, along with Belleville and Montmartre, that will save Paris!" (*Applause.*)[40]

The competitive comparisons, the irritation expressed at the errors of an outsider, and the general mistrust of the sentiments of people in other areas, especially in the center of Paris, demonstrate three things. First, those who attended the clubs saw them as the political expression of republican and patriotic activity specifically in their own districts, not in Paris as a whole. Second, the relative absence of regular contact with people in other districts caused a sense of unease about the depth of commitment to the Republic, to the idea of the Commune, and

38. Molinari, *Les clubs rouges*, p. 255.
39. Ibid., p. 155.
40. Molinari, *Les clubs rouges*, pp. 229–30.

to the war effort anywhere outside the immediately surrounding neighborhood. Third, when such contact did occur, the evidence that at least some other neighborhoods were similarly inclined to challenge the government provided the impetus for further demonstrations of local fervor so as not to be outdone. This pattern of behavior establishes the centrality of neighborhood as the principal collective identity in terms of which participation in protest during the siege was understood. More importantly, it points to the significance of the clubs themselves in crystallizing collective self-understandings at that level.

⁂ Conclusion ⁂

Liberalization of the Empire in the 1860s fostered the reemergence of militant protest in France's urban centers with a vehemence that went well beyond what Louis-Napoleon and his advisers had anticipated. Rather than accept gratefully the limited latitude the Emperor had offered them, activists in Le Creusot, Marseille, Lyon, Paris, and the industrial regions of the Nord and Alsace-Lorraine clamored angrily for a radical transformation of the political and social order. Moderate republicans, socialists, and generic revolutionaries publicly demanded that social change occur through popular action, not paternalistic reform.

Because this upsurge in opposition mobilized substantial numbers of working people, the class-formation narrative represents the ferment of the 1860s as an episode in the labor movement, a reawakening of the class awareness that had galvanized the insurgents of 1848 and was shortly to lead to yet another violent upheaval in the aftermath of the 1870–71 war with Prussia. According to partisans of this narrative, the strike waves of 1864 and 1869, together with the meeting movement of 1868–70, marked the birth of "the party of laborers."[41]

But this rendering, however appealing it may be theoretically, masks at least as much as it reveals. Industrial conflict in Paris as well as the rest of France depended on the collective action of craft groups, which in turn relied heavily on the fact that laborers—in some occupations, at least—lived, worked, and drank in the company of fellow tradesmen. Craft structured both the organization of work and social relations in such a way that groups like the Parisian tailors, iron founders, and bronze workers could see the set of their colleagues as largely coextensive with the set of their friends. This proved to be a powerful source of solidarity when employer practices provoked shop-floor protest; nonetheless, the overlap between informal social relations and workplace relations made it highly

41. Dalotel et al., *Aux origines de la Commune*, p. 371.

unlikely that militant workers would shift from the participation identity of craft to that of class in the course of mobilizing strikes. The minimally inclusive collective identity for labor militancy remained at the level of occupational groups.

On the other hand, the collective self-understanding forged in the public meetings of 1868–70 broke completely away from craft-group boundaries—but this did not mean that meeting participants now understood themselves as belonging to a social class. Because the crowds at these meetings were heterogeneous except for the fact that most lived in the immediate vicinity, and because open provocation of the Police Commissioner was easily the most dramatic aspect of the evening gatherings, the minimally inclusive collective identity for these events was the neighborhood, defined in opposition to the forces of state repression. Despite all the talk of class struggle on the part of prominent militants speaking at the meetings, it was the visible struggle between the police and local residents that repeatedly drew the crowds.

The overriding impact of the Prussian siege was to deepen and reinforce the fault line that had appeared in the public meeting movement in the last years of the Empire: a conceptual mapping of social life that pitted the residents of local urban communities against the representatives and administrative organs of the central state. Even the class rhetoric that surfaced from time to time in debates over provisions represented "the people" as an economically diverse urban population deprived of adequate nourishment by a band of largely mythical "bourgeois" composed primarily of fat, insensitive politicians and administrators. Far from improving perceptions of the state, it actually made matters worse that the Empire had been replaced by an ostensibly republican Provisional Government. After all, the latter had placed Paris under military rule and continued to deny it the right to elect its own municipal council (the *arrondissement* mayors elected in November being only a subset of the full council). Throughout the siege, this basic opposition was continually reasserted in the numerous neighborhood clubs that provided the city's population with its only form of diversion.

More schematically, neighborhood became the salient collective identity in Paris in the fall of 1870 because of three independent influences: the national transfer of political power from Empire to republic, the organizational setting in which political activity took place, and preexisting patterns of social interaction in the capital's residential districts. Unlike the February Revolution of 1848, the proclamation of the Republic on September 4, 1870, did not highlight class as a significant dimension of political conflict because the right to vote had already been permanently extended to propertyless adult men under Napoleon III; nor

was there an employment crisis that might have called attention to the organization of work.[42] On the other hand, the republican opposition had already hit upon
the idea of demanding municipal liberties in the final years of the Empire,
and the latter's collapse in 1870 provided an opening for a popular campaign to
begin the process of political decentralization—not just in Paris but in cities all
across France. The national context thus accounts for the salience (at this particular moment) of spatially defined communities as important units of political activity and, at the same time, for the insignificance of class as a conceptual basis
for political action.

Nothing about the national political context, however, pointed specifically to
neighborhoods as the level at which spatially defined communities would be
marked off; indeed, demands for the establishment of communes in cities other
than Paris were cast in terms of the autonomy of whole cities.[43] It is with reference
to the question of scale, then, that the organizational context of popular mobilization made a difference: as in the meeting movement of June 1868 to May 1870,
the fact that Parisians frequented clubs in the vicinity of their homes (often for
purely practical reasons) meant that the neighborhood was the minimally inclusive collective identity available to participants in political agitation during the
siege.

If the combination of a national political crisis and the nightly spectacle of
the clubs were sufficient to account for the process described here, then one
would have observed a Paris composed entirely of neighborhoods dedicated to
intense, localistic militancy. But this was not the case: there was substantial variation across districts in the level of political agitation for an elected municipal
council, for a *levée en masse,* or for a revolution against the Government of National Defense. The most vehement protest against the government and calls for
the establishment of the Commune came from peripheral districts like Belleville,
La Villette, Montmartre, and Batignolles—areas in which the everyday life of

42. It is worth inquiring why, given that men were already enfranchised, the fall of the Empire
did not lead to widespread calls for the extension of the suffrage to women. The answer is that it
did—up to a point. A number of feminists active in the meeting movement, including Paule Minck,
André Léo, and Elisa Gagneur, repeatedly brought up the question of the emancipation of women,
and Louise Michel and Elisabeth Dmitrieff set up organizations representing women during the Commune. But male leaders of the left, especially those affiliated with the International, were overwhelmingly condescending toward women and feminists. The events of 1870–71 did, therefore, politicize
the issue of gender in a way that 1848 did not, but only to a limited extent.

43. The next chapter will give more detail on the provincial Communes and contrast them with
the Paris Commune.

working people was structured predominantly by the social ties of neighborhood rather than craft. As I argued in chapter 4, mobilization of labor protest required the maintenance of work-based patterns of association in the artisanal center of Paris that rendered craft groups plausible as collective actors. In parallel fashion, the spirit of neighborhood solidarity that made the popular clubs worth attending night after night relied upon the prior existence of informal social relations on the Parisian periphery—relations that were predicated on residence in the same place, not employment in the same trade.

6

Neighborhood, Class, and the Commune of 1871

T HE CRITICAL EVENTS of the fall of 1870, above all the war, the Emperor's abdication, and the proclamation of the Republic, furnished the context for political activity that regarded spatially defined communities as significant collective actors. In reaction to the centralization of state power that the Second Empire epitomized, political militants across France clamored for the reinstatement of local autonomy and the mobilization of the war effort by local militia organizations. But this national political situation left indeterminate the level at which the boundaries of such spatial communities would be drawn. As I demonstrated in chapter 5, the experience of the siege and the institution of local clubs ensured that, in Paris at least, these boundaries would be set at the level of the *arrondissement*. Popular appeals for a massive military attack on the Prussian blockade focused on the solidarity of specific neighborhoods, and on the glory that would accrue to their inhabitants if they could demonstrate that their dedication to victory and to the Republic was superior to that of other districts.

Despite this pronounced neighborhood localism, I contend that the "communal" uprising of March 18, 1871, is best understood as a movement in which the city of Paris as a whole acted collectively to defend its municipal liberties.[1] It is "best understood" in this way because, as I shall demonstrate presently, this perception was shared by many of the participants in the seventy-two-day revolution that is now known as the Paris Commune: the reasons for taking part in the fighting for most of the rank and file involved membership in an urban community understood principally in spatial terms. In this chapter, I shall explain why popu-

1. In the historiography of the Commune, this view is stated most eloquently by Louis Greenberg, *Sisters of Liberty: Paris, Marseille, Lyon and the Reaction to the Centralized State* (Cambridge, MA: Harvard University Press, 1971). A number of French historians, most notably Jeanne Gaillard and Jacques Rougerie, have paid close attention to class conflict but also acknowledged the importance of municipal autonomy in the mobilizations of 1870–71. See Rougerie, *Paris libre, 1871* and *La Commune: 1871;* Gaillard, *Communes de Province, Commune de Paris* (Paris: Flammarion, 1971).

lar appeals cast on the level of the city succeeded in mobilizing tens of thousands of people for revolutionary collective action, even though preexisting social networks and organizational forms were more conducive to neighborhood-level mobilization. Examination of patterns of insurgent participation reveals that the mass mobilization of March–May 1871 depended crucially on the neighborhood-based solidarity of residentially recruited National Guard battalions. It also depended, however, on newly formed ties *across* neighborhoods—ties created by a widespread organizational network of overlapping enlistments and by the Commune's defense of Paris against the French army, which entailed the prolonged deployment of "mobile" battalions to the ring of fortresses surrounding the capital city. Insurrection on a citywide scale, ultimately framed in terms of a citywide collective identity, required the interplay of local neighborhood solidarity with extralocal organizational networks forged by the mobilization process itself.

Because its point of departure is the claim that the urban community defined in spatial terms was the fundamental unit of political action during the Commune, the argument I have just summarized entails the parallel contention that class was *not* a very important dimension of collective identity between March and May of 1871. While this claim may be relatively uncontroversial to those historians whose observations are not guided by the class-formation narrative, it will surely surprise social scientists for whom the urban uprisings of the nineteenth century formed an integral part of European workers' struggle to challenge the spread of capitalism and to forge class awareness in the process. Accordingly, before examining the connection between organizational networks and neighborhood solidarity, it is necessary to defend the premise that an urban collective identity outweighed that of class in the mobilization process. I will take up this issue after presenting a brief overview of the events of January–May 1871.

⚜ Civil War ⚜

Toward the end of December, the prospects for breaking through the blockade only got worse. A new series of French defeats brought two more Prussian armies into the vicinity of Paris, and bombardment of the capital began on January 5. These events convinced the members of the government that they had no choice but to negotiate an armistice, whereas the people of Paris became more vocal than ever in their calls for a massive assault led by the National Guard. On the day the bombardment began, the Central Committee of the Twenty Arrondissements temporarily reemerged from obscurity to placard the city with its second "red poster" (*affiche rouge*), a fiery call for a full-scale attack on the Prussians:

The municipal council or the Commune, call it what you will, is the sole protector of the people, its only recourse against death . . . Will the great People of '89, who destroyed Bastilles and overturned thrones, wait in despair for cold and famine to freeze the last drop of blood in its heart, whose every beat is counted by the enemy? No! The population of Paris will never accept this misery and this shame. It knows that there is still time, that decisive steps can be taken to ensure the ability of working people to live, and to fight.

General requisition! Free rationing! Attack *en masse!* The politics, strategy, and administration of 4 September, all continuations of the Empire, have been judged. Make way for the People! Make way for the Commune![2]

More out of fear of revolt than out of any confidence in the effectiveness of an assault, Trochu relented and ordered a sortie toward Versailles of forty thousand Guards and fifty thousand soldiers. As everyone except the Parisians had anticipated, the sortie of January 19 was a complete fiasco: the Guardsmen broke ranks as soon as their adversaries opened fire, and after five thousand casualties Trochu was forced to order a retreat. Accused of irresponsibility by the military and denounced by the Parisian public for his cowardice in calling off the attack, Trochu was forced to resign as Commander of the Army of Paris. A week later, on January 28, the Minister of Foreign Affairs signed an armistice with Bismarck; Paris was ceded to the Prussians, and the French army—though not the National Guard— was to be demobilized except for a small security force. Because Bismarck would only accept a peace treaty ratified by a duly elected National Assembly, elections were scheduled for February 8.

Paradoxically, it was only after the siege had ended, when daily life in the capital was beginning to return to normal, that anything approaching radical mass mobilization occurred in Paris. Independently of any activity on the part of professional militants—though Blanquists, Internationalists, and Jacobins once again lost no time in latching on to the movement once it had started—rank-and-file members of the National Guard elected company, battalion, and legion delegates to a citywide assembly charged with the task of constituting a National Guard Federation. In two sessions at the Tivoli-Vauxhall, one of Paris's large public meeting halls, delegates from 215 of the city's 260 battalions drew up statutes for a radical democratic organization headed by an elected Central Com-

2. *Les murailles politiques françaises*, vol. 1, pp. 490–91.

mittee and dedicated to the defense of the Republic against monarchists and foreign invaders. Apart from a single, nonspecific reference to "exploiters and oppressors who treat their equals as property," the statement of purpose enacted by the Federation appealed to the collective identity of "the people" as understood in traditional, all-inclusive republican terms. A popular militia that in principle included all adult men, the National Guard was formally and practically an organization of the Parisian citizenry, not of any particular socioeconomic stratum.[3] The collectivity represented by the Federation even crossed gender lines. Women, though excluded from active military service, were formally affiliated to their local Guard battalions as ambulance workers, *cantinières,* or uniform stitchers and as recipients of food rations and monetary subsidies accorded by battalion-level "family councils."

The National Guard Federation thus created an organizational framework for a collective self-understanding among militants that was based on neighborhoods, yet citywide in scope. The fundamental unit of participation in the Federation was the neighborhood, because battalions were recruited by residence and elected their own delegates to the Central Committee; but *arrondissement*-level concerns were linked by the regular meetings of the delegates, instituting a routine pattern of interaction across residential areas. These meetings constituted the first opportunity for large numbers of politically active Parisians to witness firsthand the comparability of their various district-level challenges to state authority. In short, the Federation lent plausibility to a collective identity on the city level, whereas the minimally inclusive identity for the clubs had been the neighborhood.

At the same time, the political context and extant organizational forms were relatively inhospitable to interpretations of the current conflict in terms of class boundaries. The distribution-oriented class rhetoric that had tinged club debate at the peak of the food and fuel shortages was already fading, as the lifting of the blockade allowed provisions to pour into Paris. Moreover, the expansion of the Guard's rank and file to include the wage-earning population could not play the key role it had played as a class-based framing device in 1848: the opening

3. Because of the varying class composition of neighborhood populations, of course, Guard battalions varied as well. Indeed, scholars of the period occasionally refer to battalions of the center as "bourgeois" battalions and those of the periphery as "popular" or "working-class" battalions. This use of shorthand obscures the fact—established by battalion registers in the Archives Historiques de l'Armée—that all Guard units mobilized employers and professionals alongside workers and white-collar employees, though in varying proportions.

of enlistment rolls had occurred months earlier, at the beginning of the siege, and in any case had not coincided with an extension of the suffrage because Bonaparte's plebiscitary Empire had preserved the electorate as it had been defined in 1848. Unlike the political crisis of 1848, then, that of February–March 1871 developed in the absence of any mobilization framed either conceptually or organizationally in class terms.

On March 3, a third assembly adopted the Federation statutes, and in a matter of weeks the Central Committee of the National Guard, composed of representatives from each *arrondissement*, acquired a popularity—one could even say legitimacy, though the committee did not arrogate to itself any functions other than the internal administration of the National Guard—that the Government of National Defense had not enjoyed except for a few optimistic days following September 4. Nonetheless, the National Guard Federation was not created as a revolutionary organization, even if a number of revolutionaries did manage to make their way into its Central Committee. It would take an overt act of aggression on the part of the government to turn this situation of dual power into an insurrection.

The National Assembly elected on February 8 was decidedly conservative in character and lost little time in demonstrating its loyalty to its predominantly rural and largely monarchist constituency—at the expense of more republican urban centers and above all of Paris. As an opening shot, the Assembly convened provisionally in Bordeaux, outside the area of Prussian occupation but also, not incidentally, far from the influence of angry crowds in the capital. (This "decapitalization" became explicit when the Assembly voted to meet permanently in Versailles.) Next, they chose Adolphe Thiers, who had been elected deputy in twenty-six departments, to head the government as *chef du pouvoir executif* ("chief of the executive power"). While Thiers had impeccable credentials as a member of the liberal opposition to the Empire and as a firm advocate of a parliamentary system, he was also no radical republican and had little fondness for the unruly masses in Paris. Most importantly, he was a leading proponent of peace negotiations, and his first duty as Chief of the Executive was to draft a treaty with Bismarck at Versailles. This task was discharged with considerable speed but at enormous cost to the nation: on February 28, Thiers announced the preliminary terms of the treaty, including the cession of the critical industrial departments of Alsace and Lorraine, a crushing indemnity of 5 billion francs, and the occupation of the capital by the Prussian army. On March 1, Prussian troops paraded down the Champs Élysées, but their occupation lasted only two days and was—wisely—restricted to the western half of the city.

These largely symbolic indignities inflicted on Paris were accompanied by measures of a more concrete sort that demonstrated, if not the antagonism, at least the insensitivity of the conservative "rural majority" toward the Parisian populace. On February 15, the government announced that the daily allocation of 1 franc 50 centimes to National Guardsmen would only be distributed to those who could prove need. At the same time, the state-owned pawnshop, or Mont-de-Piété, was reopened, which meant that Parisians were liable to lose the possessions they had pawned during the siege if they did not have the means to buy them back. Finally, the Assembly refused to extend a moratorium on rents that had gone unpaid during the military conflict and repealed another moratorium on overdue commercial bills. In each case, the burden of the Assembly's measures fell most heavily on the poorest sections of Parisian society: workers who had pawned their tools, impecunious apartment-dwellers, and small-scale artisan shopkeepers with debts to wholesale merchants.

Cognizant of the unrest created in Paris by these efforts at "normalization," the Assembly pressed Thiers to impose order in the capital. His principal obstacles in this regard were the four hundred cannon that belonged to the Paris National Guard and which the Parisians had refused to surrender after the armistice. To avert a bloody confrontation, Thiers and Vinoy, the commanding general of the army of Paris, planned a surprise seizure of the National Guard's artillery, to be followed immediately by a police roundup of the city's radicals and revolutionaries. Before dawn on March 18, two army divisions succeeded in gaining control of the two major artillery parks in the northeastern districts of Montmartre and Belleville. But a delay in the arrival of horses to haul away the cannon gave the local battalion committees time to sound the alarm, and the streets began to fill with National Guardsmen, women, and children. Surrounded by crowds in the narrow streets, the soldiers refused to fire their weapons and in some cases assisted the National Guard in taking their officers prisoner. In Montmartre, two generals were shot down in cold blood as their National Guard captors were debating what to do with them. These two deaths, along with the killing of a National Guard sentinel who had tried to sound the alarm at the army's approach, were the only casualties of the day; but the assassinations were the first of a series of popular reprisals against authority figures that Thiers and others used to justify the repression later on.

Nothing demonstrates more clearly the unplanned nature of the insurrection of March 18 than the slowness with which Paris's radical leaders became aware that they were in the midst of a revolutionary situation.[4] It was not until mid-morning that members of the National Guard Central Committee began to gather to formulate a plan of action, and it was not until the afternoon that they made any attempt to coordinate the movements of Guard battalions. By this time, Thiers had already decided to call off the operation and retreat to Versailles. In the evening, a number of Guard officers acting in the name of the Central Committee, among them the Blanquist Émile Duval and the Internationalist Jean Louis Pindy, took possession of various public buildings; finally, at midnight, the committee reconvened in the Hôtel de Ville, implicitly affirming that it was the only formally constituted body that could plausibly claim authority over Paris. Against the urging of the more military-minded of its members, who argued that Paris should immediately follow up with an attack on Versailles, the committee declined to launch a counterattack on the retreating army.

Over the next two days, the committee tried to remain within the bounds of legality as it negotiated with the Assembly through the mediation of the elected mayors of Paris's twenty *arrondissements*.[5] But these attempts at conciliation fell through when the Central Committee decided not to give up possession of the Hôtel de Ville, and the Assembly in turn refused to approve municipal elections. The committee announced that elections for a municipal council—the incarnation, for many, of the Commune—would be held in any case on March 26. The rhetoric of the announcement, and the fact that the elections were explicitly municipal, made it clear that the council was not conceived as a national government; nonetheless, the committee, and the city of Paris with it, had unequivocally broken with legality and embraced revolution. Paris was not simply going to elect a new municipal government under the auspices of the French Republic; it was now, in effect, to constitute a republic in itself.

The Commune of Paris was proclaimed on March 28 in the same atmosphere of optimism that had pervaded the capital when the Empire fell on September 4. Indeed, this optimism was not entirely unwarranted: the Central Committee had

4. This fact is especially surprising given that some militants had been acutely aware of the potential for a major political upheaval from January onward. See, for instance, the weekly deliberations of the International reproduced in *Les séances officielles de l'Internationale à Paris pendant le siège et pendant la Commune* (Paris: E. Lachaud, 1872).

5. Louis Napoleon had stripped Paris of its elected municipal council in 1851; the city government consisted of one central mayor and a mayor for each *arrondissement*, all appointed by the state. In March 1871, however, the *arrondissement* mayors held their posts by virtue of the municipal elections of the previous November.

extracted assurances of neutrality from the Prussians (in a sudden, though pragmatic, reversal of the belligerent stance that had initially triggered the conflict between Paris and the French government), and the authorities at Versailles had not yet made any active moves toward retaliation. Recognizing that one of its principal and most pressing responsibilities was the normal functioning of a city of nearly 2 million people, the Communal Council focused its attention first on ensuring that civil administration continued to operate. At the same time, it wiped out with one stroke all overdue rents from October 1870 and January and April 1871, declaring that "it is just that property should share in our sacrifices."[6] Overdue commercial bills were to be repaid over a three-year period.

On the other hand, the Commune was not to remain simply a city government: several of its visionaries, primarily the Proudhonist members of the International who had been active in clubs and workers' associations during the siege, pushed for the reorganization of society along socialist or at least social democratic lines. On April 2, the council voted the separation of church and state, and abolished the official budget for religion. The newly established Commission on Education embarked on a program of universal secular instruction, while the Commission of Labor and Exchange, headed by the Internationalists Benoît Malon and Leo Frankel, worked to define the role of the Commune in reshaping the organization of work. Following the Commune's April 16 decree authorizing the expropriation of abandoned workshops for the establishment of producers' cooperatives, the Labor and Exchange Commission appealed publicly to workers' associations for help in putting this scheme into practice. Two meetings of delegates from a variety of trade organizations took place in May, but these tentative steps were all that ever came of the Commune's project for social reform. Only one establishment, a foundry in the metalworking district of Grenelle, was actually put back into operation and run by workers; the final assault on Paris and the Commune on May 21 doomed any further attempts at the emancipation of labor.

In fact, the military situation had begun to encroach on the Commune's civil and political activities with the outbreak of overt hostilities on April 2—less than a week after the inauguration of the Communal Council. The French army, under reorganization since March 18 and reinforced (with Bismarck's permission) by fresh recruits from the provinces, launched an attack on National Guard posts to the northwest of the city; in response, the Commune ordered a massive

6. Quoted in Jacques Rougerie, *La Commune, 1871* (Paris: Presses Universitaires de France, 1988), p. 67.

sortie in the direction of Versailles, of the kind that many had clamored for unsuccessfully on March 18 and 19. But this attack on the army of Versailles fared no better than had the sortie against the Prussians: the mobile battalions of the National Guard, still untrained and lacking an able officer corps, fell apart as soon as.they encountered artillery fire from the enemy. This time, the Parisian forces retreated without waiting for anyone to give the order, leaving behind dozens of dead along with any hope of mounting a successful military offensive against the government. Hopes for a peaceful solution also vanished when Parisians learned that the army had executed several insurgents taken prisoner during the battle, including the Blanquist Battalion Commander Émile Duval and the popular revolutionary adventurer Gustave Flourens. In retaliation, the Commune passed its notorious "hostage decree," according to which anyone suspected of complicity with Versailles would be imprisoned; for every prisoner the Versailles government killed, the Commune would execute three hostages. Over the next few weeks, several dozen people, many of them clerics and public officials, were imprisoned by the Commune's Ex-Prefecture of Police[7]; but even though the army continued to shoot prisoners throughout April and May, none of the hostages was harmed until the hysteria of the final week.

Despite the initial resolve of the Commune's leaders and the intensity of Parisians' anger toward Thiers and the French government, the insurgent forces never succeeded in organizing an effective defense of the city. Over the next month, the fortresses protecting Paris fell one by one to the army of Versailles. On May 1, the Jacobin majority on the Communal Council succeeded, over the protests of the largely socialist minority, in creating a Committee of Public Safety—another allusion to the French Revolution, in this case to the Terror in particular—which would oversee the military effort while ensuring order inside the city. But this effort to create a strong executive with emergency powers only alienated the moderates and socialists on the council, and had no discernible effect on the ability of the Commune's third War Delegate—Charles Delescluze, a veteran of the Revolution of 1848 and one of the five members of the Committee of Public Safety—to organize the National Guard. On the morning of May 21, a remobilized, rearmed, and above all retrained army of over 100,000 men entered Paris at its western edge, two gates of which had been left unguarded. By that evening, and

7. This was the somewhat frivolous name used by the Commune to suggest that its police, while still operating as an instrument for maintaining order, was nevertheless somehow a negation of what the police were under an authoritarian regime.

Plate 4 Communards relaxing in the courtyard of the Ministry of Justice. (Source: Bibliothèque Historique de la Ville de Paris.)

Plate 5 Communards at the docks of La Villette, nineteenth *arrondissement.* (Source: Bibliothèque Historique de la Ville de Paris.)

Plate 6 Insurgents at a barricade in the rue de Castiglione, first *arrondissement.*
(Source: Bibliothèque Historique de la Ville de Paris.)

Plate 7 Insurgents at a National Guard post near the Seine. Note *cantinière* at center.
(Source: Bibliothèque Historique de la Ville de Paris.)

without having encountered any resistance, the army had taken possession of the entire sixteenth *arrondissement* and a large section of the adjacent fifteenth. It was not until the following morning that the general alarm was sounded.

Even at this point, however, the resistance could hardly be described as determined. Hundreds of barricades went up throughout Paris, but most were defended by only a few dozen National Guardsmen; in any case, the army avoided frontal attacks and instead attempted to take each barricade from the side or rear, or by sending troops up to the rooftops of neighboring houses.[8] For the most part, when the insurgents fought, they fought in retreat.

This did not deter the army from executing prisoners in a continuation of the practice initiated on April 2. Executions of insurgents captured inside the city began on May 22 and continued for hours after the fighting had ended on the 28th. For its part, the Commune made good on its threat to shoot hostages, beginning with the May 24 execution of six prisoners, including the Archbishop of Paris, on the orders of the Blanquist Raoul Rigault. In all, about one hundred hostages (many of them priests or bishops) were executed during the *semaine sanglante*, on official orders or at the instigation of angry crowds.

Beginning on May 23, resistance also took the form of the destruction of public buildings—a crime which, to judge from the reactionary histories that appeared immediately afterward, the party of order viewed as more heinous than the taking of lives.[9] Primarily to cover their retreat but also as a final, desperate gesture of defiance, insurgents set fire to dozens of buildings along the major streets in the center of Paris, including the Tuileries (where Louis Napoleon had lived), the Hôtel de Ville, the Prefecture of Police, and the Palais de Justice. Not all of the damage was the work of the Commune, however: many of the fires were caused by the army's artillery shells.

By the evening of May 24, the Versailles army had occupied the entire western half of the city. Progress had been slow, not because of any particular difficulty but because the experience of March 18 had made Thiers and his generals

8. Robert C. Tombs, *The War against Paris* (Cambridge: Cambridge University Press, 1981), pp. 152–62.

9. Indeed, the theme of "Paris in ruins" or "Paris in flames" occurs far more often than references to death or killing in the titles of the dozens of pamphlets and short histories that appeared between 1871 and 1873. One reason for this tendency was simply that, aside from the March 18 assassinations of Clément Thomas and Lecomte and the hostage massacre of the rue Haxo, insurgents were responsible for comparatively little bloodshed. In part, though, it reflects the fact that conservatives regarded what they perceived as the Commune's attack on the institution of private property as far more subversive than mere violence against people.

reluctant to take risks. Now, however, the army had reached areas where the insurrection was strongest; and while the piles of paving stones, metal grilles, sacks of dirt, and various sorts of debris that barricaded the narrow streets never posed a serious military challenge to the army, they nevertheless formed the focus of intense battles, most notably at the place de la Bastille and in Belleville on the right bank of the Seine, and at the place d'Italie on the left. In the fifth and thirteenth *arrondissements* on the left bank, the eleventh, nineteenth, and twentieth on the right, insurgents now fought in groups of two or three hundred, led in many cases by members of the Communal Council who had refused to take flight.

In the end, the National Guard was no match for the army of Versailles, either in numbers or in expertise. The insurgents were pushed steadily north and east, and the last pockets of resistance were overcome on May 28, in and around the Père Lachaise cemetery in the twentieth *arrondissement.* In all, the army suffered fewer than a thousand fatalities; reports on the number of insurgents killed are largely conjectural, as always in such events, but no modern historian puts the figure below twenty thousand. Most of these deaths are attributable not to the fighting itself but to the army's summary executions.

The government also detained nearly 40,000 prisoners, about one-third of them arrested after the fighting had ended. Of these, approximately 23,000 were released after spending up to a year in makeshift prisons awaiting interrogation. Those whom the investigating officers deemed suspicious after a preliminary investigation were tried by twenty-six *conseils de guerre,* or military courts—the four that had already existed as well as twenty-two new ones, hastily formed to deal with the overwhelming and unprecedented task of prosecuting 13,000 suspected insurgents. After three years, the war councils had handed down ninety-three death sentences, of which twenty-three had been carried out; 2,500 prisoners had been acquitted; 4,500 had been deported to France's penal colonies in New Caledonia; and the remaining 6,000 were serving prison or hard labor sentences ranging from a few months to twenty years. To ensure that no one had escaped notice, the military courts also condemned 3,000 insurgents in absentia—in many cases passing judgment on Parisians whose fates had already been decided on the barricades.

Class or Community?

Three aspects of the 1871 insurrection—two of which I have already touched upon—have served as justifications for its inclusion in, and interpretation in terms of, the class-formation narrative. The most straightforward and presumably prima facie evidence is the sheer predominance of manual laborers in the insurgent rank and file, insofar as this can be discerned from the pattern of arrests. Using aggregate statistics from the official army report on the repressive effort, Jacques Rougerie has estimated that 75 percent of those arrested were wage-earners (including domestic servants); individual-level data from my own archival sample of twenty-two hundred arraignees yield a figure of 78.1 percent.[10]

There was, too, a surprising—though by no means overwhelming—number of workers among the formal leaders of the revolutionary government, the elected members of the Communal Council. Of eighty-five sitting members after the March 26 elections, roughly thirty-five were wage-earners, many of them unknown prior to the events of 1871.[11] And despite the colorful red sashes they wore in the inaugural procession of March 28, these revolutionaries self-consciously declined to raise themselves above the masses whose mandate they carried: rumors in the reactionary press of wild orgies at the Hôtel de Ville notwithstanding, members of the Commune were, overall, an unassuming (if somewhat ineffectual) group. Although Marx overstated the case in claiming that the elected members earned "workmen's wages," he was not far off: the council voted to pay its members fifteen francs a day, compared with the five or six the typical handicraft worker could expect. This gesture, combined with the pro-labor and pro-tenant measures mentioned earlier, made it clear that the Commune regarded the working class as one of its major constituencies.

Third, there are the dozens of revolutionary socialist posters and pamphlets drafted by militants in the months leading up to the March 18 uprising and in the days following. I have already quoted some of the class-war rhetoric that surfaced during the siege; but the most famous document of this sort from the period is without question the article entitled "The Revolution of 18 March" that appeared in the daily journal of the government (now the journal of the Commune) on March 21, signed only "a delegate to the *Journal officiel*":

> The proletarians of the capital, amid the failures and treasons of the
> governing classes, have grasped that the hour has arrived for them

10. Rougerie, *Paris libre, 1871*, p. 259; for a description of my procedures in constructing the arraignee sample, see the methodological appendix (appendix B). The official report appears in Félix Antoine Appert, *Rapport d'ensemble de M. le Général Appert sur les opérations de la justice militaire relatives à l'insurrection du 18 mars* (Paris: Imprimerie Nationale, 1875).

11. It is impossible to be more precise because some members with handicraft occupations (tailor, shoemaker, etc.) could have been either journeymen or employers.

to save the situation by taking into their own hands the administration of public affairs. They have employed the power that the people have entrusted to them with a degree of moderation and wisdom that one cannot praise too highly.

... The laborers, those who produce everything and receive nothing, those who suffer while surrounded by a mass of accumulated riches, products of their labor and sweat—must they be forever the victims of outrage? Will they never be permitted to work for their own emancipation without becoming the target of a concert of maledictions? The bourgeoisie, their elders, having achieved their own emancipation more than three-quarters of a century ago, having preceded them on the path of revolution—do they not recognize that the time for the emancipation of the proletariat has arrived?

... May the few drops of blood that have been spilled, regrettably, fall upon the heads of the instigators of civil war and the enemies of the people who, for half a century, have been the authors of all our internecine battles and all our national catastrophes. The march of progress, interrupted for an instant, shall begin anew, and the proletariat, despite all, shall achieve its emancipation![12]

There is no evidence that this article was the product of a collective effort of the National Guard Central Committee or any other group; most historians have concluded that it was the work of a single revolutionary, either Edouard Moreau, a militant member of the Central Committee, or Charles Longuet, a Proudhonist who was to marry Jenny Marx a year later. Nonetheless, the document has been celebrated for its unabashed portrayal of the events of 1870–71 as part of the world-historical struggle of the proletariat to emancipate itself from the bourgeoisie and from capitalist production relations. Marx quoted it (erroneously attributing it to the Central Committee) in *The Civil War in France,* and Prosper-Olivier Lissagaray, the Commune's first sympathetic historian, called it "the first socialist note of the revolution," the moment at which "the movement, purely one of republican defense at the beginning, took on a social coloring under the laborer's guidance."[13]

The embarrassing fact, however, is that it is precisely the singularity of the piece that has made "The Revolution of 18 March" a beacon for scholars charting their course with reference to the idea of class formation. In contrast to the thou-

12. *Journal officiel de la Commune de Paris,* March 21, 1871.
13. Marx, *The Civil War in France,* p. 54; Prosper-Olivier Lissagaray, *Histoire de la Commune, 1871* (Paris: Maspero, [1876] 1969), p. 135.

sands of pamphlets, posters, and club announcements proclaiming or calling for the "emancipation of labor" in 1848, this article was one of only a handful to use the phrase in 1871.[14] Far more numerous were demands for municipal liberties and the safeguarding of the Republic. The Central Committee of the National Guard Federation, in its own carefully drafted announcement of elections to the Commune, made it abundantly clear that the constituency on whose behalf it saw itself as acting—the constituency, in other words, of the revolution itself—was the entire city of Paris, irrespective of class position:

> Citizens—
>
> You are called upon to elect your communal assembly (the municipal council of the city of Paris).
>
> For the first time since September 4, the Republic has been freed from a government composed of its enemies.
>
> In accordance with republican law, you have convoked yourselves, in the form of the Committee, to give the men of this council, whom you yourselves shall elect, a mandate that you yourselves shall define.
>
> Your sovereignty is hereby returned to you in its entirety, and belongs to you completely: profit from this precious, perhaps unique moment to seize the communal liberties—enjoyed by the humblest villages—of which you have been deprived for so long. In giving to your city a strong communal organization, you lay the cornerstone of your rights, the indestructible base of your republican institutions. The freedom of the city [*droit de cité*] is as imperishable as that of the nation; the city must, like the nation, have its own assembly, whether it is called municipal assembly, communal assembly, or commune . . .

14. This general characterization of the Parisian press is based on a perusal of the collected newspapers of the period March 18–May 28, 1871. (The newspapers consulted include—in addition to the *Journal officiel*—*Le cri du peuple, La patrie en danger, Le vengeur, Le rappel, Le combat,* and even *Le prolétaire.*) Most striking of all is the near-total absence of class-emancipation language in the public announcements of workers' association meetings: of the sixty or so announcements that I found in Paris newspapers during the Commune, only one mentions the "emancipation of labor." The item in question was a call for the organization of a tailors' cooperative. As chap. 4 indicated, the tailors were among the most active groups in the Parisian labor movement, and a number of the resistance society's key figures were affiliated with the International. The tailors were also, however, one of the occupational groups with the lowest participation rates in the 1871 insurgent effort (see table 6.1).

Citizens,

Paris has no desire to rule, but it wants to be free; it has no aspirations to any dictatorship but that of example; it pretends neither to impose nor to abdicate its will; it no more wishes to issue decrees than to undergo more plebiscites; it demonstrates the direction of the movement by marching forward, preparing the liberty of others by founding its own. It forces no one down the path of the Republic; it is content to be the first to take that path.[15]

The Central Committee left no doubt about the identity of the collective actor whose defiance had, in its view, made possible the insurrection of March 18: it was the entire population of Paris, or, more vividly, the city itself. In their effort to consolidate the revolution, in other words, the members of the committee had settled on a version of recent events—events in which they had been key actors—that differed sharply from the class-struggle account offered by "the delegate of the *Journal officiel*" and since distilled into the class-formation narrative.

Perhaps the last word—literally—on the participation identity most relevant to the insurgent effort came from the final call to arms published by Charles Delescluze, the War Delegate, on the day of the army's invasion of the city. While undoubtedly colored by Delescluze's own Jacobin political sympathies, the appeal was also presumably meant to present a version of the insurrection in the terms most plausible to its readers. Its purpose, after all, was to galvanize the Commune's forces for a massive defense against the Versailles army:

TO THE PEOPLE OF PARIS, TO THE NATIONAL GUARD.

Enough militarism, no more staff officers with gold-braided uniforms! Make way for the people, for fighters with their arms bared! The hour for revolutionary war has struck. The people know nothing of shrewd maneuvers, but when they have a rifle in hand, paving stones beneath their feet, they are unafraid of all the strategists of the monarchist school.

To arms, citizens, to arms! It is a matter, as you know, of winning or of falling into the pitiless hands of the reactionaries and the clerics of Versailles, of that miserable lot who, in their treachery, delivered France to the Prussians and who make us pay the ransom of their betrayals!

If you desire that the generous blood that has flowed like water

15. Poster of March 22, reprinted in *Journal officiel*, March 25, 1871.

for the past six weeks not be infertile, if you want to live free in a free and egalitarian France, if you wish to spare your children your sufferings and your misery, you will rise as one, and before your formidable resistance the enemy, who flatters himself that he shall once again have you in his yoke, will have nothing but the shame of the senseless crimes with which he has soiled himself for the past two months.

Citizens, your representatives will fight and die beside you, if necessary. But in the name of glorious France, mother of all popular revolutions, permanent home of the ideas of justice and solidarity that must and shall be the law of the globe, march upon the enemy, and let your revolutionary energy show him that one may sell Paris, but one can neither hand it over nor conquer it! The Commune counts on you, count on the Commune![16]

I have quoted the appeal in its entirety to show that there is no mention whatever of class divisions, of economic struggles apart from the general reference to "suffering," or of the question of work. "The enemy" was unambiguously the state and its attendant symbols of authority, the church and the uniformed forces of oppression; the protagonist, equally clearly, was "the people of Paris," without further social distinctions. Just as striking as the absence of class language, then, was the focus on the boundary of the city: even an inveterate republican like Delescluze took care to use "the people" in its local sense, not in the abstract universal sense of the French Revolution (though this broader collectivity might be the beneficiary of Parisians' actions) or in the working-class sense of 1848.

Never had a collective identity embracing all the inhabitants of the city (and only them) been proposed for or by the protagonists of France's earlier insurrections. The Prussian siege, the armistice of January, and the attempted seizure of National Guard artillery in March had made this innovation plausible by creating the historically unique circumstance of a national government deploying armed force in its capital city essentially on behalf of a foreign enemy.[17] The important

16. *Journal officiel,* May 22, 1871.

17. Even the Revolutionary Paris Commune of 1792–94, the radical democratic body that gave the 1871 movement its name, was rarely construed as a symbol of the city of Paris. Its constituency was either the nearly all-encompassing "people," meaning the French nation, or, just as often, the forty-eight Sections of Paris. The Section (the equivalent of *quartier*) was, for the most part, the minimally inclusive identity in terms of which the *sans-culottes* framed their political activity. See Albert Soboul, *Les sans-culottes parisiens en l'an II: Mouvement populaire et gouvernement révolutionnaire* (Paris: Clavreuil, 1958), especially part 2.

question, however, is whether the conceptual innovation (at least in nineteenth-century terms) of a "communal" identity corresponded to anything genuinely different about the way the uprising of 1871 unfolded. Answering this question requires an investigation that looks past the rhetorical flourishes of the moment to the concrete, collective actions these flourishes were intended to influence.

❧ Patterns of Mass Mobilization ❧

If the Paris Commune is to be seen as a significant moment in the formation of the French working class, then it is reasonable to expect certain broad similarities between the mobilization of insurgency in 1871 and the mobilization of industrial protest in the preceding years. The existence of such similarities has, in fact, been routinely asserted—or at least assumed—by researchers who view the Commune primarily as an episode of the French labor movement. Superficially, at least, such assertions are quite reasonable, in light of the intensification of labor militancy in France's industrial cities during the late 1860s and in light of the prominent role played by socialist activists in the meeting movement of 1868–70. As I have already demonstrated, however, class struggle was not the only thing on the minds of meeting participants at the end of the Empire, and it was far from the only thing preoccupying Parisians early in 1871.

One empirical implication that follows from the class-struggle account of the Commune is that rates of insurgent participation should have paralleled the extent of militant labor protest in Parisian craft groups. Workers with firsthand experience of industrial conflict organized through "resistance societies" would have been more inclined to join in the insurgent effort because of their familiarity with, and attachment to, the goal of emancipating the working class. According to this reasoning, the fact that successful labor protest in France relied on craft solidarity ought not to have stood in the way of insurgent participation, inasmuch as socialist militants in Paris and elsewhere had already spelled out a "federative" vision of postcapitalist society (see chap. 4) and had expended considerable energy on attempts to foster cooperation across occupational groups.[18] It follows that, if the class-formation account is right, organized, solidary crafts should have been substantially overrepresented in the insurgent rank and file.

18. Recall, too, that in 1869 the Paris chapter of the International had renewed its effort to establish a cross-trade socialist organization in the form of the Chambre Fédérale des Sociétés Ouvrières. For socialist militants in Paris, the federative vision was clearly the dominant organizing principle guiding the labor movement.

An examination of the occupations of Parisians arraigned by the military courts for participation in the insurrection casts serious doubt on the notion that insurgency should be seen as an extension of labor protest.[19] Recall from chapter 4 that the occupational groups with the most successful record of industrial militancy under the Empire were those with tightly clustered craft communities, such as tanners, cabinetmakers, tailors, bronze workers, and foundry workers. Through their clandestine organizations and newspapers, workers in these trades were—even more than the middle-class revolutionaries who made their names with dramatic speeches in public meetings—the builders of the cooperative socialist labor movement. Yet table 6.1 and figure 6.1 demonstrate that these craft groups, and others with similarly high levels of residential concentration, systematically exhibited low rates of participation in the Commune, either as rank-and-file insurgents or as officers in the National Guard. The trades that stand out as having contributed disproportionately large numbers of soldiers to the insurgent effort are those whose practitioners were widely dispersed throughout the city, and whose attempts at organizing strikes and resistance societies in the 1860s had consistently produced disappointing results: machine builders, stonemasons, painters, roofers, shoemakers.[20]

Still, even though solidary and organized crafts contributed relatively few insurgents, skilled and semiskilled craft workers overall formed the backbone of the insurgent effort (see table 6.2): artisanal wage-earners were the only group whose numerical preponderance in the arraignee population was greater than in the Parisian population as a whole. If one ignores for the moment that more than one-fifth of the arraignees were nonetheless middle-class and white-collar workers, and that unskilled workers were *not* overrepresented, the prominent role of handicraft workers could be used to justify the claim that the main participation identity on the basis of which Parisians were drawn into the fighting was that of class, just as it had been in 1848. Higher rates of participation among less solidary craft groups might be seen as reflecting the long-awaited dissolution of craft

19. See appendix B for a detailed discussion of the problems accompanying the use of the arraignee population as a sample of the insurgent population. I have presented multivariate analyses of these participation data in "Trade Cohesion, Class Unity, and Urban Insurrection: Artisanal Activism in the Paris Commune."

20. Barbers also appear to have participated at a very high rate, but the relatively small number of workers practicing this trade meant that they did not have a significant presence in the insurgent ranks.

Table 6.1 Participation Rate and Residential Concentration, by Trade

Occupational Category	Population (thousands)	Arraignment Rate[a]	Concentration[b]
Bakers, pastry workers	7.20	2.01	0.305
Butchers	4.80	1.59	0.300
Distillers, other food	2.24	2.03	0.344
Painters, plasterers	9.10	5.51	0.299
Masons, roofers	25.64	5.96	0.288
Joiners, carpenters	17.10	4.67	0.304
Other construction	17.50	5.99	0.286
Furniture workers	33.10	2.41	0.417
Tailors	14.00	2.28	0.413
Shoemakers	18.00	4.31	0.294
Other clothing, textile	14.40	4.38	0.331
Machine builders	13.70	4.44	0.307
Foundry workers	3.10	2.94	0.497
Forgers, other metal	22.10	4.13	0.365
Jewelers	15.00	3.34	0.536
Instrument makers	7.10	3.10	0.361
Ceramics, chemical	10.50	2.39	0.360
Printers, bookbinders	16.00	3.71	0.347
Luxury goods workers	7.30	1.77	0.597
Barbers	2.10	5.07	0.307
Carriage makers	7.80	3.61	0.322
Wood workers	8.00	5.03	0.401
Tanners, other leather	6.20	3.31	0.391
Service workers	13.40	3.46	0.351

[a]Total arraignees in trade i per 100 practitioners of trade i.

[b]For each trade, this measure is calculated as $\sum p_i \cdot \sum c_{ij} p_j$, where p_i is the proportion of the trade in district i, p_j is the proportion in district j, and $c_{ij} = 1$ if districts i and j are adjacent and $c_{ij} = 0$ otherwise.

boundaries posited in the class-formation narrative (though not necessary for the federative socialist program).[21]

21. This is, in fact, the claim made by Jacques Rougerie in "Composition d'une population insurgée: L'exemple de la Commune," *Le mouvement social*, no. 45 (July–September 1964), pp. 31–47. Pointing to the large numbers of metal and construction workers noted in the Appert report, Rougerie argues that these "new" trades were producing the first true proletarians in France's revolutionary history. It is true that the machine-building industry had been transformed by engineering innovations in the middle of the nineteenth century; but it is not clear what made construction trades new, other than their enormous growth under Haussmann.

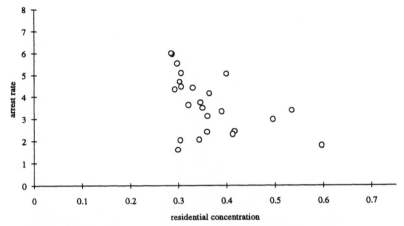

Figure 6.1 Occupational arrest rates (per 100) by residential concentration.

Table 6.2 Occupational Distribution of Paris Population and 1871 Arraignees

	Paris Population[a]	%	Arraignees[b]	%
Bourgeois/professionals	254,361	27.3	251	10.5
White-collar employees	144,007	15.4	272	11.4
Artisanal workers	396,131	42.5	1,521	63.6
Unskilled workers	137,948	14.8	347	14.5
TOTAL	932,447	100.0	2,391	100.0

[a]Population figures refer to males only (see text).
[b]Figures correspond to total number from each category in the arraignee sample, weighted to account for underrepresentation of acquittals (see appendix B).

Given the decidedly secondary role class struggle played in public discourse throughout the period of the uprising, this interpretation is already rather implausible. But the pattern of arrests by district, which invites a direct comparison with the data for the insurrection of June 1848 presented in chapter 2, is even more convincing on this point. In that earlier uprising, I demonstrated, the geographical distribution of arrests was almost completely accounted for by the class composition of districts (see chap. 2, figs. 2.2 and 2.3). In other words, the only pieces of information needed to predict the total number of arrests in an *arrondissement* were the absolute number of working-class inhabitants and their relative predominance in the district's population. It would be difficult to find more persuasive evidence of the importance of class identity for the mobilization process.

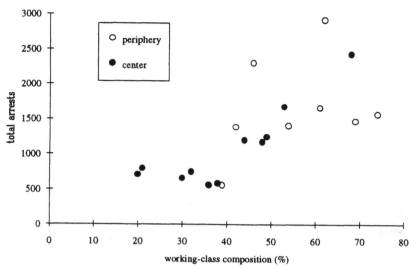

Figure 6.2 Total arrests by working-class composition of districts, May–June 1871 (peripheral and central districts shown separately).

Figure 6.2 reveals that the arrest pattern for May 1871, while still associated with the class composition of districts, was far less so than in the June Days. The amount of scatter in the graph shows that, unlike 1848, much of the variation in arrests was unrelated to the proportion of each district's population classified as wage-earners in the 1872 census. Notice in particular that it was primarily in the districts of the center that arrest rates correlated with class composition ($r = .84$); looking only at outlying *arrondissements*, which appear as hollow points in the graph, one observes a rather weak relationship ($r = .32$). Even in the center, moreover, the relationship between class composition and total arrests did not exhibit the curvilinearity observed in 1848 (see the multivariate analyses reported in appendix A). Much of the observed association, therefore, probably resulted from the simple fact that workers were more in need of the daily indemnity for Guard service—not from any self-conscious belief that the working-class sections of the city were the core of the uprising, as they had been in the insurrection of June 1848.

If class was a significant factor in mobilization at all, then, it was so only in the industrial heart of Paris, not in the more residential outlying districts. On the periphery, where support for the Commune ran deepest (see fig. 6.3), it appears that the participation identity of class played little or no part in the actual mobilization of insurgency. The implication is that many Parisians—indeed, the major-

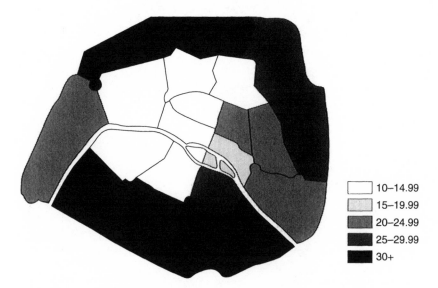

	10–14.99
	15–19.99
	20–24.99
	25–29.99
	30+

Figure 6.3 Arrest rates (per 1,000) by district, May–June 1871.

ity of those who participated in the insurrection—fought on the barricades in 1871 for reasons that had little to do with membership in the working class.[22]

In light of the lessons of the last two chapters, this result is hardly surprising. The shift in patterns of social ties during the urban renovations of 1852–70, the meeting movement and its relationship to the imperial police, and the experience of the siege had all provided the basis for a distinctive collective identity unrelated to class struggle. This identity was that of the urban community, defined and experienced explicitly as a spatially circumscribed and economically diverse collectivity in opposition to the central state authority. The preceding chapters have detailed the emergence of this opposition in the period leading up to the proclamation of the Commune and have shown why neighborhood identities meant more to Parisians dwelling on the periphery than to those in the historic city center. The question to be addressed here is how significant the community-state opposition was in the mobilization of insurgency after March 18.

22. Because there are more observations for 1871 than for 1848 (twenty districts rather than twelve), there is necessarily more variance to account for in the case of the Commune. However, the regression analyses presented in appendix A report a figure for R^2 which is adjusted for the number of cases and the degrees of freedom consumed by the estimation. The conclusion that class composition explains more of the variance in 1848 arrests than 1871 arrests is not, therefore, a mere artifact of the larger number of districts in 1871.

The answer to this question comes from firsthand reports of interactions in the streets, cafés, and clubs of Paris during the ten weeks of the Commune's existence. The sources in question are transcripts from interrogations of arrested insurgents, daily reports from spies working for the Versailles government, and reports of the Commune's own police, charged with the task of assessing the public mood in the capital. Drawn from the full range of the political spectrum, these documents furnish a striking picture of the salience of the communitarian identity—and, implicitly, the marginality of class—in the process by which Parisians were recruited to the insurgent effort.

It would be unreasonable to expect to read impassioned accounts of the revolutionary struggle in arrestee testimony; by the time they were hauled out of their makeshift prisons for interrogation, most of the thirty-six thousand suspected insurgents were far more concerned with saving their skins than with detailing their social and political views. The same story appears over and over in the trial dossiers: one after another, arrestees insisted that threats by other Guardsmen or financial desperation or both had forced them to march in the insurgent ranks.[23] (Recall that Guardsmen were paid 1 franc 50 centimes for each day they reported for duty.) Henri Delfosse, a young enameler from the twentieth *arrondissement,* testified that he "served the Commune because I could not find work" and that he "fired at the army like my comrades."[24] Louis-Eugène Foucault, a thirty-seven-year-old typesetter and National Guard captain living in the fourteenth *arrondissement,* explained his participation this way: "Having no job, and with a sizable family to support, since I have five children, I was truly forced to serve. I went to the plain of Châtillon where all of us marched like sheep. . .Most of us marched without knowing why, and I did not see the troops until the day they took possession of my street."[25] Although he was retrospectively distancing himself from his participation, Foucault nonetheless points to the essential role of example: with other members of his battalion participating, it was more difficult to justify staying home or deserting. The following excerpt of the interrogation of Louis Auguste César, an eighteen-year-old jeweler from the eleventh *arrondissement,* is even more explicit regarding the social pressure to fight:

23. One interrogating officer responded to an arrestee's story of coercion by exclaiming in frustration, "Always the same excuse! If everyone was forced to serve, who was doing the forcing?" Archives Historiques de l'Armée de Terre (AHAT), 13th *conseil de guerre,* dossier 157; interrogation of François Louis Bethemont.

24. AHAT, 14th *conseil de guerre,* dossier 504.

25. AHAT, 4th *conseil de guerre,* dossier 1208.

Q: Why did you continue to serve [in the National Guard] once the regular army had entered Paris?

A: I was forced to march if I wanted to live.

Q: ... What have you to say in your defense?

A: I marched until the very last to avoid being shot by those who wanted to fight.[26]

Similarly, Auguste Charles Mullié, a tailor, testified, "I was enrolled by force. Four armed men came to get me at my boarding-house and took me to the Caserne Napoléon to sign me up."[27]

Even if some of those claiming to have been forced to march were understating their own willingness to support the Commune, the consistency of these claims across hundreds of trial dossiers is too great not to conclude that many of the more zealous insurgents cajoled or coerced waverers into reporting for Guard duty.[28] At a minimum, it is clear that participation in the insurrection cannot be understood as the consequence of a purely individual decision process. Given the inherent risks associated with serving in the National Guard or even helping to build barricades (as many civilians did) under the artillery fire of the Versailles army, many Parisians who sympathized with the insurgent cause remained passive in the absence of further pressure to join in. For many, though, the example of their peers, often accompanied by aggressive attempts at social influence, provided this additional pressure.

There was another aspect of this process that was highly consistent across a wide range of individual stories: recruitment by example and by social influence almost invariably occurred through social relations that were based on residential proximity and explicitly construed in neighborhood terms. This was, for instance, the account given by a shoemaker from Batignolles (seventeenth *arrondissement*), Alexandre Beaumont:

Q: Why did you enlist in the Guard?

A: I had run out of money. Besides, in the building where I lived

26. AHAT, 11th *conseil de guerre*, dossier 549.

27. AHAT, 20th *conseil de guerre*, dossier 370.

28. I have not performed a systematic count, but would estimate that between one-fourth and one-third of the files contain some mention of social influence or coercion in the recruitment process. Details of this sort come not only from defendant testimony but also from that of witnesses; moreover, some of the testimony about zealous Guardsmen and local civilians prodding nonparticipants to join came from defendants who did *not* serve and thus had no reason to make up such stories.

there were a lot of *fédérés* [a common term for Guardsmen originally dating from 1790] who had threatened to make me sign up.

Q: To what battalion and company did you belong?

A: I was in the 1st company of the 91st battalion.

Q: Why did you enroll in this battalion rather than some other?

A: I signed up in my *quartier* without paying attention to which battalion it was.[29]

The fact that members of the same battalion were frequently also neighbors
proved consequential for the day-to-day mobilization of the insurgent effort, particularly because Guardsmen routinely left their posts to go home for the night
or even for a mid-day meal. When attendance flagged, those who were more willing to serve knew exactly where to find the shirkers, as the following report of a
police informant reveals:

Versailles, 10 May 1871 [report of "V.X."; no other identification]—

The aspect of Paris on 8 May, the day I left, was increasingly somber.
There is a mixture of terror and stupor—terror exists wherever hon-
est people [*honnêtes gens*, the reactionary's term for noninsurgents]
are to be found, stupor in those neighborhoods where the insurrection has taken hold.

    . . . Last Sunday in La Villette, after the general call-up had
sounded all night, the ranks of the Guard companies were still thin.
The men who had already assembled in the street shouted up at the
others, calling them cowards and do-nothings to get them to come
down.[30]

Other reports suggest that the connection between Guard battalions and neighborhoods produced a distinct sense of loyalty, at least for some:

Paris, 20 April [unsigned report to Brissand, Police Prefect]—

Reentering Paris after my tour of the surrounding areas, I saw two
wounded National Guardsmen being brought into the city on the
boulevard Courcelles. Both belonged to the 61st battalion. The
wagon stopped in front of a wine shop, and someone had just brought
them each something to drink when another Guardsman came up,
this one from the 76th battalion. The latter asked them if they knew
where his battalion was, to which they responded, "at the Pont de

29. AHAT, 19th *conseil de guerre*, dossier 371.
30. APP, BA 364/5.

Neuilly." But they saw fit to add, "Don't go if you don't want your face smashed in, citizen; it's not going well, and we heard that the men in your battalion have had enough!" Despite this wise advice, the Guardsman of the 76th went off in the direction of his comrades, saying he wished to share in their danger.[31]

This sort of solidarity worked both ways, of course: willing insurgents could be as discouraged by the lack of enthusiasm of their peers as the latter were encouraged by the efforts of the former; and the fact that members of each battalion shared their opinions about the uprising at home as well as at the barricades made their decisions doubly interdependent:

Versailles, 17 April [report of Brissand]—

The following is some information brought to me by one of my agents who has just arrived from Paris.

Yesterday morning, at the [place des] Ternes, he observed the 30th, 63rd, and 172nd battalions of the National Guard, all three of Belleville, refuse to respond to a request for volunteers for a sortie out of Paris. On the pretext that they lacked shoes, or that they were poorly armed, or that everyone should march together, they all left for home (about 600 total). Hopping on the omnibus that runs from Ternes to Belleville, my inspector overheard some of these men complain of being played for fools and of being poorly commanded. Some even claimed that if M. Thiers would "keep his promise of paying them their 30 *sous* [i.e., the 1f 50 allowance for guard service], they would be more inclined to wait for work than to go get their heads blown off."[32]

One of the Commune's police inspectors reported hearing a similar discussion take place in a Guard company returning from the Fort d'Issy, which had just been evacuated before the advancing Versailles army:

"Yesterday, there were barely 80 *fédérés* inside [the fortress] . . . We're not going back there," said two Guardsmen. "That was too close a call to try doing the impossible a second time. We won't go back, not unless everybody marches. It would be too easy, after the

31. APP, BA 364/5.
32. APP, BA 364/5.

victory, for everyone to come get his piece of cake without having helped to bake it."[33]

The insurgents of 1871 hardly needed a lesson in economics to understand the gravity of the free-rider problem they faced. But they were also keenly aware of the potential for social influence inherent in the residential recruitment system, particularly when what they were fighting for was directly tied to their understanding of what it meant to belong to an urban community. Within earshot of another of the Commune's police officers, one National Guard sergeant explained his participation to a conservative priest by exclaiming, "I can't leave; what would my comrades from the *quartier* say?"[34]

In short, by providing opportunities for interaction outside the insurgent organization, joint residence affected participation in the organization in two distinct ways. In the first place, it simplified the process of monitoring and sanctioning nonparticipation by ensuring that those who had wholeheartedly joined in the defense of the Commune knew exactly who was missing and where to find them. In the second place, it furnished a direct link between the everyday mechanism of mobilization and the conceptual framework within which this mobilization was predominantly understood—namely, the conflict between the urban community and the central state. Fellow battalion members were therefore not merely "comrades" in the sense that they belonged to the same formal unit of the insurgent organization; they also, crucially, belonged to the same social group— the neighborhood—that had constituted the basic collective identity for much of the political agitation occurring in Paris since 1868, and whose "communal liberties" had been the focus of attention since the fall of 1870. Service in the National Guard therefore came equipped with a ready-made normative appeal, reinforced by informal social relations that pre-dated the insurrection itself.

From Neighborhood to City

As I indicated earlier, one of the unique features of the 1871 insurrection was the explicit appeal not just to the *quartier* but to a collective identity that encompassed the entire city. Of course, appeals can be framed in terms of any collective identity whatever;[35] the challenge for mobilizers is to make the appeal effica-

33. Quoted in Charles Dauban, *Le fond de la société sous la Commune* (Paris: Plon, 1873), pp. 259–60.

34. Quoted in ibid., p. 104.

35. In 1848, for instance, one man from Lyon endeavored to create a republican League of Short Men, claiming that he and his ilk were systematically excluded from the heroic battles out of which

cious, to draw real people into collective action through recruitment efforts framed in terms of the identity in question. There can be little doubt that the social ties among neighbors, *understood as neighborhood ties,* made an enormous difference in the ability of local National Guard battalions to maintain a sizable, if shaky, insurgent force throughout April and May. But is there any evidence that this neighborhood-based solidarity was ever translated into a genuinely citywide collective identity, as the authors of the Commune's rhetoric clearly wished?

The conventional wisdom among historians of the Commune is that the strong identification with the *quartier* that characterized National Guard battalions ultimately proved fatal for the defense of Paris. Jacques Rougerie argues that the effect of neighborhood loyalty was "to dismantle what was left of the organized Communard troops, each one running to the defense of its *quartier* rather than forming a front." Robert Tombs explains the final defeat of the Commune in the same terms: "As [the revolutionary forces], attached to their own quarters, could not be brought together, no defensible perimeter could be formed, although there were several suitable sites."[36]

Even if it is true that neighborhood loyalties interfered with the tactical coordination of Guard battalions, however, this does not mean that the formal organization of the National Guard into a citywide insurgent force was irrelevant to the mobilization process. Prior to the uprising, as I noted earlier, the National Guard Federation had already created an organizational setting for the forging of contacts among Guard units from all over the city. The three conferences of Federation delegates had made it possible for thousands of future insurgents from diverse neighborhoods to associate with each other in the effort to work out a collective self-understanding that explicitly included all of Paris. The widespread use of the term *fédéré* during the insurrection reflected not just nostalgia for the National Guard Federation of 1792 but also a clear awareness on the part of Parisians that the conflict in which they were implicated embraced the entire city and that the fates of different neighborhoods were consequently intertwined.

The concreteness of this interdependency only increased once actual fighting had broken out between the National Guard and the army of Versailles. Throughout April and May, the Commune's Ministry of War (under the direction, first, of Gustave Cluseret, then of Louis Rossel, and finally of the veteran republican

---

history was made. To my knowledge, there is no record of a significant response to this unusual appeal to solidarity.

36. Rougerie, *Paris libre, 1871,* p. 252; Tombs, *The War against Paris,* p. 162.

Charles Delescluze) deployed Guard battalions from all over Paris to the ramparts and to the ring of fortresses surrounding the capital. National Guard records seized by the Versailles army as they swept through Paris during the Commune's final days show that at least sixty-four battalions had spent a week or more with other Guard units at the forts of Issy, Montrouge, Ivry, Bicêtre, and Vanves.[37] In view of the fact that these records pertain only to around half of the battalions, the total number of units that saw combat with battalions from other parts of the city was surely a good deal larger.

Despite the neighborhood basis of National Guard enrollment, then, the realities of active Guard service continually brought insurgents—those who reported for duty, at least—into contact with people from other areas of the city. This was true even for members of the so-called sedentary battalions (usually comprising men over the age of forty), who were not required to serve outside the city walls. These units, charged primarily with keeping order, building barricades, and guarding public buildings, were often assigned to posts outside their own neighborhoods. For instance, Louis Gaby, an excavator from the fifteenth *arrondissement,* indicated in his testimony that his Guard duty had given him a tour of the entire city:

Q: Were you in the National Guard?

A: During the siege I belonged to a company of the 81st battalion; I stayed in the battalion during the Commune because I had no money and no job. I never served outside the city; I stood guard at the Hôtel de Ville [fourth *arrondissement*], at the place Vendôme [first], bastion 75 [border of fourteenth and fifteenth], at the barracks at the Champ de Mars [seventh], at a police post in the avenue St. Charles [fifteenth], and a post at the pont de Grenelle [fifteenth]. On May 21, my company took up a position at the Hôtel de Ville; on the 22nd we were sent to the rue Richelieu [second] where we formed a column between the Théâtre Français and the fontaine Molière. We stayed there, sleeping on the sidewalk, until Thursday morning. At that point we were sent back to the place de l'Hôtel de Ville, which we left at nine o'clock as the fire broke out. I had lost my battalion; some comrades and I set off for Ménilmontant [twentieth]. I dropped my rifle somewhere as we ran. Some Guardsmen, seeing us wandering, made us follow them to a barricade. Someone gave me a *tabatière* rifle, and I stood guard until Friday evening. Then I recognized some

37. Summaries of battalion activities from March 18 to May 28 can be found in AHAT, Ly 44.

men from the 178th [another battalion from the fifteenth *arrondisse-ment*] who were passing on their way to Belleville, and followed them. I slept in the Belleville church. The next morning they posted fifty of us behind a barricade in the rue Puebla [twentieth]; we were given our allowance and some rations. That evening I escaped, and I went to sleep next to the *mairie* of the twentieth, in an alley. The next morning, around eight o'clock, I was arrested by some troops of the line.[38]

Although such peregrinations occasionally prompted complaints among Guardsmen who were especially concerned to stay near their homes,[39] they also directly exposed thousands of Parisians to events in neighborhoods outside their own. In this regard, National Guard service had an enormous impact on insurgents' experience of the uprising as a citywide phenomenon.

The most durable conduit for this sort of cross-neighborhood exposure, however, was the structure of overlapping battalion enlistments that inevitably resulted from the difficulties of administering an organization of 200,000 men. Nearly every battalion included a small contingent of men who did not live in the neighborhood from which the rest of their comrades were recruited; conversely, every neighborhood had residents who served in battalions attached to other areas of the city. (See fig. 6.4.) Whenever they reported for duty, these Guard members witnessed events outside their *quartier* to which they would otherwise have been oblivious; and their regular visits home (authorized or not) communicated this extralocal set of experiences to neighbors and family. Overlaps in National Guard recruitment patterns consequently established a stable network of social links among neighborhoods, bridging the insularity of the *quartier* that predominated in political activity during the siege.

Careful examination of death rates, size of National Guard battalions, and arrest rates demonstrates that these overlapping enlistments significantly affected the mobilization of the insurgent forces. I have presented analyses of the first two measures of mobilization in earlier work; appendix A reports comparable analyses for arrest rates, controlling for the population's class composition and the degree to which districts were residential or industrial.[40] The main conclu-

38. AHAT, 13th *conseil de guerre*, dossier 361.

39. I have given some examples of such complaints in "Multiple Networks and Mobilization in the Paris Commune," p. 719.

40. See Gould, "Multiple Networks and Mobilization in the Paris Commune," for a detailed explanation of how the analyses were performed. Battalion size is a useful measure of levels of mobilization because the number of Guardsmen reporting for duty varied significantly across neighbor-

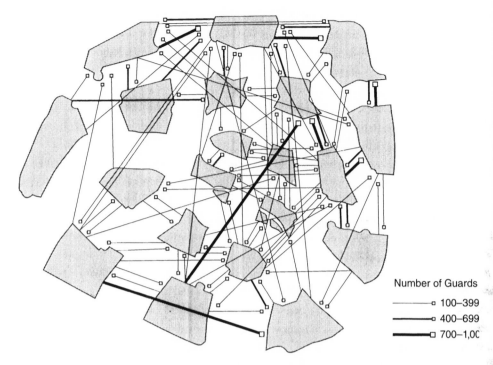

Figure 6.4 Network of cross-district National Guard enlistments (Guardsmen serving outside their area of residence), May–June 1871. Note that enlistment overlaps of fewer than 100 National Guardsmen are not shown; inclusion of such links would connect each *arrondissement* with nearly every other. Directionality is indicated by a hollow square; i.e., if 150 inhabitants of district A served in a National Guard battalion from district B, this would appear as a thin line from A ending in a square near B.

sion the data yield is that levels of resistance, measured in three completely different ways, exhibited a substantial amount of contagion across districts. Moreover, this contagion occurred through the social ties created by overlapping enlistments: each district's resistance level was substantially influenced by the resistance levels of other districts in whose Guard units its residents were enrolled. Mere spatial adjacency of neighborhoods was not associated with contagion, highlighting the importance of the organizational network.

It is important to be precise about what this finding means. Above all, it does

hoods. Likewise, both arrests and deaths during the final week occurred chiefly where the army encountered military resistance; these measures, therefore, likewise furnish useful information about which districts supported the insurgent effort most energetically.

not mean that overlapping battalion enrollments necessarily enhanced the over-all level of mobilization (though that may have been the case—it is just not pos-sible to tell from these data). Contagion in the sense intended here implies that high levels of mobilization in one area contributed to high levels elsewhere when enlistment patterns provided a conduit for communication and social interaction. Conversely, areas of low participation dampened resistance in neighborhoods that were linked closely to them. This sort of interdependence, which succinctly captures the commonsense notion of "solidarity," was thus a double-edged sword: enthusiastic participation in one area influenced the behavior of insurgents in other districts (at least when overlapping enlistments permitted), but so did apa-thy. In any instance of collective action, individuals' decisions about whether to contribute are interdependent because the perceived risks are lower if the participation of others is assured, and because normative appeals are strength-ened by example. By the same token, though, the perception of widespread reluc-tance to join can weaken resolve. Social contacts within and across neighbor-hoods could thus communicate optimistic as well as pessimistic impressions: the network of interaction created by Guard enlistments made pockets of insurgency vulnerable to areas of inactivity as well as providing channels for encouragement. The point, then, is not that overlapping National Guard enrollments ensured that there were more people fighting than would otherwise have been the case; it is that these linkages made the rates of participation in some districts relevant for the choices about participation that were being made in other districts. The orga-nizational network, in short, prompted an increase in the scale at which the "col-lective" in "collective action" was understood.

A final detail that requires attention is that the observed interdependence is not strictly reciprocal: National Guardsmen with news of activity outside their own districts made a difference for their neighbors' behavior, but their news about activity in their own districts did not alter the behavior of the Guardsmen in whose battalions they served. This finding suggests that neighborhood solidar-ity had an impact not only on the local process of recruitment and mobilization, but on the process of cross-district social influence as well. Insurgents fighting outside their own areas could change the way their neighbors saw the overall insurgent effort when they returned home, but did not influence the actions of those insurgents whom they knew only through Guard service. The National Guard enlistment network thus underlay the jump in scale from neighborhood to citywide collective action, but it did not supplant neighborhood social ties as a major element in mobilizing participation.

As far as it is possible to tell from the documentary record, the vast network of overlaps shown in figure 6.4 was not the product of any plan but simply emerged from a three-month process of shifting battalion memberships by restless Guardsmen and confused enlistment officers.[41] But by creating a network of organizational linkages that spanned all twenty *arrondissements*, this process achieved what the inspired pleas of revolutionary leaders could never accomplish alone: the coalescence of a patchwork of urban neighborhoods into a single, citywide collective actor. Just as the Luxembourg Commission and the National Workshops had made it possible for workers in disparate crafts to act collectively as a class, the National Guard enabled residents of isolated neighborhoods to act collectively as the people of Paris. In both cases, new collective identities emerged because formal organizations cut across the indigenous boundaries of interaction rather than respecting them. In both cases, too, the only reason these organizations existed in the first place was so that political elites could keep a lid on mass mobilization. Evidently they did not have their intended effect.

❧ Paris and the Provinces ☙

A sudden twist in national politics, the grinding hardship of a winter siege, and a dawn military attack jointly formed the backdrop and precondition for an urban insurrection framed as a struggle for municipal autonomy from the centralized state. As I have noted several times, the movement for municipal liberties was a national phenomenon, triggered by the abdication of the Emperor and the September 4 proclamation of the Republic. During the fall of 1870 and on into the winter, activists in a variety of French cities pressed for the same rights. Following the Paris uprising of March 18, revolutionary communes were formed in Toulouse, Narbonne, Lyon, Marseille, Le Creusot, and St. Etienne, in some cases before the formal proclamation of the Commune of Paris on the 26th.

The national scope of the communal movement naturally raises the issue of whether it is reasonable to account for the events in Paris in terms of specifically Parisian factors. If similar events occurred in a variety of urban centers, none of which had experienced transformations like those that had taken place in Paris

---

41. To cite just one instance, a young day-laborer named Charles Delaplace reported to the authorities that he had originally belonged to the 231st battalion, which was formed in his own *arrondissement*, the nineteenth. He testified, however, that "after a disagreement with our captain, who refused to distribute to us some equipment we needed and which he had at his disposal, I and fifteen others quit the 231st and joined the 208th"—a battalion recruited over a mile away, in the fifteenth *arrondissement*. AHAT, 11th *conseil de guerre*, dossier 534.

under the Empire, the changes in the capital city's residential and industrial geography would be irrelevant to an explanation of the urban character of the Commune of 1871. With such a diverse group of local settings for uprisings based on spatial collective identities, the contrast with 1848 would suggest only the significance of national political context in determining what collective identities are pertinent for mobilization. There would be no basis for the claim that either preexisting or organizational networks made a difference.

However, even a rather brief examination of the provincial Communes points to the opposite conclusion. Despite very similar beginnings, the communal movements outside Paris ended in a manner quite different from that in the capital. They thus demonstrate the importance of local factors, rather than the national situation, in determining outcomes. I shall explain why after presenting a short summary of events in the provinces.

At Le Creusot, a major industrial center that had been the site of a bloody strike in 1870, a self-appointed "republican socialist committee" staged a demonstration before the town hall on March 24, demanding communal elections to follow the example of Paris. The demonstrators were greeted warmly by the city's mayor, as well as by the National Guard, and the Commune was proclaimed. One day later, though, the prefect of the Saône-et-Loire entered the city with one thousand troops, seized the town hall, and restored order within a few hours. The National Guard, whose rank and file had enthusiastically shouted *"Vive la Commune!"* a day earlier, put up no resistance. The story at Narbonne was nearly identical, though it lasted a few days longer.[42]

Much the same can be said for St. Etienne, another French city that owed most of its nineteenth-century growth to the development of heavy industry. Following an autumn and winter in which popular clubs resounded, as in other cities, with demands for the establishment of a Commune, National Guard militants occupied the Hôtel de Ville on March 23. Here, too, a sympathetic mayor promised municipal elections and persuaded the activists to withdraw from the town hall; but they retook the building on March 25, after a demonstrator was killed in the square outside, and imprisoned the departmental prefect, whose office was also located in the Hôtel de Ville. Later that night, the prefect was shot and killed during a dispute between two groups of Guardsmen. Although the insurgents announced the formation of a Commune the next morning, the vio-

42. Edwards, *The Paris Commune, 1871*, pp. 176–77; Gaillard, *Communes de province, Commune de Paris*, pp. 64–66.

lence of the day before had already alienated a large segment of the population. Army troops arrived to reestablish order on March 27 and arrested the few dozen insurgents who still occupied the town hall. As in Le Creusot and Narbonne, then, the revolutionary version of the movement for municipal autonomy faded away at the first threat of armed confrontation.

In the department of the Haute-Garonne, Toulouse had experienced a situation of dual power beginning in October, with the establishment by radicals of a Committee of Public Safety that was intended to supplant the more moderate municipal council. In this case, militants even had the support of the department's prefect, a veteran republican named Armand Duportal, who stubbornly refused to follow the directives of the Interior Ministry. Once again, news of insurrection in Paris provoked militant action. Word came on March 23 that the reactionary Comte de Kératry (formerly the police prefect for Paris) was to take over the post of prefect, and Duportal, concerned that the revolutionary forces were getting out of hand, duly stepped down. Unwilling to accept such a quick defeat, National Guardsmen from several battalions marched the reluctant Duportal from the prefecture to the town hall, more or less forcing him to sign a formal proclamation of the Commune. A few days later, moderate republicans negotiated a settlement with the insurgents whereby Kératry would take office, the Commune would be dissolved, and a National Guard commander would temporarily occupy the post of mayor. Of course, not everyone was happy with the agreement, and when troops arrived on April 8 to enforce it, an angry crowd built barricades in the area surrounding the town hall. They did not last long, however, and the streets emptied after soldiers fired a few shots into the air.[43]

The case of Lyon, France's second city and a long-established center both of republican politics and of labor activism, is most informative as a lesson in how civil war in Paris might have been avoided.[44] In September 1870, activists at the Hôtel de Ville in Lyon had hoisted the red flag, symbol of the revolutionary re-

43. Ronald Aminzade, *Ballots and Barricades: Class Formation and Republican Politics in France, 1830–1871* (Princeton: Princeton University Press, 1993), pp. 216–23.

44. The extensive labor movement that developed in Lyon and the surrounding industrial region in the latter half of the nineteenth century is described in breathtaking detail in Yves Lequin, *Les ouvriers de la région lyonnaise, 1848–1914*. Given that his central interest is the formation of the working class as a self-conscious collective actor, it is striking that Lequin pays almost no attention to the events of 1870–71. In my opinion, this is an entirely reasonable decision: it reflects the disjuncture between workers' struggles against the growth of capitalism and the issue of urban autonomy that dominated the communal movement.

public, even before the new government had been formed in Paris. Constituting themselves as a Committee of Public Safety, they immediately sent a telegram to the Interior Ministry in Paris, requesting the right to hold municipal elections. The new prefect of the Rhône, just arrived with his letter of appointment from the capital, somewhat unexpectedly championed the committee's demands for local autonomy. Moreover, he was successful: on September 16, with the permission of the Government of National Defense, Lyon held its first local elections since 1851. The elected council, to demonstrate its republican leanings, continued to fly the red flag over the city hall throughout the fall and winter. In effect, Lyon had been given its Commune, only through nonrevolutionary means.

The result was a largely peaceful, yet politically active city. In an effort to take advantage of what they perceived as an opportunity for revolution, socialists and anarchists led by Mikhail Bakunin and affiliated with the Lyon section of the International pushed for more radical change, announcing the abolition of the state administrative machinery and the courts. Faced with derision from the republican municipal council, they assembled several thousand National Guardsmen to march on city hall, turning into an attempted coup what was initially advertised as a protest against the reduction in the daily cash indemnity for Guard duty. The remaining National Guard battalions, both from working-class districts and others, responded promptly to the mayor's summons, and the incipient insurrection was quickly routed. This widespread support for the mayor and the elected council indicated that, for most inhabitants of the city, the current state of affairs already reflected what they wanted from the Republic.

It was not much of a surprise, then, that when insurgents tried again to radicalize the communal movement after the March uprising in Paris, very little happened in Lyon. Following the armistice, the government had replaced the prefect with a more conservative one and the red flag had been taken down. But republican National Guard officers organized an effort to force the city council to denounce Versailles and proclaim its solidarity with the insurrection in Paris. Despite their open sympathy with the Parisians' call for municipal elections, the mayor and the council declared their reluctance to defy the duly elected National Assembly at Versailles. On March 22, two or three National Guard units arrested the prefect, took control of the Hôtel de Ville, and formed a Communal Commission to be led by five of the more radical members of the elected council. The latter refused to serve, and one day later it was again clear that popular support was lacking for an insurrection. Only a hundred insurgents remained in the city hall, with the majority of National Guard battalions now declaring their solidarity with the prefect, the mayor, and the council. On the morning of March 24, sensing their isolation, the leaders of the Lyon Commune surrendered without bloodshed.[45]

Things went furthest in Marseille, another stronghold of republican opposition under the Empire, and the only city other than Paris to have voted in the negative (that is, against the Empire) in the plebiscite of May 1870. Unlike Lyon and Paris, Marseille had an elected municipal council, which had pressed for enhanced control over local affairs as soon as the Republic had been proclaimed in Paris. Under the leadership of a local radical, Alphonse Esquiros, republicans in Marseille even became the center of the Ligue du Midi, an association that was meant to unite the departments of southern France for a coordinated regional defense against the Prussians. Socialists and republican leaders were much more closely allied, moreover, than in Lyon or even in Paris.

The insurrection in Marseille resulted from the misguided effort of the prefect of the Bouches-du-Rhône to forestall one: soon after receiving news of the uprising in Paris, he called out the National Guard on March 23 for a public demonstration of support for Versailles. A number of battalions declared their support for Paris instead, invaded the prefecture, and announced the creation of a Revolutionary Departmental Commission to be led by a prominent local republican, Gaston Crémieux. Rather than challenge local authorities in addition to the central government, they invited the municipal council to join forces with the commission. Hoping to steer the insurgents toward moderation, the council agreed. Within a few days, however, this alliance became strained, as delegates from Paris pushed the commission to adopt a more revolutionary stance.[46] When the Parisian delegates arrested the mayor and the bishop as hostages, the council decided that further cooperation was senseless and appealed to the Versailles government to restore order. Six thousand regular army troops arrived on the morning of April 3, surrounded the prefecture (which still housed the Departmental Commission) by noon, and controlled the city by nightfall. Figures for the dead and wounded show that the revolutionaries holed up in the prefecture had only scant support from the National Guard battalions that had put them in

---

45. The most detailed account of these events is given by Greenberg, *Sisters of Liberty*, pp. 215–61.

46. One of the three delegates, Bernard Landeck, had already made a name for himself in the capital as an exceptionally nasty revolutionary. Some historians have argued that he was sent to Marseille because other activists in Paris wanted him out of the way. See Antoine Olivesi, *La Commune de 1871 à Marseille* (Paris: Marcel Rivière, 1950), p. 137.

power: the government suffered only 80 casualties (including 30 deaths), the insurgents 150.[47]

One might have expected that the decentralist movement would have taken root far more readily in cities like Lyon, Marseille, and St. Etienne than in Paris. After all, administrative, political, and cultural centralization were practically synonymous with the influence Paris exerted over the rest of France.[48] In addition, as Aminzade has pointed out in his examination of Rouen, Toulouse, and St. Etienne, communal uprisings were more likely in cities in which republicans and socialists controlled municipal offices.[49] Yet the single most salient fact about the series of uprisings in the provinces is that, unlike the Paris insurrection, none of them produced a period of sustained mass collective action. Government troops were able in each case to suppress the revolts with a minimum of force; even in Marseille, where some street fighting did take place, nothing even approaching the level of mobilization in Paris occurred. The events of 1870–71 thus constitute a uniquely informative natural experiment: militant leaders in most of France's major cities attempted almost simultaneously to provoke popular uprisings invoking the principle of municipal liberties. In only one of the cities—Paris—did this attempt meet with a massive popular response. It was only in the capital that the movement for municipal liberties turned into a bloody civil war, as tens of thousands of women and men took up arms and fought against a military assault that proved far more savage than that of the Prussian army.

It is tempting to attribute the difference of outcomes to the brutal privations the Prussian siege had inflicted on Parisians, resorting to the traditional tactic of explaining protest in terms of misery and anger. But such an explanation seems highly suspect. If events had gone in the opposite direction—that is, if the mass uprisings had occurred in the provinces and not in Paris—would it not have been just as easy to account for quiescence in the capital by arguing that the population was too weary and exhausted after a grueling winter siege to resist further affronts by the government? Arguments from misery alone do not generate unambiguous predictions about outcomes and therefore do not suffice as explanations.

47. Greenberg, *Sisters of Liberty*, pp. 184–213.

48. For instance, the communal movement in Marseille was closely tied to the resurgence of a Provençal cultural identity, epitomized in the writings of Frédéric Mistral. The theme of Parisian dominance has a long pedigree in interpretations of French society since the revolution. See Alexis de Tocqueville, *The Old Regime and the French Revolution* (Garden City, NY: Anchor Books, 1955); Eugen Weber, *Peasants into Frenchmen: The Modernization of Rural France, 1870–1914* (Stanford: Stanford University Press, 1976).

49. Aminzade, *Ballots and Barricades*, chap. 7.

A more reasonable account, given the stark pattern observed in the spatial distribution of insurgent participation, is that social life in the capital was fundamentally different from that of other major metropolitan centers. The rebuilding projects of the 1850s and 1860s had changed Paris in a way and on a scale that neither it nor any other French city had ever experienced. The product of these changes was not, however, the class-divided city feared by liberal critics of the Empire; the barricades of 1848 had drawn the class boundary between east and west far more clearly than it would ever be drawn again. What the renovations in the center and annexations on the periphery had created, rather, was a city of residential neighborhoods—urban villages in which the relative absence of industrial production permitted social attachments to place, to the spatially defined community, rather than to craft or class. That was the reason that the neighborhood meetings on the edge of Paris were so much more contentious than those of the center; and it was the reason the people of Belleville, Montmartre, La Villette, and Charonne formed the core of political agitation during the siege. In other large cities, such as Lyon and Marseille, some renovation had occurred since 1851, and large factories sprang up in the surrounding suburbs, but no new residential neighborhoods had been created in between. In Lyon, the *faubourgs* of La Croix-Rousse and La Guillotière continued to house most of the city's workers along with their places of employment.[50] In Marseille, industrial expansion increased the scale and level activity of the harbor, but most of the city's workers continued to live in areas close by.[51] In the major industrial towns of the Nord, Alsace-Lorraine, and the Loire valley, factory workers were often scattered across the countryside or lived in *cités ouvrières* built by paternalistic employers, while handicraft workers remained tied to their artisanal communities.[52] For both groups, when places of residence were clustered sufficiently to constitute a community, it was a community wedded to the world of work.

The creation of primarily residential neighborhoods separated from places of work, and housing sufficiently numerous and diverse populations to permit cross-

50. Lequin, *Les ouvriers de la région lyonnaise*, pp. 159–82; Pierre Cayez and Martine Chevalier, "Approche du phénomène d'urbanisation de la rive gauche du Rhône (1852–1894)," pp. 55–68, in *Construire la ville, XVIIIe–XXe siècles* (Lyon: Presses Universitaires de Lyon, 1983); Vincent Féroldi, "Le Quartier Saint-Louis de la Guillotière au XIXe siècle," pp. 69–82, in ibid.

51. William H. Sewell, Jr., "Uneven Development, the Autonomy of Politics, and the Dockworkers of Nineteenth-Century Marseille," *American Historical Review* 93, no. 3 (July 1988): 604–37; Marcel Roncayolo, *L'imaginaire de Marseille: Port, ville, pôle* (Marseille: Chambre de Commerce et d'Industrie, 1990).

52. Hanagan, *The Logic of Solidarity*, esp. pp. 87–201.

class social relationships, occurred only in Paris. Together with a set of events pitting the city politically against the state, this rearrangement of social networks provided a new basis for a geographically defined collective identity corresponding to the notion of the urban community—a collective identity that, though salient in the radical phase of the Revolution of 1789, had been occluded in the nineteenth century by profound changes in the nature of work and an increasingly vociferous protest movement based on craft solidarities. And, much as the key organizations of 1848 briefly created social ties among workers that bridged craft boundaries, the National Guard in 1871 created ties among Parisians that bridged neighborhood boundaries.

The overlaying of these organizational ties onto a multitude of informal ties rooted in residential neighborhoods made a vast difference in the way the communal movement unfolded in Paris. In every other city where it arose, the demand for municipal liberties turned out to be a brief and largely costless flirtation with an unusual and ill-fitting collective identity; in Paris, on the other hand, the parallels between the communal identity and concrete patterns of social relations were only too real. The all-too-real consequence was one of the greatest social catastrophes in modern European history.

7

Conclusion

NEARLY THREE DECADES of scholarship in what was once called "the new social history" have radically reshaped our view of protest in nineteenth-century Europe. The combination of raw data and theoretical insight that has emerged from this body of scholarship has, moreover, left no part of the political spectrum untouched. On the one hand, the conservative view of militants as groups of unruly, misguided (and usually drunk) workers under the sway of subversive middle-class hotheads has been discarded in favor of a more sympathetic perspective: the strikes, demonstrations, and insurrections that once counted as evidence of workers' irrationality are now more often seen as instances of organized and purposive collective action. The participants can now be viewed as self-consciously political actors endowed not only with relatively well defined interests, but even with the capacity to elaborate and articulate those interests. The radicalism and occasional violence that characterized their actions resulted not from the psychology of the mob but from their systematic and forcible exclusion from the arenas of institutionalized politics; indeed, the preponderance of the evidence indicates that most of the violence that occurred in Europe during these turbulent times was instigated by those in power, not by the powerless. The conservative perspective, it seems, has had to retract a number of its most pointed claims.

On the other hand, the orthodox Marxist understanding of the period, according to which the wave of militancy that swept across western Europe at midcentury represented the coming of age of the industrial proletariat, has also undergone deep revisions. Painstaking research on economic development and working-class protest in Britain, France, and Germany has repeatedly shown that unskilled factory workers constituted only a small segment of the working population of industrializing Europe and an even smaller segment of the labor movement. The key partisans of working-class activism, in both absolute and relative terms, were skilled handicraft workers—artisanal laborers trained and socialized in a traditional craft, often through long apprenticeships, and employed in

small workshops. Indeed, the corporate traditions and informal patterns of association that sustained craft communities furnished the main organizational un-
derpinning for industrial militancy for most of the century.

Despite the now thorough regnancy of this portrait of "artisanal activism,"
however, most scholars still make use of the story of working-class formation as
a pivotal device for interpreting long-term developments in European social history. This is especially true for discussions of France, where political and social
unrest remained closer to the surface than in any other early industrializing nation. The revolutionary uprisings that occurred in Paris, Lyon, and other cities
tend to be seen as integral parts of the broader labor movement in nineteenth-
century France and as transformative moments pushing this movement ever
closer to universal class consciousness. In the class-formation story, in other
words, the class unity expressed in revolutionary mobilization increasingly predominated in smaller-scale protest actions as well.

I have pointed out elsewhere that there is something paradoxical in the claim
that craft solidarities underpinned labor protest throughout the 1800s even as
craft boundaries dissolved to make way for a generalized class consciousness.[1]
It is worth stressing in addition that, however widespread this general class
awareness might be said to have become, it never again attained the intensity of
1848. Instead, the evidence I presented in chapter 4 pointed resolutely to the
conclusion that the resurgent working-class activism of 1864–70 retained few
of the traits that had made 1848 such an extraordinary year. Even though the
cooperative vision persisted as the central theme in the ideology of labor protest,
the notion of federation across trades did not produce major changes in the labor
movement that workers created in their quotidian struggles with employers. Under the Second Empire, the mobilization of actual industrial protest remained
reliant upon, and thus continued to be segmented by, an enduring pattern of
craft-specific social relations.

1. Gould, "Trade Cohesion, Class Unity, and Urban Insurrection," pp. 722–23. Ronald Aminzade, one of the authors most closely tied to the class-formation narrative in historical sociology, has
recently adopted a more cautious stance on the issue. He now argues—quite rightly, I think—that
the emergence of class consciousness among French workers was a highly contingent affair, depending in particular on local histories of industrial conflict and republican political activity. Nonetheless, he maintains a strong attachment to the supposition that urban uprisings in 1871 reflected
class-formation "successes" in the municipalities where they occurred, as compared with cities
where communal insurrections failed to take place. In contrast, I have tried to show in the preceding
chapter that, across France, the mobilizations of 1871 had relatively little to do with class awareness.
See Aminzade, *Ballots and Barricades*, chap. 7.

To be sure, the discussion in chapter 4 was based on the Parisian experience, and therefore does not by itself license generalizations on a national scale. But where could one expect to find signs of eroding trade boundaries if not in the city that witnessed firsthand the searing class war of 1848? If Paris was atypical, it was most likely in the direction of greater class solidarity, not less; and in any case the historical record does not present any major instances of cross-trade cooperation, even in France's most heavily industrialized regions, until the 1890s. The essential problem came down to this: during the Second Empire, no organization existed—in Paris or anywhere else in France—that forged social ties across trade boundaries as the National Workshops and the Luxembourg Commission had done, albeit briefly, in 1848.

Even more significant than the labor movement's departure from the class unity of 1848 is the fact that conflict during the Commune of 1871 was in many respects not about work at all. Researchers looking for signs of growing comprehension among working-class militants that their local struggles formed part of some larger battle of labor against capital can at least take heart in the fact that, during the 1860s, French workers active in the labor movement and in the working-class press often spoke of "the emancipation of labor" and "the exploitation of the worker by the capitalist"—even if industrial protest was still in practice deeply craft-divided. As I showed in chapter 6, they can take far less comfort in the words and actions of the insurgents of 1871.

This conclusion does not merely refer to the fact that municipal autonomy, rather than the right to work, became the focus of political agitation and public debate prior to and during the insurrection. The truly significant lesson of the preceding chapter is that the mobilization process itself—recruitment of rank-and-file insurgents and social sanctioning of participation—occurred through and was explicitly understood in terms of social relations among neighbors. To be sure, the Prussian siege and the terms of the armistice (in particular, the issue of disarming the National Guard) provided the political preconditions for conflict between the government and the city of Paris, making Guard service during the uprising synonymous with loyalty to a spatially defined urban community. But it is essential to keep in mind that actual mass mobilization based on this urban collective identity was possible only because the mapping of the Paris National Guard's organizational structure onto residential areas meant that failure to serve could be construed as a betrayal of one's neighbors and because organizational linkages across districts facilitated—again, briefly—solidarity on a citywide scale.

It is this dependence of the mobilization process on neighborhood social relations and their interplay with the formal insurgent organization that warrants reconsideration not only of structural Marxist and radical humanist interpretations of the Commune, but of any master narrative that relies on a class-struggle account of French insurrections. As I noted in chapter 1, radical geographers have offered two strategies for understanding the "urban turn" of the 1871 insurrection. David Harvey, for one, proposes to reduce the "communal" struggle to class struggle by arguing that conflicts over urban space in Paris were determined by the logic of capital circulation in an industrial metropolis—a logic that, by forcing the state to intervene massively in land markets to forestall a financial crisis, ultimately produced "communities of class" on the Parisian periphery. For their part, humanists like Henri Lefebvre and Manuel Castells have seen in the Commune a popular attack on the version of "urban meaning" represented by the imperial state and the city planning projects of Haussmann and Napoleon III.

The structural Marxist interpretation fails, however, on two counts. First, as I demonstrated in chapter 3, patterns of informal association among Parisians in the annexed zone show no sign of class homogeneity in social networks; middle-class Parisians were, in fact, more likely to act as witnesses to working-class marriages than one would expect on the basis of their prevalence in the population of peripheral neighborhoods. This cross-class inclusiveness makes it difficult to describe the annexed zone, where the Commune unquestionably achieved its greatest success in mobilizing insurgency, as a hotbed of working-class solidarity. Second, arrest rates showed that the class composition of neighborhoods was only faintly related to levels of insurgent activity, in contrast to the striking relationship observed for 1848. Indeed, there was no association whatever between arrest rates and the *relative* size of the working-class population in peripheral districts—precisely the areas where, if the structural Marxist account were right, the "community of class" should have been the strongest.

The humanist version of the 1871 uprising does not fare much better in light of these findings. While the disruption caused by eighteen years of annexation, demolition, and new construction was undeniable, one searches in vain for signs of the "loss of community" lamented by both nineteenth- and twentieth-century critics of Haussmann's projects. In fact, Parisians dwelling in the annexed zone led social lives that were considerably more structured by neighborhood relationships than those remaining in the center. And the insurrection itself bore grim witness to this difference: in an insurgent effort whose mobilization depended fundamentally on solidarity among neighbors, outlying districts made the strongest showing, to their very great cost. These insurgents did not die on the Commune's barricades as dispossessed denizens of the city center, but as inhabitants of Grenelle, Montrouge, Charonne, Belleville, Montmartre, and Batignolles. Immediate political circumstances and the National Guard organization permitted the (temporary) construction of a citywide collective identity; but mobilization of a large-scale insurgent movement based on this identity could occur only because of preexisting social relations and collective identities tied to local neighborhoods. The relationship between Haussmann's projects and the Commune was thus far more ironic than that posited by the humanist account: far from destroying the community basis of life in the capital, Haussmann brought into the city an entire set of residential communities that became home to thousands of Parisians previously tied to craft groups in the center. Without this vast increase in the number of people living in urban villages, a mass uprising based on neighborhood solidarity would scarcely have been possible.

In place of a single thread of class formation linking each protest episode to the next, then, the evidence suggests a more multidimensional world of crossed purposes and digressions. The major insurrections that form the endpoints of the period covered in this book were distinct in several significant respects both from each other and from the "labor movement," at least insofar as this phrase refers to collective struggles about wages, hours, and control over shop-floor practices. The combination of organizations and events that drove the radical period of the 1848 revolution to its violent close made class far more salient as a participation identity than at any other moment in the nineteenth century. Subsequently, the rebuilding of Paris by Haussmann, the growth of large industry in the suburbs but *not* the peripheral districts within Paris, the 1870–71 war, and the National Guard together produced a revolution that depended crucially on the collective identity of an urban community defined in opposition to the state. And throughout this period, from 1830 until well after the Commune, labor militancy—even when it explicitly adhered to socialist ideology—relied on the collective identity of craft as it was durably reproduced in the social lives of workers and their struggles with employers. These disparate social movements were founded on distinct kinds of social ties and understood in terms of distinct participation identities; they should not be brought together under the single rubric of class formation.

While in no way questioning the significance of working-class solidarity as a powerful mobilizing mechanism at various points in French history, I have shown that it is misleading to think of this mechanism as exerting an increasingly dominant force as the nineteenth century progressed. Relatively short-term political and organizational circumstances, in conjunction with more long-term shifts in patterns of urban social relations, ensured that protest and insurgency would be tied at different moments to radically different collective identities.

This argument should not be read as an attempt to dispense with the use of theory in historical sociology and to elevate pure contingency to the status of a theoretical framework. The implication of my research is, rather, that the particular theoretical standpoint embodied in the class-formation narrative is inadequate if the goal is to understand the full range of political and social protest in nineteenth-century France. Nor is my argument reducible to the mere claim that there are details of the story that the class-formation narrative ignores; what makes a theoretical framework powerful, after all, is precisely the fact that it ignores some features of the world without forfeiting coherence or consistency with the features it treats as relevant. My point has been that, even on its own terms, the class-formation narrative is inconsistent with evidence about French social conflict during the 1800s.

ᐳᐸ Identities, Networks, and Protest ᐳᐸ

What sort of theoretical framework, then, *is* adequate to the task of explaining the diverse forms of militancy described in the foregoing chapters? In chapter 1, I offered a sketch of what I believe is the right way to think about how identities shape and are shaped by the mobilization of social protest. That sketch focused on the connection between the various collective self-understandings available to groups of potential insurgents and the pattern of social relationships in which they are implicated. In the presence of a preexisting distribution of institutional attachments and material interests, any given instance of political or social conflict—a wage dispute, an assassination, a foreign invasion, or a clash with police—will render salient only one or a few identities out of a wide range of candidates. In February 1848, massive unemployment and the expansion of the franchise suddenly made a meaningful collectivity out of male laborers by giving them both a common interest and the institutional means to pursue it; and after the failure of working-class electoral organization to produce a socialist parliament, the focus on the National Workshops made plausible a collective identity embracing both male and female wage-earners. In 1870–71, on the other hand, the government's callousness during the winter siege and subsequent seizure of the National Guard's artillery gave the collective identity of "Parisian" an urgency (and an adversary) it had not previously possessed. In the interval, capitalist development in various industries accentuated the importance of craft identities, while the experience of public meetings in the late 1860s gave many residents of the capital a sense of their neighborhoods as collective political actors.

Short-term events highlight certain collective identities at the expense of others but rarely in a completely unambiguous way. That is why, during moments of political turmoil or state collapse, hundreds or even thousands of would-be shapers of events compete to provide definitive interpretations of what is going on—interpretations that invariably include statements about who the relevant collective actors are. Revolutions and insurrections are enormously generative of this sort of interpretive activity precisely because they seem to permit the construction of so many more versions of what is happening than is usually the case with institutionalized politics.

But if major events and quick-witted activists set the stage for particular collective identities to emerge as salient, networks of social ties determine who sees fit to take part in the action. For any one person to join in protest on the basis of a given participation identity, she or he must be convinced that the identity also applies to a sufficiently large group of others. As I observed in chapter 1, this is not simply a matter of efficacy, in the sense that participation by one person is useless without the simultaneous participation of many others. It is also a matter of norms or of normative social pressure: because collective identities define sets of people who are equally interested in the outcome of collective action, all are entitled to insist that others participate if they do, and to refuse to participate if others do not.[2]

It is this interdependence of individual actions, based both on practical and normative concerns, that makes networks of social relations crucial for the mobilization of protest. Collective identities draw conceptual boundaries around the set of people who are similarly affected by specific political circumstances; but these conceptual maps have no consequence in the absence of social ties that make some identities more plausible than others through social comparison and enable people to draw one another into collective action through normative appeals.

The dual role of social relations—as a means for assessing the validity of a

2. If norms did not play a role by allowing people to persuade (or even force) others to contribute their share, the knowledge that others were already committed to the cause would encourage idleness, not action.

collective identity, and as a means for acting on it or pushing others to do so—accounts for the fact, observed repeatedly in this study, that formal and informal ties act together in the mobilization of protest. Apart from their obvious effects on efficiency and coordination, organizations are enormously consequential for mobilization because, often during the process of mobilization itself, they forge contacts among people who are not already linked by informal relations. The grand scale of urban uprisings owes much, to be sure, to the sudden opening of political opportunity occasioned by state breakdown; but it owes at least as much to the inclusiveness of the collective identities that insurgent organizations are capable of sustaining.

Some Generalizations

Until now, I have focused almost unswervingly on nineteenth-century France. But if that were the only context in which I hoped my argument would shed some light, there would have been little purpose in setting up an abstract theoretical framework in the first chapter. The reason for rendering a concrete empirical case in conceptual terms is that the insights gained by studying one context in these terms may thereby be transferred to other situations. (Or they may not. But that is an empirical issue and can only be decided if one is willing to abstract from particular contexts.) Accordingly, in the few pages remaining, I shall point to a number of ways in which the theoretical argument I have defended in this book either makes sense of or makes predictions about other empirical settings.

In schematic form, the findings I have presented are consistent with four general propositions implied by the theoretical model sketched in chapter 1. First, a collective identity is plausible to particular individuals to the degree that the map it proposes of the relations among collective actors is both congruent with those individuals' own patterns of social relations and salient in light of current political circumstances. Second, a collective identity that is plausible in this sense will only sustain collective action if the people to whom it refers are also tied socially to one another in sufficient numbers to facilitate (1) mutual awareness of its general applicability and (2) the use of normative appeals (or coercion justified normatively) reinforced by concrete social obligations. Third, identities that actually succeed in mobilizing collective action, which I have referred to as participation identities, are those that optimize on the trade-off between comprehensiveness (offering the advantage of a broad-based constituency) and social integration (ensuring sufficient levels of internal social linkage to make mobilization possible). Fourth, formal organizations increase the scale at which this trade-off is resolved by establishing social contacts across the boundaries established by everyday life, although mobilization continues to depend on the preexisting social integration of the smaller-scale collectivities defined by these boundaries.

The extant literature on collective action of various kinds offers empirical material that is broadly consistent with these generalizations.[3] I will limit my attention to two prominent examples. To begin in a context close to that considered in this book, histories of labor struggles (*not* insurrections) in industrializing Europe demonstrate almost monolithically that small-scale artisanal communities were the mainstay of labor protest in both cities and towns, and that craft was the dominant participation identity in these struggles even into the twentieth century. Given that artisanal economies throughout western Europe are known to have exhibited high levels of father-to-son occupational persistence, husband-to-father-in-law occupational endogamy, and craft-specific social interaction, it is clear that moving from the collective identity of craft to that of class would have entailed a sharp drop in network connectivity. The definitive emergence of class as a collective self-understanding with the real potential to mobilize political action had to await the formation of national trade-union federations and workers' parties. Though weak at the outset, these institutions were the first to provide the framework for regular and sustained social contact across trade lines. Even then, as numerous writers have observed, mass workers' parties and union federations have consistently been reformist rather than revolutionary. Moreover, the world has never witnessed a truly international workers' movement, despite the salience of internationalism in socialist rhetoric and the determined efforts in this direction on the part of such organizations as the Comintern. Both observations point to the difficulty of mobilizing radical collective action when the level at which collective identities are defined is so high that sustained social contact across subgroups is severely restricted.[4]

---

3. By pointing this out, I am not suggesting that the theory set out here offers a better explanation of any particular case studied by other authors. But there is something to be gained by observing that each of these studies yields conclusions consistent with my argument: it shows that they are particular instances of a more general phenomenon.

4. I am assuming here that, other things being equal, more radical collective action requires stronger social relations. The intuitive justification for this supposition is that, if overcoming the free-rider problem depends in general on recruitment and mobilization through preexisting social relationships among potential beneficiaries, then collective action carrying a very high risk must depend on very close relations, such as kinship or long-term friendship. In other words, while activ-

A second instructive case is feminism, which has emerged several times in the modern era, with mixed results. Research on feminism in the nineteenth-century United States points consistently to the role of religious associations in forging crucial contacts among otherwise isolated middle-class women. Despite the sharply conservative intent of the male pastors who encouraged these local associations, the women who participated in them achieved a sense of solidarity through the mutual recognition of their quasi-imprisonment in a "separate sphere." The same can be said of the thousands of feminist consciousness-raising groups that sprang up across the United States and Europe during the 1960s and 1970s.[5]

As with labor protest, though, patterns of social relations have placed severe limits on the kind of collective identity that could convince women to participate in protest. With the exception of radical (and, particularly, lesbian) separatists, women in the West have maintained close social relations with men, whether as fathers, sons, spouses, lovers, brothers, or friends. The continued presence in the lives of most women of strong social connections to males (however asymmetrical or even exploitative these connections might be from the feminist point of view) stands in the way of any collective identity based on a fundamental antagonism between the sexes. The result is an abiding moderation in both the ideology and tactics of feminist collective action—again, with the instructive exception of those feminists whose social networks almost completely exclude men. Though civil war between the sexes is by no means logically impossible (indeed, much feminist thinking endeavors to show that contemporary society is precisely a war waged on women), nothing even approaching such a conflict has ever occurred

---

ists might have little trouble persuading a casual acquaintance to sign a petition, they would have great difficulty convincing such a person to risk injury, death, or imprisonment. They would be more successful with a sibling or a close friend, even controlling for the latter's prior sympathy with the movement in question. I am unaware of any systematic attempt to verify this hypothesis but am quite confident that it will turn out to be correct. In any case, it leads to a further empirical prediction, which seems to be consistent with what is generally known about protest. Given that most people have few very intimate social ties, radical, violent collective action should be associated more often with small, close-knit groups than with large organizations; collective action involving large numbers of people, conversely, should be relatively moderate and nonviolent.

5. Nancy F. Cott, *The Bonds of Womanhood: "Woman's Sphere" in New England, 1780–1835* (New Haven: Yale University Press, 1977); Barbara L. Epstein, *The Politics of Domesticity: Women, Evangelism, and Temperance in Nineteenth-Century America* (Middletown, CT: Wesleyan University Press, 1981); Judith Hole and Ellen Levine, *Rebirth of Feminism* (New York: Quadrangle Books, 1971).

between the sexes. The main reason, I submit, is that the thicket of social obligations linking men to women and women to men renders such an idea totally implausible, or downright unacceptable, to most ordinary people.[6]

Finally, an even broader implication of my argument is that the disappearance of spatially defined collective identities should not be anticipated in the
near future. Despite the recent fascination in some circles with such phenomena
as globalization and the "compression" of time and space by means of digital
communication technology, most strong personal relationships in both Western and non-Western societies continue to rely on fairly regular physical co-
presence. Financial obligations are much easier to transmit electronically than
social ones. More importantly, spatially bounded relationships have a significant
property not shared by most social ties with nonspatial bases: an intrinsic tendency toward transitivity. If I associate primarily with my neighbors and most of
those with whom I associate do the same, then my friends' friends are necessarily
(at least) my neighbors.[7] This simple fact means that social networks founded on
spatial proximity provide fertile ground for the emergence of plausible collective
identities: individuals with ties to neighbors can readily observe numerous others
whose patterns of social interaction match their own. In contrast, when social
ties are based not on joint residence but on diverse interests (shared schooling,
athletics, amateur pursuits), people are likely to see their associates' social networks as distinct from their own, discouraging the formation of broad collective

6. It might be countered that the peaceful history of the women's movement has nothing to do
with social ties but, rather, derives from the fact that feminists (or women in general) are simply
averse to the violence that the conceptual map of total hostility between the sexes implies. This may
be so; but there are numerous examples of radical feminists plainly advocating violent collective
action against men. See, for example, the manifesto of S.C.U.M (the Society for Cutting Up Men),
excerpted in Robin Morgan, ed., *Sisterhood Is Powerful* (New York: Vintage Books, 1970). Another
objection is that the interaction between women and men might be a consequence, not a cause, of
the moderate form that feminist collective identity usually takes. This line of argument is sensible
but does not rule out the possibility of reciprocal influence. I conjecture that women who subscribe
to the radical separatist view of gender relations are disproportionately likely to have experienced
harmful or exploitative interactions with men *prior* to their adoption of the separatist standpoint. It
would be entirely consistent with my argument (as well as unsurprising) to find in addition that
adoption of the separatist identity led to further social isolation from men.

7. This pattern is an example of weak transitivity: a strong link from A to B and from B to C
implies *at least* a weak tie from A to C. (In this case, the weak tie consists of living in the same place.)
One might predict, in addition, that my friend's friend will be more likely to become my friend as
well if we cross paths regularly—which will be the case if we are neighbors. In contrast, I am unlikely
to become friendly with my friend's sibling if the latter lives far away.

identities. Other situations may produce widespread structural similarity but without the accompanying opportunities for mutual awareness: for instance, holidays that call for adult offspring to gather in their parents' homes generate enormous numbers of isomorphic interactions but in closed settings.[8]

Two related predictions follow from this straightforward observation. First, as long as social interaction is structured by propinquity, collective identities based wholly or partly on space—including neighborhood, region, nation, and even ethnicity—will continue to play a significant role in social conflict. Second, in settings where social ties are freed from the constraints of space, collective identities that convincingly encompass large numbers of people will be hard to find. If "communities" are constructed on the basis of individual tastes for specific voluntary activities, with each activity yielding a distinct grouping, broad comparability of egocentric social networks will be a near impossibility. Any given collective self-understanding will refer to a tiny set of individuals and have relatively little political significance. Mass mobilization will be rare.

If it is true that human beings make their own identities, they nonetheless do not make them in circumstances of their own choosing. What this book offers, if anything, is an account of the kinds of constraints circumstances place on the identities that shape and inform collective action. It is an account that focuses not on predetermined historical scripts but on the disciplined improvisations that result when political events map—sometimes in surprising and unrepeatable ways—onto existing patterns of social relations. The purveyors of revolutionary ideas may say what they like, but their followers have to answer to neighbors and friends.

8. Kinship is another example of a type of social relation which is often intrinsically transitive: in most systems, ego's kin's kin are also ego's kin. The predominance of nonprescriptive marriage in Western societies weakens this tendency, however, by ensuring that ego's blood relations will rarely be related to other kin (e.g., in-laws) in the same way that ego is. Little wonder, then, that the extended family has less importance as a source of collective identity in the West than in traditional societies.

Statistical Analyses

Table A1 Regression of June 1848 Total Arrests (logarithmic scale) on Class Composition (by *arrondissement;* N = 12; *t*-values in parentheses)

Independent Variable	Model 1	Model 2	Model 3	Model 4
Number leaving	.050*	.015⁺		
no estate	(2.971)	(2.043)		
Percent leaving		.085**		
no estate		(8.480)		
Number receiving				
bread rations,			.066**	.042*
1847			(7.314)	(2.718)
Percent receiving				
bread rations,				1.669⁺
1847				(1.840)
Constant	4.721	−.406	5.040	4.771
R^2 (adjusted)	.416	.928	.827	.860

$^+p < .10.$
$^*p < .05.$
$^{**}p < .01.$

NOTE: The denominator for percentages is the male population, as arrested insurgents were overwhelmingly men. The logarithm of total arrests is used to reduce the impact of two extreme values on the coefficient estimates; using absolute number of arrests as the dependent variable slightly reduces the proportion of variance explained but yields the same statistical inferences.

Table A2 Regression of Paris Commune (1871) Total Arrests on Class Composition (by *arrondissement;* N = 20; *t*-values in parentheses)

Independent Variable	Model 1	Model 2	Model 3
Number of wage-earners	33.423**	25.917*	34.717**
	(5.476)	(2.814)	(3.892)
Percent wage-earners		10.085	2.016
		(1.085)	(.227)
Ratio of industrial establishments			−221.785*
to residences			(−2.406)
Constant	358.802	97.045	588.013
R^2 (adjusted)	.604	.608	.694

*$p < .05$.
**$p < .01$.
NOTE: Logarithmic scale is not used in these analyses because there are no outliers on the dependent variable, as in the 1848 data. The contrast between the two events (i.e., the lack of an independent effect of proportion wage-earners in 1871) is not, however, an artifact of the scale used (see note to table A1).

Table A3 Network Autocorrelation Models of Arrest Rates, May–June 1871

Independent Variable	Model 1	Model 2	Model 3
Autocorrelation (ρ)	.494*	.215*	.284**
Poverty rate (per 1000)	.075**		.051
Percent wage-earners	.198*	.271**	.233*
Percent white-collar employees	.414	.342	.476
Ratio of industrial to			
residential buildings		−2.580**	−1.821
Constant	−13.602	−2.665	−8.418
Fit[a]	.786	.800	.846
N	20	20	20

*$p < .05$ (one-tailed).
**$p < .01$ (one-tailed).
[a]"Fit" is the square of the correlation between the observed and predicted values of the dependent variable. While it corresponds roughly to R^2 in standard regression analysis, it is not strictly comparable and should not be interpreted as the percentage of variance explained.

Table A4 Network Autocorrelation Models, Enlistment Network Transposed

Independent Variable	Model 1	Model 2	Model 3
Autocorrelation (ρ)	−.136	.071	−.447
Poverty rate	.081**		.060
Percent wage-earners	.185	.269**	.225*
Percent white-collar employees	.366	.338	.444
Ratio of industrial to residential buildings		−2.674*	−2.110
Constant	−2.923	−.057	3.552
Fit[a]	.782	.799	.842
N	20	20	20

*$p < .05$ (one-tailed).
**$p < .01$ (one-tailed).
[a]See note to table A3.

Table A5 Occupational Categories Used in Analysis of Marriage Documents and Insurgent Participation

Class Category	Occupations
Skilled worker	BAKER(*boulanger, pâtissier, confiseur, chocolatier*)
	BUTCHER(*boucher, charcutier*)
	OTHER FOOD(*distillateur, raffineur de sucre, cuisinier*)
	PAINTER, PLASTERER(*peintre en bâtiments, plâtrier, peintre-vitrier, glazier*)
	MASON, ROOFER(*maçon, marbrier, tailleur de pierre, couvreur, plombier-zingeur*)
	JOINER, CARPENTER(*menuisier, charpentier, cintreur, scieur de bois*)
	OTHER CONSTRUCTION(*briquetier, fumiste, ornémaniste, sculpteur, serrurier en bâtiments, carreleur, parqueteur*)
	FURNITURE WORKER(*ébéniste, lampiste, menuisier-ébéniste, tourneur, mouleur, bronzier, fondeur en bronze, monteur en bronze, doreur sur bronze, imprimeur sur papiers peints, sculpteur en bois, modeleur, tapissier*)
	TAILOR(*tailleur, tailleur d'habits, tailleur à façon*)
	SHOEMAKER(*cordonnier, bottier, sabotier, galochier, piqueur(se) de bottines, coupeur en chaussures*)

Table A5 continued

Class Category	Occupations

CLOTHING, TEXTILE WORKER(*passementier, brodeur, dentellier, chapelier, casquettier, bonnetier, boutonnier, blanchisseur(se), teinturier, couturièr(e), tisserand, imprimeur sur étoffes, gantier*)

MACHINE BUILDER(*mécanicien, serrurier-mécanicien, ajusteur, dessinateur-mécanicien, tourneur en fer, tourneur sur cuivre, tourneur-mécanicien, lamineur sur métaux, tôlier, chauffeur-mécanicien, polisseur*)

FOUNDRY WORKER(*fondeur en fer, fondeur en métaux, fondeur en cuivre*)

FORGER, OTHER METAL(*forgeron, frappeur sur fer, ferblantier, chaudronnier, estampeur, cloutier, boulonnier, tailleur de limes, taillandier*)

JEWELER(*bijoutier, orfèvre, joaillier, sertisseur, monteur en bijoux, doreur sur métaux, plaqueur en argent, émailleur, nacrier*)

INSTRUMENT MAKER(*horloger, opticien, facteur de pianos, facteur d'instruments*)

CERAMIC, CHEMICAL WORKER(*porcelainier, faïencier, verrier, fondeur en suif, fondeur en graisse*)

PRINTER, BINDER(*imprimeur, typographe, fondeur en caractères, lithographe, graveur, photographe, papetier, relieur, brocheur, correcteur d'imprimerie*)

LUXURY GOODS WORKER(*bimbelotier, ouvrier en peignes, brossier, billardier, ouvrier en fleurs artificielles, plumassier, éventailliste, encadreur*)

BARBER(*coiffeur, perruquier*)

CARRIAGE MAKER(*carrossier, charron, serrurier en voitures, menuisier en voitures, sellier-carrossier*)

WOOD WORKER(*cartonnier, layetier, emballeur, tourneur en bois, tonnelier, vannier*)

TANNER, LEATHER WORKER(*tanneur, mégissier, corroyeur, maroquinier*)

SERVICE WORKER(*garçon de restaurant, garçon de café, garçon d'hôtel, concierge, valet de chambre, domestique, jardinier, cocher, charretier, porteur*)

Unskilled worker DAY LABORER, EXCAVATOR(*journalier, terrassier, homme de peine, manoeuvre, manouvrier*)

Table A5 continued

Class Category	Occupations
White collar worker	EMPLOYEE, CLERK(*employé de commerce, commis de commerce, commissionnaire, voyageur de commerce, clerc, clerc d'huissier, clerc d'avoué*)
	ACCOUNTANT(*comptable, caissier, teneur de livres, employé-comptable*)
Bourgeois/ professional	PROFESSIONAL(*avocat, médecin, pharmacien, chimiste, dentiste, professeur, ingénieur, géomètre, dessinateur*)
	ARTS AND LETTERS(*journaliste, homme de lettres, artiste peintre, éditeur*)
	PROPERTY OWNER(*rentier, propriétaire*)
	MERCHANT(*négociant, courtier, commerçant, marchand en gros*)
	SHOPKEEPER(*marchand de vins, restaurateur, limonadier, traiteur, herboriste, fruitier, fleuriste, loueur de voitures*)
	SMALL EMPLOYER(*fabricant, fabricant de parapluies, fabricant de bronzes, maître teinturier, maître boulanger, maître tailleur, gérant d'hôtel*)

Methodological Concerns

Data and Sources

It is typical of popular uprisings that the most visible traces they leave do not derive from the actions of insurgents but, rather, from the operations of the repressive forces. In the aftermath of both the insurrection of June 1848 and the Commune, the authorities were particularly diligent in this respect, with the result that primary materials concerning these mass uprisings are uncommonly rich. The 1848 data used in this study are taken from the Tilly and Lees (1975) study; they provide detailed information on their procedures in the two articles cited in the bibliography to this book. (The codebook for these data was generously provided by Mark Traugott.) The dossiers for the thirteen thousand prisoners who were ultimately put on trial for participation in the Commune are preserved in the French Army Historical Archives, along with more than one hundred cartons of documents concerning the administration of Paris and of the National Guard between March and May of 1871. (Although the army also compiled dossiers on the prisoners who were released without a trial, these files were destroyed in the 1950s.)

Each trial dossier contains transcripts from the interrogations of the accused and any witnesses, a summary report filed by the interrogating officer, and the judgment of the court. The last two documents together provide information on each prisoner's age, occupation, place of birth, address, marital status, number and type of previous encounters with the law, and any other details that seemed relevant to the investigating officers. Although these dossiers were the basic source for the army's official report to the French National Assembly (Appert 1875), they have never been used in a systematic way by modern scholars. The one existing attempt to make empirical generalizations about the rank and file of the 1871 revolution (Rougerie 1964a) bases its conclusions exclusively on the official statistical report, which, though admirable in its apparent thoroughness and attention to detail, suffers from arithmetic errors and contradictions as well as more subtle forms of bias and distortion. (For a thoughtful critique of the Appert report, see Maitron 1972.) The only relatively reliable sources of information on the Parisian insurgents of 1871 are the dossiers themselves.

Accordingly, the data for this study come from a 10 percent sample of the dossiers preserved in the French army archives. An initial list of insurgents was drawn up by selecting every tenth name from the *Dictionnaire biographique du mouvement ouvrier fran-*

çais (Maitron 1968)[1]. But because the *Dictionnaire biographique* is based on dossiers constituted at the Ministry of Justice when convicted prisoners applied for pardons, this initial list excluded anyone who was acquitted by the military courts. Since it was desirable to have information on acquittals, both to compare more active with less active participants and to uncover any biases that might have influenced the judicial process, a separate sample of acquitted prisoners was drawn directly from the records in the army archives. Because of limitations on public access to trial dossiers in these archives, it was impossible to draw a random or systematic sample of acquittals; consequently, this sample was constructed by selecting two letters of the alphabet at random and consulting all the dossiers for acquitted prisoners whose last names began with one or the other of these letters. The final sample consisted of 945 insurgents who received guilty verdicts, 177 who were acquitted, and 283 who were tried (and invariably convicted) in absentia.[2] In total, this yielded a sample of 1,405 people who were formally charged with participation in the insurrection. For each individual, the data recorded included the basic demographic information listed above as well as details about the defendant's role in the Commune. Specifically, each record contains a variable indicating whether the defendant was enrolled in the National Guard and, if so, whether he had held a rank above sergeant. Another variable indicates whether the defendant had held a civilian administrative post under the Commune. Finally, the verdict was recorded (acquittal, conviction, or conviction in absentia) and in the case of conviction the sentence was noted as well. These data are used both in the individual-level analyses reported in this appendix and in aggregated form in chapter 6 and appendix A, where the units of analysis are occupational groups and geographical areas. (For occupational groups, it was necessary to increase the size of the sample to permit a sufficiently fine-grained division into professional categories; thus the figures for occupational distribution of arrests reported in chap. 6 are based on the initial sample as well as an additional 795 arraignees for whom occupation only was recorded.)

Many of the questions addressed in this study also require information about the Parisian population in general. For instance, comparing occupational groups or neighborhoods

1. The enumeration process was actually somewhat more complicated, since the volumes of the *Dictionnaire biographique* that include participants in the Paris Commune also contain entries for participants in the various revolutionary Communes that arose elsewhere in France in 1871, and for other labor militants who were active between 1864 and 1871. Consequently, the only entries used in the sampling frame were those that specifically concerned people tried by the *conseils de guerre* for participation in the Parisian uprising.

2. Appert reported that the military courts convicted 10,137 prisoners, acquitted 2,445, and sentenced 3,330 in absentia. Some of the discrepancy between the number of insurgents in the sample and what one would expect given these figures probably results from losses of dossiers over the past 120 years; on the other hand, the smaller number of acquittals is simply the result of the sampling procedure, which did not guarantee a fixed percentage. Finally, there are only 283 absentee defendants in the sample in part because many of these trials were redundant: about five hundred convictions in absentia were annulled after 1875 when it was discovered that the defendants had already appeared before other military courts.

with respect to their rates of participation in the uprising naturally entails reasonably accurate estimates of the sizes of these groups in the overall population. Similarly, if variation in these rates is to be explained in terms of occupation- or neighborhood-level characteristics, then it is preferable to obtain information on these characteristics from a source other than the insurgent sample itself. In the context of late-nineteenth-century Paris, the problem facing the researcher is not scarcity but, rather, an abundant supply of occasionally conflicting sources. At the very least, it is difficult to reconcile censuses and other official sources with each other because of variations in the way different data-gathering organizations classified people and professions.

This lack of standardization does not affect population counts across specific areas of Paris, since administrative boundaries within the capital did not change between 1860 and 1872. The figures for the population of each district used here are taken from the 1872 census to minimize the possibility of distortions due to changes over time. Data on the social characteristics of different districts are also drawn from the 1872 census. (For tabular and graphic presentation of 1872 census results for Paris, see Loua 1873.)

Divergent data collection practices do pose a problem in estimating the sizes of occupational groups. First, no two sources classify all occupations together in exactly the same way; thus joiners and carpenters might be counted as a single group in one source, while another source lists carpenters separately and counts joiners with floor-layers. Such overlaps frequently make it impossible to compare different sources for consistency.

Second, published sources vary with respect to the way their data were collected. The 1872 industrial survey conducted by the Paris Chamber of Commerce (Chambre de Commerce de Paris 1875) is exceptionally detailed, but its figures are based on questionnaires distributed to proprietors at their workshops; consequently, trades in which domestic outwork or subcontracting were common practices, such as tailoring and construction, are subject to severe undercounting. In addition, figures for the number of workers employed in each industry do not distinguish between white-collar employees and manual workers, or for that matter between skilled and unskilled labor. By contrast, the 1866 census (Statistique Générale de la France 1869) gives a less fine-grained breakdown of occupational categories, but reports white-collar employees separately from manual workers and does not exclude domestic outworkers or subcontracted laborers. (The 1872 population census recorded broad social categories such as "worker" or "professional," but did not record specific occupations.)

Given these various difficulties, the most reasonable strategy is to generate independent estimates of occupational group sizes and rely on published sources only as a corrective to flaws in archival materials. The estimates used in later chapters are derived from a systematic 2 percent sample of Parisians registered to vote in the national elections of July 1871; data on age, place of birth, and occupation were recorded for every fiftieth voter (beginning with a randomly chosen entry among the first fifty) in the alphabetical electoral lists preserved in the Archives de Paris. To obtain estimates of the actual number of male residents of Paris exercising each profession, the number of sampled voters in each occupational category was first multiplied by 50 to match the size of the sampling frame; then these figures were adjusted to account for differential rates of voter registration across social classes. For example, the number of people in the sample classified as bourgeois or professional was multiplied by 1.29, whereas the number of people in each skilled artisanal occupation was multiplied by 2.04.[3] This procedure ensures that social groups are not overrepresented in the sample simply because their members were more likely to be registered voters.

Careful data collection practices are essential, but they leave unanswered one central question that is too often ignored in historical studies of social protest: to what extent are repressive authorities to be trusted in their evaluations of who did and who did not participate in protest activities? Arrest and trial records are, after all, the only source available to scholars interested in identifying the social bases of large-scale social upheavals; there is no independent information on participants in insurrections and revolts that can be used to check the validity of official documents. Moreover, it is obvious that no government, however conscientious and thorough in its efforts, could ever succeed in arresting all the people—and only those people—who were involved in a specific protest activity. Even if a clear set of criteria for the notion of involvement could be set forth, errors of both inclusion and omission would be inevitable.

What, then, justifies the use of the sample described above in a study of insurgency? The standard response to such questions—that the data may not be perfect but they should be used because they are the only data available—is not satisfactory in the present context, since it is conceivable that the sample of arraignees differed from the general Paris population in ways that have nothing to do with the differences between insurgents and noninsurgents. Comparisons between the arraignee sample and the Parisian population will be meaningless from the point of view of this study unless the authorities made a genuine and on the whole successful effort to sort prisoners according to the degree to which they took an active role in the insurrection.[4] The principal task of the next section, then, is to determine the extent to which this effort was successful and—just as important—to pinpoint the ways in which it fell short.

3. This procedure assumes, of course, that professional groups *within* social classes do not vary with respect to registration rates. Ideally, we would want to know the exact rate for each occupational category within each social class; for example, if jewelers were more likely to register to vote than other skilled workers, the procedure used here would result in an overestimation of the number of jewelers in the city. Of course, the only way rates could be known for each category would be to have complete census data whose categories matched those used in this study. But if this were the case, then there would be no need for a sample based on electoral lists. In cases where census figures *are* available for well-defined occupational groups (for instance, tailors and shoemakers), the rate of voter registration generally does not vary appreciably from the overall figure of .49, which appears to justify the assumption made here. When the electoral list estimate for a specific category differs markedly from estimates based on census data, suggesting some kind of occupation-specific under- or overcounting, census figures have been used.

4. This is not to say that the authorities would have had to be correct in every instance, only that on average their decisions about whom to try and whom to release corresponded to real differences in prisoners' extent of participation.

Validity of Arrestee Documents

Historical research on protest movements is severely constrained insofar as the documentary sources that make such research possible cannot be counted on to portray people and events in the way most scholars would like. First, the kinds of information necessary for the practice of political repression are simply not the same as those required for social science research. Second, it is possible that the people involved in repressive efforts collect information and make decisions in ways that depend on their own prejudices and presuppositions about collective protest. To the extent that this is the case, official assessments of the extent of a person's involvement in protest activities will reflect these presuppositions rather than the person's actual behavior.

To put the issue more concretely, in the present context the central question is whether it is reasonable to suppose that the thirteen thousand people represented in what I have called an "insurgent sample" were in any sense more active in the 1871 insurrection than anybody else. Now, it *is* reasonable to believe that many of the thirty-six thousand people initially detained by the army did play some real part in the armed struggle against the French government. More than three thousand people were arrested during clashes between the army and the National Guard outside Paris, and over nineteen thousand more were arrested during the street fighting between May 21 and May 28 (Appert 1875). Most of the remaining thirteen thousand were picked up in June by police officers acting on tips from private citizens; given that the police actually received over three hundred thousand denunciations, this last figure suggests that the authorities were fairly selective in deciding which reports to take seriously. On the whole, it seems likely that the group of initial arrestees included a sizable cross-section of those who had participated in the fighting.

The difficulty stems from the fact that twenty-three thousand of these prisoners were released after an initial investigation persuaded the military courts either that these suspects had been completely uninvolved or that their role in the fighting had been minimal. The dossiers for these more fortunate arrestees, which contained the same information as did the dossiers for arraignees, no longer exist. As a result, detailed data are unavailable for about two-thirds of what would otherwise be a pretty representative sample of Parisian insurgents.

These missing data in themselves would not pose a problem if it could be assumed that arraignees were simply randomly chosen from the population of arrestees, or if the only difference between arraignees and nonarraignees was their extent of participation in the insurrection. In the former case, the arraignee sample would be thoroughly representative of arrestees; in the latter case, the sample would be representative of participants in the insurrection according to a stricter definition of participation. But the first assumption is clearly untenable, since the decision to release or charge each arrestee occurred after several months of investigation into his or her whereabouts and activities during the Commune. Whatever the arraignment decision was based on, it was certainly not random.

On the other hand, the second assumption is probably not much more defensible than the first. This is not to say that arraignees were not on average more involved in the insurrection than nonarraignees; on the contrary, the documents in each prisoner's dossier make it clear that army officers did try to distinguish between people who had participated actively in the uprising and people who had not. Most of the questions they posed while interrogating prisoners and witnesses involved the accused's activities during the Commune's ten weeks of existence; specifically, the authorities wanted to know if accused persons had taken part in any of the National Guard's sorties, if they had helped to build or defend any barricades, if they had ever been armed, and whether they had participated in the fighting during the week of May 21–28. To the degree that these questions received accurate answers, arraignment did indeed depend on the level of participation of those accused.

Unfortunately, it is highly unlikely that arraignment depended *only* on this factor. Few people among the party of order felt that the role of the *conseils de guerre* was simply to locate and prosecute the people who had taken up arms against the government; the repression of the Commune was to fulfill the second function of cleansing Paris of its dangerous and subversive elements.[5] Accordingly, part of the prearraignment inquiry was oriented toward gathering information on each prisoner's "morality," generally by requesting a report from the local police commissioner on his or her neighborhood reputation. While not bearing directly on the question of insurgency, these reports nevertheless influenced army officers' assessments of the evidence that did bear on this question. For instance, both in face-to-face interrogations and in their summary reports, officers repeatedly expressed the belief that a criminal record or a police report that mentioned excessive drinking constituted strong evidence of participation in the insurrection; at the very least, such characteristics were grounds for discounting an arrestee's testimony. As a result, even if the authorities made a good-faith attempt to make each arraignment decision based only on the arrestee's (imputed) degree of involvement in insurgent activities, arraignees may still have differed from nonarraignees along other dimensions.

The real danger is not, therefore, that the sample to be used in this study does not tell us anything about insurgency. Some of the evidence I will present below shows quite clearly that what arraignees had done during the insurrection had a direct effect on the outcomes of their trials. In any case, there are strong a priori reasons to believe that the arraignee sample does in fact represent a group of people who on average were more involved in the insurrection than the general population. Whatever other motives and prejudices the authorities may have harbored, they were surely also quite keen on locating and punishing the people who really had taken up arms against the government. It is certainly possible that the repression fulfilled functions other than the explicit one of imposing sanctions on insurgents and that as a result people other than insurgents were occasionally put on trial; still, it is unlikely that the fulfillment of these other goals would have so dominated the process of repression that actual insurgents were systematically excluded from the arraignee population.

5. In one sense, of course, these were not perceived as two separate tasks, since insurrection and radical politics were hardly distinguished from straightforward crime. It was not simply that thieves and vagabonds were to be disposed of along with the insurgents; they were thought to have *been* the insurgents.

But it is clear that serious problems remain even if it is accepted that the arraignee sample represents a population of people who on average participated more actively in the uprising than other Parisians. In this study, data from the sample are used to compare arraignees with the general population on a variety of variables and these comparisons provide the basis for inferences about the determinants of participation in the insurrection. If, as seems likely, selection into the arraignee population was determined by a variety of criteria aside from participation in insurgent activities, such inferences will be difficult to make. For instance, if the authorities acted on the presumption that people with past criminal convictions were ipso facto more suspect than those without a criminal record, we would observe a higher proportion of people with criminal records in the arraignee sample than in the general population even if criminal convictions were not related to insurgency itself. Conversely, if people with past convictions were actually less likely to have participated in the insurrection, then the simultaneous effect of this relationship and of official prejudice might make past criminal convictions appear to be unrelated or only weakly related to participation.

In short, there is a considerable risk that the sample used in chapter 6 suffers from selection bias; and standard techniques used to correct for selection bias are not an option because the data required for such techniques—that is, data that would make it possible to model the selection process itself—are not available. This means that any conclusions about the determinants of insurgency based on data from the sample may be inaccurate.

There is a way out of this dilemma, however. That is, it is possible to make reasonably firm statements about what kinds of bias underlay the selection process that sorted thirty-six thousand prisoners into arraignees and nonarraignees, despite the fact that no individual-level data survive for the latter group. The reason is that the arraignee sample contains information about a sorting process that is strictly analogous to the initial process of holding some prisoners for trial and releasing others—namely, the military court's decision on whether each defendant was guilty or not guilty. Aggregate data on the prearraignment population of prisoners make it possible to draw some conclusions about the extent to which the arraignment/release decision depended on the same criteria as the conviction/acquittal decision. Insofar as it did, then an analysis of the determinants of the trial verdict will reveal quite a bit about the determinants of arraignment—or, in other words, about selection into the population represented by the arraignee sample. More precisely, an analysis of trial verdicts will tell us something about the effect of factors other than insurgent activities on inclusion in the arraignee population and about what these factors were.

This is the approach I shall adopt here. Using data on trial verdicts, social characteristics of arraignees, and more or less objective indicators of extent of participation in insurgent activities, I will defend the claim that it is reasonable to make inferences from the arraignee sample to the population of insurgents. At the same time, I will argue that there is clear evidence of selection bias in the sample but that this bias can for the most part be controlled for. In brief, I will show that the data used in chapter 6 (and, by extension, the arrest data from 1848 with which they are compared) merit the attention I am giving them not simply because they are the only data available but, more importantly, because they represent a valuable and—when used with care—reliable source of information about insurgent behavior.

Much depends, therefore, on the analogy between the initial decision to release or try suspected insurgents and the subsequent trial verdict. Only if the former decision was based on substantially the same criteria as the latter is it possible to identify and take account of selection bias in the arraignee sample. In other words, the problem of selection bias is manageable only if a reasonably strong case can be made that arraignees differed from released prisoners in the same way (that is, along the same dimensions and in the same direction) that the prisoners who were convicted differed from those who were acquitted.

The aggregate data on all thirty-six thousand arrestees that are included in the army's official report to the National Assembly (Appert 1875) make it possible to draw basic comparisons between these two stages of selection. Percentage distributions within each group for age, marital status, place of birth and place of residence (Paris region or elsewhere), and record of past criminal convictions appear in table B1.

It is immediately apparent that differences between the first and second groups are by and large reproduced in the differences between the third and fourth. That is, arrestees were more likely to be between the ages of twenty-one and forty than nonarraignees; but arraignees who were ultimately convicted of participation in the insurrection were also more likely to be in this age group than arraignees who were ultimately acquitted. Similarly, arrestees who were unmarried (or living with someone out of wedlock) were more likely to be arraigned than married arrestees and subsequently more likely to be convicted. Natives of Paris were more likely to be convicted as well as arraigned, as were arrestees with a criminal record. In brief, for all four variables, groups that were disproportionately likely to remain in the population of prisoners at the first stage of selection were also disproportionately selected (though not necessarily at the same rate) at the second stage.

This pattern constitutes persuasive—though admittedly circumstantial—evidence that the process by which arrestees were either held for trial or released was broadly similar to the process by which arraignees themselves were either acquitted or convicted. If selection at each of the two stages had depended on *different* sets of factors, we should expect to observe differences between group 1 and group 2 that do not match the differences between group 3 and group 4. The fact that these mismatches do not appear strongly suggests that the factors involved in selection at the arraignment stage were the same as those involved in selection at the trial stage.

But this conclusion is only half the battle (or perhaps a third). Just because army officers applied the same criteria at arraignment and at trial does not mean that these criteria had anything to do with the arrestees' participation or nonparticipation in the insurrection. Moreover, it is virtually certain that the decisions to arraign and convict did not depend only on participation in insurgent activities. Officers involved in the repressive effort operated from preformed notions about what kinds of people were likely to join in insurrections; these notions affected both their prior appraisals of the guilt or innocence of suspected insurgents and their interpretation of evidence.

To get around this problem, then, it is first necessary to find some fairly good reasons for believing that selection into the arraignee population depended at least in part on actual involvement in the insurrection. The second task is to isolate the factors that contributed to an individual's inclusion in the arraignee population independent of his or her insurgent activities—in other words, to identify the sources of selection bias. Clearly, fulfillment of these goals requires some kind of multivariate analysis, since the central difficulty is the possibility of multiple influences on the single variable of selection into or out of the arraignee population.

The process of sifting through the data using logistic regression is tedious, so I will limit myself to reporting the general inferences these analyses yield. To begin with, multivariate analyses confirm the bivariate results in table B1; that is, effects on trial verdict do not appear to be confounded by intercorrelations among the independent variables. Overall, arraignees between the ages of twenty-one and forty were more likely to be convicted than those under twenty-one or over forty. Again as in table B1, unmarried arraignees were more likely to be convicted than those who were married but less likely to be convicted than arraignees who lived with someone out of wedlock. In addition, the number of previous criminal convictions on a defendant's record exerted a positive effect on likelihood of a guilty verdict. Finally, likewise, arraignees in different socioeconomic·categories experienced significantly different chances of conviction: specifically, for both skilled and unskilled workers the odds of conviction were approximately three times the odds for bourgeois and professional arraignees.

Analysis of the odds of conviction shows, then, that army officers may have been influenced by preconceptions regarding the criminality and marital behavior of suspected insurgents. But it also demonstrates that the decision to convict also depended on actual insurgent participation. For instance, trial dossiers include information about the formal position each arraignee occupied in the National Guard, if any, as well as information about civil service functions performed under the Commune. These records make it possible to evaluate whether an unambiguous measure of level of participation in the insurrection was associated with the chances of a guilty verdict. As it turns out, the odds of conviction for officers are more than twice the odds for nonofficers. Occupants of civilian posts were not significantly more likely to be convicted than other arraignees, indicating that participation in the administration of the revolutionary government was not sanctioned to the same degree as military insurgency. This difference most likely reflects a line of reasoning on the part of the courts-martial according to which occupancy of a civil post was interpreted as evidence that an arraignee had made a conscious attempt to avoid serving the Commune in a military capacity.[6] Army officers were thus specifically interested in convicting people who had participated directly in the armed struggle against the

6. The *conseils de guerre* did not, however, apply such an interpretation to the occupation of a *political* office under the Commune—least of all to serving as a member of the elected Communal Council. Rather, it was those who fulfilled the more or less mundane clerical functions of registering births and marriages, administering public assistance, and rationing food and the like who were treated with relative leniency.

French government—people who had, in other words, engaged in insurrection in the narrow sense of the term.

It is clear, then, that official decisions about arraignees' degree of involvement in the insurgent movement were at least partially dependent on concrete differences in behavior, not simply on preformed ideas about what kind of people were most suspect. Indeed, not many other factors appeared to have exerted a strong direct effect on the verdict reached in each case. Apart from the officer rank in the National Guard, only past criminal convictions and socioeconomic background exhibit a statistically significant association with trial verdict. Given that other forms of social marginality (lack of employable skills, recent arrival in Paris) were actually negatively related to conviction rates, it seems likely that the effect of criminal record resulted not from an actual association of criminality with insurgent participation but of a *belief* about this association on the part of army officers.

If socioeconomic differences were related to trial outcomes primarily through army officers' bias against workers, we should expect to see more than just a direct association of social background with verdicts. That is, officers' predisposition to view working-class people as more likely candidates for insurgency would have manifested itself not simply as a greater propensity to find workers guilty, but also as a tendency to weigh and interpret evidence in different ways depending on the social category the defendant fell into. These differences in turn should be observable as contingent differences in the effects of other variables on the likelihood of conviction (i.e., as interactions between socioeconomic group and other factors).

The most noticeable interaction observed is that, when officer rank is controlled, marital status is associated with trial outcomes for working-class arraignees, but not for middle-class and white-collar arraignees. Specifically, working-class defendants who were married were significantly less likely to be convicted than those who were unmarried. By contrast, the coefficient estimate for marital status among middle-class defendants is near zero.

It is possible that being married affected people's behavior during the insurrection, which in turn influenced their chances of receiving a guilty verdict. It is also conceivable that marital status influenced the military courts' verdict independent of its connection with insurgent behavior. Finally, it may be the case that the coefficient for marital status reflects both mechanisms and that the fact of class differences in the size of this coefficient corresponds to a different mix of the two processes.

Other considerations suggest that the third possibility is the most likely. In the first place, for working-class arraignees at least, the effect on trial verdict of cohabiting is not significantly different from zero at the .05 level. But if the effect of marital status on trial outcomes were only due to its relationship with participation in insurgent activities, these two estimates should be roughly the same: cohabitation out of wedlock was essentially equivalent to marriage among the working class and should therefore have had essentially the same effect on behavior. Consequently, an interpretation of the effect of marital status solely in terms of its relation to insurgent activity cannot account for the difference. The contrast results from the fact that army officers considered married arraignees to be respectable people on the whole, whereas they regarded cohabitation as immoral. They thus behaved differently toward arraignees in these two types of marital situation. In general, then, it appears that the negative effect of being married on the likelihood of a guilty verdict stems from leniency on the part of the *conseils de guerre*. Arraignees with spouses or whole families to support were viewed as more deserving of sympathy; moreover, they could more easily justify having served in the National Guard on the basis of financial need. In contrast, arraignees who lived with someone out of wedlock were less likely to receive merciful treatment because their liaisons were regarded as illegitimate.

It might seem that the differential effect of marital status depending on whether arraignees were middle class or working class favors the conclusion that class differences in trial outcomes resulted from class bias against workers and not from class differences in insurgent behavior. But if this were the case, why would the military courts have been inclined to show leniency toward married *workers* and not toward married *bourgeois?* If the authorities wished to apply stricter standards of guilt or innocence to working-class defendants, it would not make much sense to offer them a form of indulgence that was not also available to middle-class defendants; yet being married did not reduce the likelihood of conviction for the latter group. It seems more sensible, then, to conclude that the contingent effect of marital status resulted from a genuine effort by the military tribunals to take account of extenuating circumstances: working-class arraignees who were married were clearly in a better position than their middle-class counterparts to plead economic misery both as a justification for having served in the National Guard under the Commune and as a reason for clemency.[7]

Essentially the same argument applies to the second major interaction effect— namely, the fact that number of prior convictions increased the chances of conviction more sharply for middle-class defendants than for workers. Again, if army personnel were predisposed to convict people of lower socioeconomic status regardless of their actual degree of involvement in the Commune, it would be surprising if the military courts did not weigh criminal records at least as heavily when judging workers as when they were judging middle-class arraignees; yet the data reveal precisely the opposite pattern. The observed difference may reflect the fact that past convictions were simply more commonplace among workers (the mean number of prior convictions was .71 among workers versus .29 among bourgeois and white-collar arraignees) and thus played a correspondingly less decisive role in their trials; but this interpretation only reinforces the conclusion that the higher likelihood of a guilty verdict among working-class arraignees was not due to prejudicial treatment in court.

For the most part, then, it is fair to attribute the difference in chances of conviction

7. By the same logic, being married probably *was* more compelling for workers than for middle-class Parisians as a reason to serve in the National Guard during the insurrection. That is, if level of participation could be measured accurately and comprehensively, one would most likely observe that being married exerted a positive effect on participation and that this effect was more pronounced among workers than among the middle class. Such a result would not, however, change the interpretation of the interaction observed in the data; indeed, it would imply that, if extent of participation were completely controlled in the analyses presented here, the difference between the terms for marital status among working-class and middle-class arraignees would be even larger.

between working-class and middle-class defendants to real behavioral differences between the two groups rather than to bias on the part of the military tribunals. In other words, workers were more likely to receive a guilty verdict not because army officers were predisposed to find them guilty of having participated in the insurrection but because they actually were more likely to have participated. Workers were disproportionately represented in the arraignee population, and even more disproportionately represented among those found guilty, because they had been overrepresented in the ranks of insurgents.

Discussion

While studies of large-scale popular protest in nineteenth-century Europe have invariably been based on arrest records (see, e.g., Pinkney 1972b; Sewell 1974; Tilly and Lees 1975; Traugott 1985), researchers working in this area have generally refrained from asking explicit questions about the reliability of such sources. The consequence of this practice is that the conclusions reached in these studies are trustworthy only insofar as we take it on faith that the officials charged with repressing popular protest were conscientious and universalistic in their attempts to ferret out dissidents and insurgents. Yet few scholars would seriously maintain that the army and police in nineteenth-century Europe went about the business of political repression in an evenhanded and objective manner.

The more detailed one wants to be in analyzing data from arrest records, the more serious the problem of official bias becomes. Since the research I am reporting in this study is at times quite detailed, it is impossible to proceed without some sense of the ways in which data on arrests might be distorted; the objective of this appendix was to inspect the data set itself for information of this kind.

On the whole, the results are quite encouraging. First of all, there are good reasons to think that the sorting process that produced the population of thirteen thousand arraignees really was used to distinguish insurgents from noninsurgents. Even if other considerations sometimes entered into the decision, and even if the fact of an arraignee's participation or nonparticipation could not always be established firmly, the population from which the sample is drawn represents a group of people who were on average more active in the uprising than the general Paris population. All other things being equal, differences between arraignees and the general population therefore corresponded to differences between insurgents and noninsurgents.

Of course, other things are not equal to the degree that the selection into the arraignee population did not depend exclusively on participation in insurgent activities; and the analyses discussed here show pretty clearly that insurgent behavior was not the only factor that entered into the selection process. In particular, arraignees with criminal records faced significantly higher chances of conviction—independent of their actual extent of involvement in the insurrection—because army officers believed that a pattern of past criminal activity predisposed people to participate in revolutionary movements.

But it also appears that differential treatment of people with criminal records nearly exhausts the phenomenon of official prejudice in the repressive effort. Apart from marital status, whose negative effect for wage-earners suggests that workers fared somewhat better at trial if they were (legally) married, other variables affected trial outcomes only weakly and not in directions that suggest official bias. The apparently greater likelihood of conviction for arraignees between the ages of twenty-one and forty suggests that people in this age group really were more active in the insurrection: the military tribunals could be expected to exercise greater indulgence with younger prisoners, but there is no obvious reason why they should have taken pity on defendants over forty. Similarly, it is hard to see what sort of prior beliefs about insurgency could have motivated army officers to find native Parisians guilty at a higher rate than nonnatives (among working-class defendants, $p < .10$ for Paris natives).

In general, then, the arraignee sample does show signs of selection bias but in ways that are straightforward, not subtle. Some arrestees were inappropriately selected into the population of arraignees because they fit the stereotypical profile of insurgents as dangerous riffraff; others were inappropriately selected out because they invited sympathy as struggling workers with families to support. Aside from these two factors, inclusion in the arraignee population seems to have depended principally on the information the military courts were able to gather about arrestees' activities during the Commune.

This finding has major implications for the use of information on overall arrest patterns (a key element of the evidence presented in chaps. 2 and 6). Because the biases uncovered in the trial processes depended on details that could only be obtained *after* arrest and interrogation, the geographical distribution of arrests should be a valid measure of levels of insurgent mobilization. Troops deployed in the streets during the street fighting of 1848 and 1871 could not have known the particular facts about their prisoners that would eventually become important in the process of judging them. Inferences based on arrest rates (as opposed to conviction rates) should therefore be relatively free of the distortions described in this appendix.

Although this discussion has been aimed at the essentially methodological goal of diagnosing data problems, it has also produced substantive findings whose implications deserve some attention. First, the results discussed above shed some light on the process of political repression in nineteenth-century France. Pitiless as the army of Versailles had been during the fighting of May 21–28, the *conseils de guerre* appear to have made a genuine effort to adhere to the rule of law once order had been restored in the capital. Indeed, the contrast between the treatment of insurgents during the "bloody week" and after the fighting had ended is quite striking: after thousands were summarily shot in the streets of Paris, the military tribunals handed down only ninety-six death sentences, seventy-three of which were later commuted. This comparative moderation (even by twentieth-century standards, it is admittedly unusual to characterize as "moderate" any aspect of a repressive operation in which nearly forty thousand civilians were incarcerated) can presumably be attributed to the heightened level of formal accountability associated with the judicial process.

At the same time, it would be grossly misleading to portray the trials as fair or impartial. Arrestees spent months in prison without being formally charged and were frequently arraigned and convicted on the basis of circumstantial or even irrelevant evidence. For those who were convicted, sentencing depended as much on the whim of the court as on the nature of the crime committed. In general, prisoners with criminal records or unfavorable police reports received considerably more severe treatment than those who fit the approved image of the hard-working, sober, and respectable French citizen. Arrestees in the former category were viewed as drunkards, thieves, and vagabonds who had seized on the insurrection as an opportunity to make mischief; in judging the latter group, on the other hand, the military courts frequently interpreted participation in the insurgent effort as a momentary—albeit serious—digression of the kind that occurs when naive but well-meaning working-class people allow themselves to be carried away by the outlandish ideas of subversives and revolutionary agitators.

Table B1 Comparison of Released, Arraigned, Acquitted, and Convicted Prisoners

	Released[a]	Arraigned[b]	Acquitted[b]	Convicted[b]
Age				
< 16	1.7	1.1	4.0	.3
16–20	10.5	10.7	8.6	11.2
21–40	49.7	63.5	58.3	64.8
41–60	35.3	23.5	27.8	22.5
60+	2.9	1.1	1.3	1.1
N	23727	1143	151	916
Marital status				
Unmarried	49.1	54.5	50.7	55.4
Married	49.0	37.6	44.4	35.9
Cohabiting	1.9	7.9	4.9	8.7
N	23727	1089	144	873
Birthplace				
Paris	23.3	27.3	24.7	27.9
Elsewhere	76.7	72.7	75.3	72.1
N	23556	1136	150	910
Prior convictions				
None	83.1	72.5	85.5	69.3
1 or more	16.9	27.5	14.5	30.7
N	23727	1147	152	919

NOTE: The total number arraigned does not equal acquittals plus convictions because the data in column 2 are weighted to account for the fact that acquittals are underrepresented in the sample. Columns 3 and 4 are unweighted.

[a]Source: Appert (1875).

[b]Source: Arraignee sample (Archives de l'Armée).

Table B2 Logistic Regression of Trial Verdict on Social Background Variables

Variable	Model 1	Standard Error	Model 2	Standard Error
Age	0.0737	.0467	0.0496	.0482
Age^2	−0.0009	.0006	−0.0006	.0006
Married	−0.2880	.2240	−0.3561	.2278
Cohabiting	0.4179	.4321	0.4391	.4355
Paris native	0.2021	.2169	0.1887	.2193
Convictions	0.4590**	.1410	0.4897**	.1431
White collar	0.4849	.3618	0.4025	.3695
Skilled worker	1.0623**	.2714	1.2862**	.2844
Unskilled	0.9439**	.3185	1.1403**	.3307
Officer	—	—	0.7494**	.2474
Civil post	—	—	0.4958	.4886
Constant	−0.5851	—	−0.4627	—
Log-likelihood	−389.571		−380.340	
N	998		981	

**p < .01.

Table B3 Logistic Regression of Trial Verdict on Social Background Variables, Working-Class Arraignees Only

Variable	Model 1	Standard Error	Model 2	Standard Error
Age	0.1219*	.0565	0.0914	.0579
Age^2	−0.0015	.0008	−0.0011	.0008
Married	−0.4577	.2781	−0.5579*	.2820
Cohabiting	−0.0811	.4509	−0.1391	.4529
Paris native	0.5065	.2653	0.4771	.2664
Convictions	0.3735**	.1401	0.3932**	.1415
Unskilled	−0.1355	.2480	−0.1570	.2495
Officer	—	—	0.6486*	.3212
Civil post	—	—	0.9763	1.0440
Constant	−0.3386	—	0.1113	—
Log-likelihood	−293.448		−287.686	
N	825		810	

*p < .05.
**p < .01.

Table B4 Logistic Regression of Trial Verdict on Social Background Variables, Bourgeois and White-Collar Arraignees Only

Variable	Model 1	Standard Error	Model 2	Standard Error
Age	−0.0526	.1132	−0.0820	.1220
Age^2	0.0005	.0014	0.0008	.0015
Married	0.0465	.3955	0.1210	.4170
Cohabiting	9.2309	44.6600	9.6174	44.2900
Paris native	−0.5827	.4276	−0.5389	.4484
Convictions	1.0240	.5349	1.1571*	.5408
White collar	0.3579	.3805	0.2030	.4048
Officer	—	—	1.1069**	.4042
Civil post	—	—	0.4350	.6241
Constant	1.9348	—	1.9759	—
Log-likelihood	−88.790		−84.173	
N	173		171	

*$p < .05$.
**$p < .01$.

Bibliography

Archival Sources

ARCHIVES DE L'ARMÉE DE TERRE, VINCENNES.
Series Ly—Commune de 1871.
Conseils de guerre—trial dossiers.

ARCHIVES NATIONALES, PARIS.
Series F⁷—Police Générale.
Series F¹²—Ministère du Commerce, Ministère de l'Intérieur.
Series BB²⁴—Ministère de la Justice: Demandes de grâces.

ARCHIVES DE PARIS.
Series V⁴E—Actes de mariage.
Listes Electorales.

ARCHIVES DE LA PRÉFECTURE DE POLICE.
Series Ba—Réunions publiques; insurrection de 1871.

Newspapers

Le cri du peuple
Journal officiel de la Commune de Paris
Le journal des travailleurs
Le mot d'ordre
La nouvelle république
L'organisation du travail
L'ouvrier de l'avenir
Paris libre
Le Père Duchêne
Le peuple souverain, journal des travailleurs
Le progrès (Lyon)
Le rappel
La révolution démocratique et sociale
Le tocsin des travailleurs
Le travail

Published Sources

Abbott, Andrew. 1990. "Conceptions of Time and Events in Social Science Methods: Causal and Narrative Approaches." *Historical Methods* 23:140–50.

Aguet, Jean-Pierre. 1954. *Les grèves sous la monarchie de juillet: Contribution à l'étude du mouvement ouvrier français.* Geneva: Droz.

Agulhon, Maurice. 1973. *1848 ou l'apprentissage de la république, 1848–1852.* Paris: Editions du Seuil.

Agulhon, Maurice, Françoise Choay, Maurice Crubelhier, Yves Lequin, and Marcel Roncayolo. 1983. *Histoire de la France urbaine.* Vol. 4, *La ville et l'âge industriel.* Paris: Editions du Seuil.

d'Alméras, Henri. N.d. *La vie parisienne pendant le Siège et sous la Commune.* Paris: Albin Michel.

———. N.d. *La vie parisienne sous le Second Empire.* Paris: Albin Michel.

Amann, Peter. 1975a. "The Paris Club Movement in 1848." Pp. 115–32 in *Revolution and Reaction,* edited by Roger Price. New York: Barnes and Noble.

———. 1975b. *Revolution and Mass Democracy: The Paris Club Movement in 1848.* Princeton: Princeton University Press.

Aminzade, Ronald A. 1981. *Class, Politics, and Early Industrial Capitalism: A Study of Mid-Nineteenth-Century Toulouse, France.* Albany: State University of New York Press.

———. 1993. *Ballots and Barricades: Class Formation and Republican Politics in France, 1830–1871.* Princeton: Princeton University Press.

Annuaire du commerce et de l'industrie pour la ville de Paris. 1869, 1870. Paris: Société Didot-Bottin.

Appert, Félix Antoine. 1875. *Rapport d'ensemble de M. le Général Appert sur les opérations de la justice militaire relatives à l'insurrection de 1871.* Paris: Imprimerie Nationale.

Assemblée Nationale. 1849. *Compte rendu des séances.* Paris: Imprimerie de l'Assemblée Nationale.

———. 1872. *Enquête parlementaire sur l'insurrection du 18 mars.* 3 vols. Paris: Imprimerie Nationale.

Berlanstein, Lenard R. 1984. *The Working People of Paris, 1871–1914.* Baltimore: Johns Hopkins University Press.

———. 1992. "The Distinctiveness of the Nineteenth-Century French Labor Movement." *Journal of Modern History* 64:660–85.

Bertillon, Jacques. 1889. *Atlas de statistique graphique de la ville de Paris.* Paris: Service de la Statistique Municipale.

Bezucha, Robert. 1974. *The Lyon Uprising of 1834: Social and Political Conflict in the Early July Monarchy.* Cambridge, MA: Harvard University Press.

Blau, Peter M. 1975. "Parameters of Social Structure." Pp. 220–53 in *Approaches to the Study of Social Structure,* edited by Peter M. Blau. New York: Free Press.

Boehm, Christopher. 1984. *Blood Revenge: The Anthropology of Feuding in Montenegro and Other Tribal Societies.* Lawrence: University Press of Kansas.

Boorman, Scott A., and Harrison C. White. 1976. "Social Structure from Multiple Networks. II. Role Structures." *American Journal of Sociology* 81:1384–1446.

Bruhat, Jean, Jean Dautry, and Emile Tersen. 1970. *La Commune de 1871.* Paris: Editions Sociales.

Cable, Sherry, Edward J. Walsh, and Rex H. Warland. 1988. "Differential Paths to Political Activism: Comparisons of Four Mobilization Processes after the Three Mile Island Accident." *Social Forces* 66:951–69.

Calhoun, Craig. 1982. *The Question of Class Struggle: Social Foundations of Popular Radicalism during the Industrial Revolution.* Chicago: University of Chicago Press.

————. 1983. "The Radicalism of Tradition: Community Strength or Venerable Disguise and Borrowed Language?" *American Journal of Sociology* 88:886–914.

————. 1993. "'New Social Movements' of the Early Nineteenth Century." *Social Science History* 17:385–428.

Canfora-Argandoña, Elsie, and Roger-Henri Guerrand. 1976. *La répartition de la population: Les conditions du logement des classes ouvrières à Paris au 19e siècle.* Paris: Centre de Sociologie Urbaine.

Castells, Manuel. 1983. *The City and the Grassroots.* Berkeley: University of California Press.

Cayez, Pierre, and Martine Chevalier. 1983. "Approche du phénomène d'urbanisation de la rive gauche du Rhône (1852–1894)." Pp. 55–68 in *Construire la ville, XVIIIe–XXe siècles,* edited by Maurice Garden and Yves Lequin. Lyon: Presses Universitaires de Lyon.

Ceaux, Jean. 1974. "Rénovation urbaine et stratégie de classe: Rappel de quelques aspects de l'haussmanisation." *Espaces et sociétés* 13–14:19–31.

Chambre de Commerce de Paris. 1851. *Statistique de l'industrie à Paris, résultant de l'enquête faite par la chambre de commerce pour les années 1847–1848.* Paris: Guillaumin.

————. 1875. *Enquête sur les conditions du travail en France, pendant l'année 1872. Département de la Seine.* Paris: Chambre de Commerce.

Chevalier, Louis. 1950. *La formation de la population parisienne au XIXe siècle.* Paris: Presses Universitaires de France.

————. 1958. *Classes laborieuses et classes dangereuses à Paris pendant la première moitié du dix-neuvième siècle.* Paris: Plon.

Chorley, Katharine. 1943. *Armies and the Art of Revolution.* London: Faber and Faber.

Choury, Maurice. 1967. *La Commune au coeur de Paris.* Paris: Editions Sociales.

Clapham, J. H. 1968. *The Economic Development of France and Germany, 1814–1914.* Cambridge: Cambridge University Press.

Clark, T. J. 1984. *The Painting of Modern Life: Paris in the Art of Manet and His Followers.* New York: Alfred A. Knopf.

Clifford, Dale L. 1975. "Aux Armes Citoyens! The National Guard in the Paris Commune of 1871." Ph.D. dissertation, Department of History, University of Tennessee, Knoxville.

Cobban, Alfred. 1963. *A History of Modern France.* 3 vols. Middlesex: Penguin Books.

Cohen, Jean L. 1985. "Strategy or Identity: New Theoretical Paradigms and Contemporary Social Movements." *Social Research* 52:663–716.

Colin, Auguste. 1831. *Le cri du peuple*. Paris: Imprimerie de Démonville. Reprinted in 1974, *Les révolutions du XIXe siècle*. Vol. 4: *Naissance du mouvement ouvrier, 1830–1834*. 12 vols. Paris: EDHIS.

Commune de Paris. 1871. *Journal officiel*. Paris.

Coons, Lorraine. 1987. *Women Home Workers in the Parisian Garment Industry, 1860–1915*. New York: Garland Publishing.

Cott, Nancy F. 1977. *The Bonds of Womanhood: "Woman's Sphere" in New England, 1780–1835*. New Haven: Yale University Press.

Cottereau, Alain. 1986. "The Distinctiveness of Working-Class Cultures in France, 1848–1900." Pp. 111–54 in *Working-Class Formation: Nineteenth-Century Patterns in Western Europe and the United States*, edited by Ira Katznelson and Aristide Zolberg. Princeton: Princeton University Press.

Dalotel, Alain, Alain Faure, and Jean-Claude Freiermuth. 1980. *Aux origines de la Commune: Le mouvement des réunions publiques à Paris, 1868–1870*. Paris: Maspero.

Dauban, Charles. 1873. *Le fond de la société sous la Commune*. Paris: Plon.

Daumard, Adéline. 1963. *La bourgeoisie parisienne de 1815 à 1848*. Paris: SEVPEN.

———. 1965. *Maisons de Paris et propriétaires parisiennes au XIXe siècle, 1809–1880*. Paris: Editions Cujas.

Daumas, Maurice. 1968. *Histoire générale des techniques*. 3 vols. Paris: Presses Universitaires de France.

Daumas, Maurice, and Jacques Payen. 1976. *Evolution de la géographie industrielle à Paris et de sa proche banlieue au XIXe siècle*. 2 vols. Paris: Centre de Documentation d'Histoire des Techniques.

Dautry, Jean, and Lucien Scheler. 1960. *Le Comité Central Républicain des vingt arrondissements de Paris*. Paris: Editions Sociales.

Découflé, André. 1969. *La Commune de Paris (1871): Révolution populaire et pouvoir révolutionnaire*. Paris: Editions Cujas.

Delvau, Alfred, ed. 1868. *Les murailles révolutionnaires de 1848*. 2 vols. Paris: E. Picard.

Département de la Seine. 1882. *Résultats statistiques du dénombrement de 1881 pour la ville de Paris*. Paris: Masson.

———. 1887. *Résultats statistiques du dénombrement de 1886 pour la ville de Paris et le département de la Seine*. Paris: Masson.

———. 1889. *Cartogrammes et diagrammes relatifs à la population parisienne et à la fréquence des principales maladies à Paris pendant la période 1865–1887*. Paris: G. Masson.

Doreian, Patrick. 1980. "Estimating Linear Models with Spatially Distributed Data." Pp. 359–88 in *Sociological Methodology, 1981*, edited by Samuel Leinhardt. San Francisco: Jossey-Bass.

Duclos, Jacques. 1970. *La Commune de Paris à l'assaut du ciel*. Paris: Editions Sociales.

Dusolier, Alcide. 1866. *Les spéculateurs et la mutilation du Luxembourg*. Paris: Librairie du Luxembourg.

Duveau, Georges. 1946. *La vie ouvrière en France sous le Second Empire*. Paris: Gallimard.

———. 1967. *1848: The Making of a Revolution*. New York: Vintage Books.

Edmonson, James M. 1987. *From Mécanicien to Ingénieur: Technical Education and the Machine Building Industry in Nineteenth-Century France*. New York: Garland.

Edwards, Stewart. 1971. *The Paris Commune, 1871*. London: Eyre and Spottiswoode.

Epstein, Barbara L. 1981. *The Politics of Domesticity: Women, Evangelism, and Temperance in Nineteenth-Century America*. Middletown, CT: Wesleyan University Press.

Erbring, Lutz, and Alice A. Young. 1979. "Individuals and Social Structure: Contextual Effects as Endogenous Feedback." *Sociological Methods and Research* 7:396–430.

Evans-Pritchard, E. E. 1940. *The Nuer*. Oxford: Oxford University Press.

Fanon, Frantz. 1963. *The Wretched of the Earth*. New York: Grove Press.

Fantasia, Rick. 1988. *Cultures of Solidarity*. Berkeley: University of California Press.

Faure, Alain. 1974. "Mouvements populaires et mouvement ouvrier à Paris, 1830–1834." *Le mouvement social*, no. 88:51–92.

Fernandez, Roberto M., and Roger V. Gould. 1994. "A Dilemma of State Power: Brokerage and Influence in the National Health Policy Domain." *American Journal of Sociology* 99:1455–91.

Fernandez, Roberto M., and Douglas McAdam. 1988. "Social Networks and Social Movements: Multiorganizational Fields and Recruitment to Mississippi Freedom Summer." *Sociological Forum* 3 (May): 357–82.

———. 1989. "Multiorganizational Fields and Recruitment to Social Movements." In *Organizing for Change: Social Movement Organizations across Cultures*, edited by Bert Klandermans. Greenwich, CT: JAI Press.

Féroldi, Vincent. 1983. "Le Quartier Saint-Louis de la Guillotière au XIXe siècle." Pp. 69–82 in *Construire la ville, XVIIIe–XXe siècles*, edited by Maurice Garden and Yves Lequin. Lyon: Presses Universitaires de Lyon.

Ferry, Jules. 1868. *Comptes fantastiques d'Haussmann: Lettre adressée à MM. les membres de la commission du Corps Législatif chargés d'examiner le nouveau projet d'emprunt de la ville de Paris*. Paris: Le Chevalier.

Fireman, Bruce, and William A. Gamson. 1979. "Utilitarian Logic in the Resource Mobilization Perspective." Pp. 8–44 in *The Dynamics of Social Movements*, edited by Mayer N. Zald and John D. McCarthy. Cambridge, MA: Winthrop Publishers.

Flamand, Jean-Paul. 1989. *Loger le peuple: Essai sur l'histoire du logement social en France*. Paris: Editions La Découverte.

Foster, John. 1974. *Class Struggle and the Industrial Revolution*. London: Weidenfield and Nicolson.

Freymond, J. 1962. *La Première Internationale: Recueil de documents*. 2 vols. Geneva: Droz.

Gaillard, Jeanne. 1960. "Les usines Cail et les ouvriers métallurgistes de Grenelle." *Le mouvement social*, no. 33:35–53.

———. 1965. "Les associations de production et la pensée politique en France (1852–70)." *Le mouvement social*, no. 52: 59–84.

———. 1977a. *Communes de province, commune de Paris, 1870–1871*. Paris: Flammarion.

————. 1977b. *Paris, la ville, 1852–1870.* Paris: Editions Honoré Champion.

Galignani's Paris Guide. 1867. Paris: Galignani.

Gamson, William A. 1990. *The Strategy of Social Protest.* 2d ed. Homewood, IL: Dorsey.

Gandhi, Mohandas K. 1922. *Indian Home Rule.* Madras: Ganesh.

Garrioch, David. 1986. *Neighborhood and Community in Paris, 1740–90.* New York: Oxford University Press.

Gennep, Arnold van. 1960. *The Rites of Passage.* Chicago: University of Chicago Press.

Giedion, Siegfried. 1977. *Space, Time, and Architecture: The Growth of a New Tradition.* Cambridge, MA: Harvard University Press.

Girard, Louis. 1952. *La politique des travaux publics du Second Empire.* Paris: Armand Colin.

Gossez, Rémi. 1956. "Diversité des antagonismes sociaux vers le milieu du XIXe siècle." *Revue économique* 7:439–57.

————. 1967. *Les ouvriers de Paris: Bibliothèque de la Révolution de 1848.* La Roche-sur-Yonne: Société de l'Histoire de la Révolution de 1848.

Gould, Roger V. 1990. "Social Structure and Insurgency in the Paris Commune, 1871." Ph.D. dissertation, Department of Sociology, Harvard University, Cambridge, MA.

————. 1991. "Multiple Networks and Mobilization in the Paris Commune, 1871." *American Sociological Review* 56:716–29.

————. 1993a. "Collective Action and Network Structure." *American Sociological Review* 58:182–96.

————. 1993b. "Trade Cohesion, Class Unity, and Urban Insurrection: Artisanal Activism in the Paris Commune." *American Journal of Sociology* 98:735–38.

Greenberg, Louis. 1973. *Sisters of Liberty: Marseille, Lyon, Paris and the Reaction to the Centralized State, 1868–1871.* Cambridge, MA: Harvard University Press.

Grignon. 1974. *Réflexions d'un ouvrier tailleur sur la misère des ouvriers en général, la durée des journées de travail, le taux des salaires, les rapports actuellement établis entre les ouvriers et les maîtres d'ateliers, la nécessité des associations d'ouvriers comme moyen d'améliorer leur condition.* Reprinted in *Les Révolutions du XIXe siècle.* Vol. 4, *Naissance du Mouvement Ouvrier, 1830–1834.* 12 vols. Paris: EDHIS.

Guerrand, Roger-Henri. 1987. *Propriétaires et locataires: Les origines du logement social en France, 1850–1914.* Paris: Quintette.

Halbwachs, Maurice. 1909. *Les expropriations et le prix des terrains à Paris, 1860–1900.* Paris: Cornely.

————. 1928. *La population et les tracés de voies à Paris depuis un siècle.* Paris: Presses Universitaires de France.

Hanagan, Michael P. 1977. "Artisans and Skilled Workers: The Problem of Definition." *International Labor and Working-Class History* 12:28–31.

————. 1980. *The Logic of Solidarity: Artisans and Industrial Workers in Three French Towns, 1871–1914.* Urbana: University of Illinois Press.

————. 1982. "Urbanization, Worker Settlement Patterns and Social Protest in Nineteenth-Century France." Pp. 208–29 in *French Cities in the Nineteenth Century,* edited by John M. Merriman. London: Hutchinson.

Harvey, David. 1985. *Consciousness and the Urban Experience.* Baltimore: Johns Hopkins University Press.

Hattam, Victoria. 1993. *Labor Visions and State Power: The Origins of Business Unionism in the United States.* Princeton, NJ: Princeton University Press.

Haupt, Georges. 1980. "La Commune comme symbole et comme exemple." Pp. 45–76 in *L'historien et le mouvement social.* Paris: Maspero.

Hechter, Michael. 1987. *Principles of Group Solidarity.* Berkeley: University of California Press.

Hobsbawm, E. J., and Joan W. Scott. 1980. "Political Shoemakers." *Past and Present* 89:86–114.

Hole, Judith, and Ellen Levine. 1971. *Rebirth of Feminism.* New York: Quadrangle Books.

Horne, Alistair. 1965. *The Fall of Paris: The Siege and the Commune, 1870–71.* London: Macmillan.

Jacquemet, Gérard. 1982. "Belleville ouvrier à la Belle Époque." *Le mouvement social,* no. 118:61–77.

———. 1984. *Belleville au XIXe siècle: Du faubourg à la ville.* Paris: Éditions de l'École des Hautes Études en Sciences Sociales.

Jenkins, J. Craig. 1982. "Why Do Peasants Rebel? Structural and Historical Theories of Modern Peasant Rebellions." *American Journal of Sociology* 88:487–514.

———. 1983. "Resource Mobilization Theory and the Study of Social Movements." *Annual Review of Sociology* 9:527–53.

Johnson, Chalmers. 1966. *Revolutionary Change.* Boston: Little, Brown.

Johnson, Christopher. 1975. "Economic Change and Artisan Discontent: The Tailors' History, 1800–1848." Pp. 88–114 in *Revolution and Reaction: 1848 and the Second French Republic,* edited by Roger Price. New York: Barnes and Noble.

———. 1979. "Patterns of Proletarianization: Parisian Tailors and Lodève Woolens Workers." Pp. 65–84 in *Consciousness and Class Experience in Nineteenth-Century Europe,* edited by John M. Merriman. New York: Holmes and Meier.

Jones, Gareth Stedman. 1983. *Languages of Class: Studies in English Working-Class History, 1832–1982.* Cambridge: Cambridge University Press.

Jordan, David P. 1995. *Transforming Paris: The Life and Labors of Baron Haussmann.* New York: Free Press.

Joyce, Patrick. 1991. *Visions of the People: Industrial England and the Question of Class, 1848–1914.* Cambridge: Cambridge University Press.

Judt, Tony. 1986. *Marxism and the French Left: Studies on Labour and Politics in France, 1830–1981.* Oxford: Clarendon Press.

Katznelson, Ira. 1981. *City Trenches: Urban Politics and the Patterning of Class in the United States.* New York: Pantheon.

———. 1986. "Working-Class Formation: Constructing Cases and Comparisons." Pp. 3–44 in *Working-Class Formation: Nineteenth-Century Patterns in Western Europe and the United States,* edited by Ira Katznelson and Aristide Zolberg. Princeton: Princeton University Press.

———. 1992. *Marxism and the City.* Oxford: Clarendon Press.

Katznelson, Ira, and Aristide Zolberg. 1986. *Working-Class Formation: Nineteenth-Century Patterns in Western Europe and the United States.* Princeton: Princeton University Press.

Kuhn, Philip A. 1971. *Rebellion and Its Enemies in Late Imperial China: Militarization and Social Structure, 1796–1864.* Cambridge, MA: Harvard University Press.

Landes, David. 1968. *The Unbound Prometheus: Technological Change and Industrial Development in Western Europe from 1750 to the Present.* Cambridge: Cambridge University Press.

Lavedan, Pierre. 1975. *Histoire de l'urbanisme à Paris.* Paris: Hachette.

Lazare, Louis. 1869. *Les quartiers pauvres de Paris.* Paris: Bureau de la Bibliothèque Municipale.

———. 1870. *Les quartiers de l'est de Paris.* Paris: Bureau de la Bibliothèque Municipale.

Lefebvre, Georges. 1970. *La grande peur de 1789.* Paris: Armand Colin.

Lefebvre, Henri. 1965. *La Proclamation de la Commune.* Paris: Gallimard.

———. 1970. *La révolution urbaine.* Paris: Gallimard.

———. 1973. *La production de l'espace.* Paris: Gallimard.

Leibman, Robert. 1980. "Repressive Strategies and Working-Class Protest, Lyon, 1848–1852." *Social Science History* 4:33–55.

Lenin, V. I. 1969. *What Is to Be Done?* New York: International Publishers.

Léon, Pierre, Maurice Lévy-Leboyer, et al. 1976. *Histoire économique et sociale de la France.* Vol. 3, *L'avènement de l'ère industrielle, 1789–années 1880.* Paris: Presses Universitaires de France.

Lequin, Yves. 1977. *Les ouvriers de la région lyonnaise, 1848–1914.* 2 vols. Lyon: Presses Universitaires de Lyon.

L'Huillier, Ferdinand. 1957. *La lutte ouvrière à la fin du Second Empire.* Paris: Librairie Armand Celin.

Lissagaray, Prosper-Olivier. [1876] 1969. *Histoire de la Commune de 1871.* 2 vols. Paris: Maspero.

Loua, Toussaint. 1873. *Atlas statistique de la population de Paris.* Paris: J. Dejey.

Lowe, Stuart. 1986. *Urban Social Movements: The City after Castells.* New York: St. Martin's Press.

McAdam, Doug. 1982. *Political Process and the Development of Black Insurgency, 1930–1970.* Chicago: University of Chicago Press.

———. 1983. "Tactical Innovation and the Pace of Insurgency." *American Sociological Review* 48:735–54.

———. 1986. "Recruitment to High-Risk Activism: The Case of Freedom Summer." *American Journal of Sociology* 92:64–90.

———. 1989. "The Biographical Consequences of Activism." *American Sociological Review* 54:744–60.

McCarthy, John D., and Mayer N. Zald. 1973. *The Trend of Social Movements in America: Professionalization and Resource Mobilization.* Morristown, NJ: General Learning Press.

———. 1977. "Resource Mobilization and Social Movements: A Partial Theory." *American Journal of Sociology* 82:1212–41.

McDougall, Mary L. 1978. "Consciousness and Community: The Workers of Lyon, 1830–1850." *Journal of Social History* 12:129–45.

McKay, Donald. 1933. *The National Workshops: A Study in the French Revolution of 1848.* Cambridge, MA: Harvard University Press.

Maitron, Jean, ed. 1968. *Dictionnaire biographique du mouvement ouvrier français. 2e partie. 1864–1871.* 6 vols. Paris: Editions Ouvrières.

———. 1972. "Etude critique du rapport Appert: Essai de 'contre-rapport.'" Pp. 95–118 in *La Commune de 1871: Colloque universitaire.* Paris: Editions ouvrières.

Maneglier, Hervé. 1990. *Paris Impérial: La vie quotidienne sous le Second Empire.* Paris: Armand Colin.

Margadant, Ted W. 1979. *French Peasants in Revolt: The Insurrection of 1851.* Princeton: Princeton University Press.

Markoff, John. 1986. "Literacy and Revolt: Some Empirical Notes on 1789 in France." *American Journal of Sociology* 92:323–49.

Marwell, Gerald, and R. E. Ames. 1979. "Experiments on the Provision of Public Goods. I. Resources, Interest, Group Size, and the Free Rider Problem." *American Journal of Sociology* 84:1335–60.

———. 1980. "Experiments on the Provision of Public Goods. II. Provision Points, Stakes, Experiences, and the Free Rider Problem." *American Journal of Sociology* 85: 1356–75.

Marwell, Gerald, Pamela E. Oliver, and Ralph Prahl. 1988. "Social Networks and Collective Action: A Theory of the Critical Mass. III." *American Journal of Sociology* 94 (November): 502–34.

Marx, Gary, and John L. Wood. 1975. "Strands of Theory and Research in Collective Behavior." *Annual Review of Sociology* 1:363–428.

Marx, Karl. [1871] 1940. *The Civil War in France.* New York: International Publishers.

———. 1963a. *The Eighteenth Brumaire of Louis Bonaparte.* New York: International Publishers.

———. [1847] 1963b. *The Poverty of Philosophy.* New York: International Publishers.

———. [1856] 1978a. "Address of the Central Committee to the Communist League." Pp. 570–86 in *The Marx-Engels Reader,* edited by Robert C. Tucker. New York: Norton.

———. [1844] 1978b. "Critical Marginal Notes on 'The King of Prussia and Social Reform.'" Pp. 128–29 in *The Marx-Engels Reader,* edited by Robert C. Tucker. New York: Norton.

———. [1856] 1978c. "Wage Labor and Capital." Pp. 203–17 in *The Marx-Engels Reader,* edited by Robert C. Tucker. New York: Norton.

Marx, Karl, and Friedrich Engels. [1848] 1967. *The Communist Manifesto.* New York: Penguin Books.

Mason, Edward S. 1930. *The Paris Commune: An Episode in the History of the Socialist Movement.* New York: Macmillan.

Massey, Douglas S., and Nancy A. Denton. 1988. "The Dimensions of Residential Segregation." *Social Forces* 67:281–315.

Melucci, Alberto. 1989. *Nomads of the Present.* Philadelphia: Temple University Press.

Merriman, John. 1975. "Radicalisation and Repression: A Study of the Demobilisation of the '*Démoc-Socs*' during the Second French Republic." Pp. 210–35 in *Revolution and Reaction,* edited by Roger Price. New York: Barnes and Noble.

———. 1978. *The Agony of the Republic: The Repression of the Left in Revolutionary France, 1848–1851.* New Haven: Yale University Press.

———, ed. 1979. *Consciousness and Class Experience in Nineteenth-Century Europe.* New York: Holmes and Meier.

———, ed. 1981. *French Cities in the Nineteenth Century.* New York: Holmes and Meier.

———. 1985. *The Red City: Limoges and the French Nineteenth Century.* New York: Oxford University Press.

———. 1991. *On the Margins of City Life: Explorations on the Urban Frontier, 1815–1851.* New York: Oxford University Press.

Ministère du Commerce, de l'Industrie, des Postes, et des Télégraphes—Office du Travail. 1904. *Les associations professionnelles ouvrières.* 4 vols. Paris: Imprimerie Nationale.

Molinari, Gustave de. 1872. *Le mouvement socialiste et les réunions publiques avant la révolution du 4 septembre 1870.* Paris: Garnier Frères.

———. 1874. *Les clubs rouges pendant le siège de Paris.* Paris: Garnier Frères.

Morgan, Robin, ed. 1970. *Sisterhood Is Powerful.* New York: Vintage Books.

Moss, Bernard. 1976. *The Origins of the French Labor Movement, 1830–1914: The Socialism of Skilled Workers.* Berkeley: University of California Press.

Les murailles politiques françaises. 1874. Vol. 2. Paris: Lechevalier.

Nadel, S. F. 1957. *The Theory of Social Structure.* London: Cohen and West.

Nakajima, Toshikatsu. 1985. "L'industrie mécanique à Paris, 1847–1914." Thèse de 3e cycle, Université de Paris-Sorbonne. Paris.

Noiriel, Gérard. 1986. *Les ouvriers dans la société française, XIXe-XXe siècle.* Paris: Editions du Seuil.

Odland, John. 1988. *Spatial Autocorrelation.* Newbury Park, CA: Sage Publications.

Oliver, Pamela E., and Gerald Marwell. 1988. "The Paradox of Group Size in Collective Action: A Theory of the Critical Mass. II." *American Sociological Review* 53:1–8.

Oliver, Pamela E., Gerald Marwell, and Ruy Texeira. 1985. "A Theory of the Critical Mass. I. Interdependence, Group Heterogeneity, and the Production of Collective Action." *American Journal of Sociology* 91:522–56.

Olivesi, Antoine. 1950. *La Commune de 1871 à Marseille.* Paris: Marcel Rivière.

Olson, Mancur. 1965. *The Logic of Collective Action.* New York: Schocken.

Ozouf, Mona. 1971. "Le cortège et la ville: Les itinéraires parisiens des cortèges révolutionnaires." *Annales: Economies, sociétés, civilisations,* no. 26:1061–91.

———. 1976. *La fête révolutionnaire.* Paris: Gallimard.

Payne, Howard. 1966. *The Police State of Louis Bonaparte*. Seattle: University of Washington Press.

Perrot, Michelle. 1974. *Les ouvriers en grève, 1871–90*. 2 vols. Paris: Mouton.

———. 1986. "On the Formation of the French Working Class." Pp. 71–110 in *Working-Class Formation: Nineteenth-Century Patterns in Europe and the United States*, edited by Ira Katznelson and Aristide Zolberg. Princeton: Princeton University Press.

Persigny, Victor Fialin. 1896. *Mémoires du duc de Persigny*. Paris: Plon.

Pinkney, David. 1958. *Napoleon III and the Rebuilding of Paris*. Princeton: Princeton University Press.

———. 1972a *The French Revolution of 1830*. Princeton: Princeton University Press.

———. 1972b. "The Revolutionary Crowd in Paris in the 1830s." *Journal of Social History* 5:512–20.

Plessis, Alain. 1979. *De la fête impériale au mur des fédérés*. Paris: Editions du Seuil.

———. 1985. *The Rise and Fall of the Second Empire, 1852–1871*. London: Cambridge University Press.

Poulot, Denis. [1870] 1980. *Le sublime, ou le travailleur comme il est en 1870 et ce qu'il peut être*. Paris: Maspero.

Préfecture de la Seine—Service de la Statistique Municipale. 1881. *Annuaire statistique de la ville de Paris. Deuxième année—1881*. Paris: Imprimerie Nationale.

Price, Roger, ed. 1975a. *1848 in France*. Ithaca: Cornell University Press.

———, ed. 1975b. *Revolution and Reaction: 1848 and the Second French Republic*. New York: Barnes and Noble.

———. 1987. *A Social History of Nineteenth-Century France*. London: Hutchinson.

Radcliffe-Browne, A. R. 1965. *Structure and Function in Primitive Society*. New York: Free Press.

Reddy, William M. 1984. *The Rise of Market Culture: The Textile Trade and French Society, 1750–1900*. Cambridge: Cambridge University Press.

Reid, Donald. 1984. "Night of the Proletarians." *Radical History Review* 30:445–63.

———. 1991. *Paris Sewers and Sewermen: Realities and Representations*. Cambridge, MA: Harvard University Press.

Rihs, Charles. 1955. *La Commune de Paris, sa structure et ses doctrines*. Geneva: Droz.

Roche, Daniel. 1981. *Le peuple de Paris: Essai sur la culture populaire au XVIIIe siècle*. Paris: Aubien Montaigne.

Roncayolo, Marcel. 1990. *L'Imaginaire de Marseille: Port, ville, pôle*. Marseille: Chambre de Commerce et d'Industrie.

Rougerie, Jacques. 1964a. "Composition d'une population insurgée: L'exemple de la Commune." *Le mouvement social*, no. 45:31–47.

———. 1964b. *Procès des Communards*. Paris: Julliard.

———. 1968. "Remarques sur l'histoire des salaires à Paris au XIXe siècle." *Le mouvement social*, no. 63:71–108.

———. 1971. *Paris libre 1871*. Paris: Editions du Seuil.

———. 1972. "1871." *Le mouvement social,* no. 78:3–77.

———. 1973. "L'A.I.T. et le mouvement ouvrier à Paris pendant les événements de 1870–1871." Pp. 3–102 in *1871: Jalons pour une histoire de la Commune de Paris,* edited by Jacques Rougerie. Assen: Van Gorcum.

———. 1977. "Espace populaire et espace révolutionnaire: Paris, 1870–1871." *Institut d'histoire economique et sociale: Recherches et travaux,* no. 5:48–83.

———. 1988. *La Commune 1871.* Paris: Presses Universitaires de France.

Rouleau, Bernard. 1985. *Villages et faubourgs de l'ancien Paris: Histoire d'un espace urbain.* Paris: Editions du Seuil.

Rudé, George. 1959. *The Crowd in the French Revolution.* Oxford: Oxford University Press.

———. 1964. *The Crowd in History.* New York: Wiley.

Saalman, Howard. 1971. *Haussmann: Paris Transformed.* New York: George Braziller.

Schulkind, Eugene W. 1960. "The Activity of Popular Organizations during the Paris Commune of 1871." *French Historical Studies* 1:394–415.

Schwartz, Michael. 1976. *Radical Protest and Social Structure: The Southern Farmers' Alliance and Cotton Tenancy, 1880–1890.* New York: Academic Press.

Scott, Joan W. 1974. *The Glassworkers of Carmaux: French Craftsmen and Political Action in a Nineteenth-Century City.* Cambridge, MA: Harvard University Press.

———. 1987a. *Gender and the Politics of History.* New York: Columbia University Press.

———. 1987b. "On Language, Gender, and Working-Class History." *International Labor and Working-Class History,* no. 31:1–13.

———. 1987c. "A Reply to Criticism." *International Labor and Working-Class History,* no. 32:37–46.

Les Séances officielles de l'Internationale à Paris pendant le siège et pendant la Commune. 1872. Paris: E. Lachaud.

Serman, William. 1986. *La Commune de Paris (1871).* Paris: Fayard.

Sewell, William H., Jr. 1971. "La classe ouvrière à Marseille sous la Seconde République: Structure sociale et comportement politique." *Le mouvement social,* no. 76:27–65.

———. 1974. "Social Change and the Rise of Working-Class Politics in Nineteenth-Century Marseille." *Past and Present* 65:75–109.

———. 1980. *Work and Revolution in France: The Language of Labor from the Old Regime to 1848.* Cambridge: Cambridge University Press.

———. 1986. "Artisans, Factory Workers, and the Formation of the French Working Class, 1789–1848." Pp. 45–70 in *Working-Class Formation: Nineteenth-Century Patterns in Western Europe and the United States,* edited by Ira Katznelson and Aristide Zolberg. Princeton: Princeton University Press.

———. 1988. "Uneven Development, the Autonomy of Politics, and the Dockworkers of Nineteenth-Century Marseille." *American Historical Review* 93:604–37

Shapiro, Ann-Louise. 1985. *Housing the Poor of Paris, 1850–1902.* Madison: University of Wisconsin Press.

Shorter, Edward, and Charles Tilly. 1974. *Strikes in France, 1830–1968.* London: Cambridge University Press.

Skocpol, Theda. 1979. *States and Social Revolutions.* New York: Cambridge University Press.

Smelser, Neil. 1963. *Theory of Collective Behavior.* New York: Free Press.

Snow, David A., Louis A. Zurcher, and Sheldon Ekland-Olson. 1980. "Social Networks and Social Movements: A Microstructural Approach to Differential Recruitment." *American Sociological Review* 45:787–801.

Soboul, Albert. 1958. *Les sans-culottes parisiens en l'an II: Mouvement populaire et gouvernement révolutionnaire.* Paris: Clavreuil.

Somers, Margaret R. 1992. "Narrativity, Narrative Identity, and Social Action: Rethinking English Working-Class Formation." *Social Science History* 16:591–630.

Statistique Générale de la France. 1869. *Résultats généraux du dénombrement de 1866.* Strasbourg: Imprimerie Nationale.

Steinmetz, George. 1992. "Reflections on the Role of Social Narratives in Working-Class Formation: Narrative Theory in the Social Sciences." *Social Science History* 16:489–516.

Sutcliffe, Anthony. 1970. *The Autumn of Central Paris: The Defeat of Town Planning, 1850–1970.* London: Edward Arnold.

Tarrow, Sidney. 1988. "National Politics and Collective Action: Recent Theory and Research in Western Europe and the United States." *Annual Review of Sociology* 14:421–40.

Thomas, Emile. 1848. *Histoire des ateliers nationaux.* Paris: Michel Lévy.

Thompson, E. P. 1963. *The Making of the English Working Class.* New York: Vintage Books.

———. 1978. *The Poverty of Theory and Other Essays.* London: Merlin Press.

Tilly, Charles. 1978. *From Mobilization to Revolution.* Reading, MA: Addison-Wesley.

———. 1982. "Charivaris, Repertoires and Urban Politics." Pp. 73–91 in *French Cities in the Nineteenth Century,* edited by John M. Merriman. London: Hutchinson.

———. 1984. "Social Movements and National Politics." Pp. 297–317 in *Statemaking and Social Movements: Essays in History and Theory,* edited by Charles Bright and Susan Harding. Ann Arbor: University of Michigan Press.

———. 1985. "Models and Realities of Popular Collective Action." *Social Research* 52:717–47.

———. 1986. *The Contentious French: Four Centuries of Popular Struggle.* Cambridge, MA: Harvard University Press.

Tilly, Charles, and Lynn Lees. 1974. "Le peuple de juin 1848." *Annales: Économies, sociétés, civilisations* 29:1061–91.

———. 1975."The People of June, 1848." Pp. 170–209 in *Revolution and Reaction,* edited by Roger Price. New York: Barnes and Noble.

Tilly, Charles, Louise Tilly, and Richard Tilly. 1975. *The Rebellious Century, 1830–1930.* Cambridge, MA: Harvard University Press.

Tilly, Louise A. 1981. "Women's Collective Action and Feminism in France, 1870–1914." Pp. 207–31 in *Class Conflict and Collective Action,* edited by Louise A. Tilly and Charles Tilly. Beverly Hills: Sage.

Tilly Louise A., and Joan W. Scott. 1978. *Women, Work, and Family*. New York: Holt, Rinehart, and Winston.

Tocqueville, Alexis de. 1861. *Oeuvres complètes*. 2 vols. Paris: Michel Lévy Frères.

———. 1955. *The Old Regime and the French Revolution*. Garden City, NY: Anchor Books.

Tombs, Robert. 1982. *The War against Paris, 1871*. Cambridge: Cambridge University Press.

Touraine, Alain. 1981. *The Voice and the Eye*. New York: Cambridge University Press.

Traugott, Mark. 1980. "Determinants of Political Orientation: Class and Organization in the Parisian Insurrection of June 1848." *American Journal of Sociology* 86:32–49.

———. 1985. *Armies of the Poor: Determinants of Working-Class Participation in the Parisian Insurrection of June 1848*. Princeton: Princeton University Press.

Tudesq, André-Jean. 1964. *Les grands notables en France (1840–1849)*. 2 vols. Paris: Presses Universitaires de France.

Turgan, Émile. 1871. *Les grandes usines: Études industrielles en France et à l'étranger*. 2 vols. Paris: Michel Lévy Frères.

Vial, Jean. 1967. *L'industrialisation de la sidérurgie française, 1814–64*. 2 vols. Paris: Mouton.

Vigier, Philippe. 1982. *La vie quotidienne en province et à Paris pendant les journées de 1848*. Paris: Hachette.

Ville de Paris. 1872. *Bulletin de statistique municipale, 1871*. Paris: Imprimerie Municipale.

Vitu, Auguste. 1869. *Les réunions publiques à Paris, 1868–1869*. Paris: E. Dentu.

Voss, Kim. 1992. "Disposition Is Not Action: The Rise and Demise of the Knights of Labor." *Studies in American Political Development* 6:272–321.

———. 1993. *The Making of American Exceptionalism: The Knights of Labor and Class Formation in the Nineteenth Century*. Ithaca: Cornell University Press.

Walzer, Michael. 1965. *The Revolution of the Saints: A Study in the Origins of Radical Politics*. Cambridge, MA: Harvard University Press.

Weber, Eugen. 1976. *Peasants into Frenchmen: The Modernization of Rural France, 1870–1914*. Stanford: Stanford University Press.

White, Michael J. 1986. "Segregation and Diversity Measures in Population Distribution." *Population Index* 52:198–221.

Willbach, Daniel. 1977. "Work and Its Satisfactions: Origins of the French Labor Movement, 1864–1870." Ph.D. dissertation, University of Michigan.

Wolf, Eric R. 1969. *Peasant Wars of the Twentieth Century*. New York: Harper and Row.

Wolfe, Robert D. 1968. "The Parisian *Club de la Révolution* of the 18th arrondissement, 1870–1871." *Past and Present* 39 (April): 81–119.

Zolberg, Aristide. 1986. "How Many Exceptionalisms?" Pp. 397–455 in *Working-Class Formation: Nineteenth-Century Patterns in Western Europe and the United States*, edited by Ira Katznelson and Aristide Zolberg. Princeton: Princeton University Press.

Index

Note: Italic numbers indicate pages with illustrations